THE FORM OF POLITICS

McGILL-QUEEN'S STUDIES IN THE HISTORY OF IDEAS
Series Editor: Philip J. Cercone

1 Problems of Cartesianism
Edited by Thomas M. Lennon, John M. Nicholas, and John W. Davis

2 The Development of the Idea of History in Antiquity
Gerald A. Press

3 Claude Buffier and Thomas Reid: Two Common-Sense Philosophers
Louise Marcil-Lacoste

4 Schiller, Hegel, and Marx: State, Society, and the Aesthetic Ideal of Ancient Greece
Philip J. Kain

5 John Case and Aristotelianism in Renaissance England
Charles B. Schmitt

6 Beyond Liberty and Property: The Process of Self-Recognition in Eighteenth-Century Political Thought
J.A.W. Gunn

7 John Toland: His Methods, Manners, and Mind
Stephen H. Daniel

8 Coleridge and the Inspired Word
Anthony John Harding

9 The Jena System, 1804–5: Logic and Metaphysics
G.W.F. Hegel
Translation edited by John W. Burbidge and George di Giovanni
Introduction and notes by H.S. Harris

10 Consent, Coercion, and Limit: The Medieval Origins of Parliamentary Democracy
Arthur P. Monahan

11 Scottish Common Sense in Germany, 1768–1800: A Contribution to the History of Critical Philosophy
Manfred Kuehn

12 Paine and Cobbett: The Transatlantic Connection
David A. Wilson

13 Descartes and the Enlightenment
Peter A. Schouls

14 Greek Scepticism: Anti-Realist Trends in Ancient Thought
Leo Groarke

15 The Irony of Theology and the Nature of Religious Thought
Donald Wiebe

16 Form and Transformation: A Study in the Philosophy of Plotinus
Frederic M. Schroeder

17 From Personal Duties towards Personal Rights: Late Medieval and Early Modern Political Thought, c. 1300–c. 1650
Arthur P. Monahan

18 The Main Philosophical Writings and the Novel *Allwill*
Friedrich Heinrich Jacobi
Translated and edited by George di Giovanni

19 Kierkegaard as Humanist: Discovering My Self
Arnold B. Come

20 Durkheim, Morals, and Modernity
W. Watts Miller

21 The Career of Toleration: John Locke, Jonas Proast, and After
Richard Vernon

22 Dialectic of Love: Platonism in Schiller's Aesthetics
David Pugh

23 History and Memory in Ancient Greece
Gordon Shrimpton

24 Kierkegaard as Theologian: Recovering My Self
Arnold B. Come

25 Enlightenment and Conservatism in Victorian Scotland: The Career of Sir Archibald Alison
Michael Michie

26 The Road to Egdon Heath: The Aesthetics of the Great in Nature
Richard Bevis

27 Jena Romanticism and Its Appropriation of Jakob Böhme: Theosophy – Hagiography – Literature
Paolo Mayer

28 Enlightenment and Community: Lessing, Abbt, Herder, and the Quest for a German Public
Benjamin W. Redekop

29 Jacob Burckhardt and the Crisis of Modernity
John R. Hinde

30 The Distant Relation: Time and Identity in Spanish-American Fiction
Eoin S. Thomson

31 Mr Simson's Knotty Case: Divinity, Politics, and Due Process in Early Eighteenth-Century Scotland
Anne Skoczylas

32 Orthodoxy and Enlightenment: George Campbell in the Eighteenth Century
Jeffrey M. Suderman

33 Contemplation and Incarnation: The Theology of Marie-Dominique Chenu
Christophe F. Potworowski

34 Democratic Legitimacy: Plural Values and Political Power
F.M. Barnard

35 Herder on Nationality, Humanity, and History
F.M. Barnard

36 Labeling People: French Scholars on Society, Race, and Empire, 1815–1849
Martin S. Staum

37 The Subaltern Appeal to Experience: Self-Identity, Late Modernity, and the Politics of Immediacy
Craig Ireland

38 The Invention of Journalism Ethics: The Path to Objectivity and Beyond, Second Edition
Stephen J.A. Ward

39 The Recovery of Wonder: The New Freedom and the Asceticism of Power
Kenneth L. Schmitz

40 Reason and Self-Enactment in History and Politics: Themes and Voices of Modernity
F.M. Barnard

41 The More Moderate Side of Joseph de Maistre: Views on Political Liberty and Political Economy
Cara Camcastle

42 Democratic Society and Human Needs
Jeff Noonan

43 The Circle of Rights Expands: Modern Political Thought after the Reformation, 1521 (Luther) to 1762 (Rousseau)
Arthur P. Monahan

44 The Canadian Founding: John Locke and Parliament
Janet Ajzenstat

45 Finding Freedom: Hegel's Philosophy and the Emancipation of Women
Sara MacDonald

46 When the French Tried to Be British: Party, Opposition, and the Quest for Civil Disagreement, 1814–1848
J.A.W. Gunn

47 Under Conrad's Eyes: The Novel as Criticism
Michael John DiSanto

48 Media, Memory, and the First World War
David Williams

49 An Aristotelian Account of Induction: Creating Something from Nothing
Louis Groarke

50 Social and Political Bonds: A Mosaic of Contrast and Convergence
F.M. Barnard

51 Archives and the Event of God: The Impact of Michel Foucault on Philosophical Theology
David Galston

52 Between the Queen and the Cabby: Olympe de Gouges's Rights of Women
John R. Cole

53 Nature and Nurture in French Social Sciences, 1859–1914 and Beyond
Martin S. Staum

54 Public Passion: Rethinking the Grounds for Political Justice
Rebecca Kingston

55 Rethinking the Political: The Sacred, Aesthetic Politics, and the Collège de Sociologie
Simonetta Falasca-Zamponi

56 Materialist Ethics and Life-Value
Jeff Noonan

57 Hegel's *Phenomenology*: The Dialectical Justification of Philosophy's First Principles
Ardis B. Collins

58 The Social History of Ideas in Quebec, 1760–1896
Yvan Lamonde
Translated by Phyllis Aronoff and Howard Scott

59 Ideas, Concepts, and Reality
John W. Burbidge

60 The Enigma of Perception:
D.L.C. Maclachlan

61 Nietzsche's Justice: Naturalism in Search of an Ethics
Peter R. Sedgwick

62 The Idea of Liberty in Canada during the Age of Atlantic Revolutions, 1776–1838
Michel Ducharme
Translated by Peter Feldstein

63 From White to Yellow: The Japanese in European Racial Thought, 1300–1735
Rotem Kowner

64 The Crisis of Modernity
Augusto Del Noce
Edited and translated by Carlo Lancellotti

65 Imprinting Britain: Newspapers, Sociability, and the Shaping of British North America
Michael Eamon

66 The Form of Politics: Aristotle and Plato on Friendship
John von Heyking

THE FORM OF POLITICS

Aristotle and Plato on Friendship

John von Heyking

McGill-Queen's University Press
Montreal & Kingston • London • Chicago

ISBN 978-0-7735-4755-1 (cloth)
ISBN 978-0-7735-4756-8 (paper)
ISBN 978-0-7735-9928-4 (ePDF)
ISBN 978-0-7735-9929-1 (ePUB)

Legal deposit second quarter 2016
Bibliothèque nationale du Québec

Printed in Canada on acid-free paper that is 100% ancient forest free (100% post-consumer recycled), processed chlorine free

This book was first published with the help of a grant from the Canadian Federation for the Humanities and Social Sciences, through the Awards to Scholarly Publications Program, using funds provided by the Social Sciences and Humanities Research Council of Canada.

McGill-Queen's University Press acknowledges the support of the Canada Council for the Arts for our publishing program. We also acknowledge the financial support of the Government of Canada through the Canada Book Fund for our publishing activities.

Library and Archives Canada Cataloguing in Publication

Heyking, John von, author
The form of politics: Aristotle and Plato on friendship / John von Heyking.

(McGill-Queen's studies in the history of ideas; 66)
Includes bibliographical references and index.
Issued in print and electronic formats.
ISBN 978-0-7735-4755-1 (cloth). – ISBN 978-0-7735-4756-8 (paper). – ISBN 978-0-7735-9928-4 (ePDF). – ISBN 978-0-7735-9929-1 (ePUB)

1. Aristotle – Criticism and interpretation. 2. Plato – Criticism and interpretation. 3. Friendship – Political aspects. 4. Political science – Philosophy. I. Title. II. Series: McGill-Queen's studies in the history of ideas; 66

JA71.H49 2016 320.01 C2016-901012-0
C2016-901013-9

This book was typeset by Interscript in 10/12 New Baskerville.

Contents

Abbreviations

The Perseus Digital Library (Classics Department, Tufts University) has been used for the Greek texts used in this study (http://www.perseus.tufts.edu/hopper/). For the main texts examined that are cited in-line, I have used the English translations listed below.

Laws	Plato. *The Laws of Plato.* Translated by T.L. Pangle. Chicago: University of Chicago Press, 1988.
Lysis	Plato. *Lysis.* In *Plato's Dialogue on Friendship: An Interpretation of the* Lysis, *with a New Translation*, translated by D. Bolotin, 17–61. Ithaca, NY: Cornell University Press, 1979.
NE	Aristotle. *Nicomachean Ethics.* Translated by J. Sachs. Newburyport, MA: Focus Publishing, 2002.
Poetics	Aristotle. *Poetics.* Translated by Joe Sachs. Newburyport, MA: Focus Publishing, 2006.
Politics	Aristotle. *Politics.* Translated by C. Lord. Chicago: University of Chicago Press, 1984.
Republic	Plato. *Republic.* Translated by Joe Sachs. Newburyport, MA: Focus Publishing, 2007.

Preface

My wife reminds me that the idea of writing this book came to me as a godsend in the summer of 2002 or 2003 – I cannot remember which. I was conducting a reading group with some students on either Plato's *Lysis* or Aristotle's *Nicomachean Ethics.* At one point I put down my book and announced that I must write a book about friendship, because there is no other topic in politics, or ethics, that really matters. It has taken me over a dozen years to prepare this book on Plato and Aristotle because the task of understanding a philosopher's views on friendship obliges one to try to understand nearly everything else about that philosopher. Aristotle seems to tell us this when he suggests that friendship is not simply a particular virtue, but the entirety of virtue. If you want to understand friendship, you had better understand everything that goes into it. This book is a meagre attempt to convey a sense of that "everything," and, as such, necessarily fails at the task. But I hope the reader will come away from it with a better sense of why friendship is central to our constitution as human beings and as political animals.

The governing insight of the book concerns what Aristotle calls *sunaisthesis,* which can be translated as common, or mutual, perception of the good. I behold the good while beholding you behold the good; we behold the good together while beholding one another. Put in simpler terms: my delight in beholding a beautiful painting is enhanced and enlivened by my beholding it together with my friend, and my beholding it is inseparable from my beholding you. The sunaisthetic moment is surely momentary, but it may still anchor a life that is lived, as Aristotle says, "conversing together and thinking." Virtue-friendship, which is considerably more beautiful than a painting, consists of mutually beholding the good, and also telling stories with one another. Telling stories frequently takes the form of recollection – both of events, and of those shared epiphanies that punctuate and orient our lives together.

This book describes Aristotle's account of it, and then Plato's. I reverse their historical order on the grounds that Aristotle's account of friendship and politics remains within the bounds of common sense, while Plato's horizon is wider because it is daimonic. The meaning of this claim will be elaborated over the course of this book.

Sunaisthetic moments. Beholding the beauty of a lake under Mount Assiniboine when we immediately recognize the smell of Lagavulin from the other backpacker's newly opened flask. Your rendition of Sinatra attracting the carabinieri above a lake in the Swiss "Riviera." Learning to die in the bullpen on the seventh floor. Getting mistaken for Canadians in a Philadelphia hotel. Wearing tour shirts for "The Raw Sexual Energy of Harvey Keitel." Just talking at Lula's where time seemed to stand still. Learning to love your "fish songs" while you learned the wisdom of Johnny Cash. Having you point out to me that death is not necessarily an evil. Enjoying you ridiculing the nagging street signs of Toronto that tell pedestrians to obey the pedestrian signs. Seeing you fall off the curb by the Penny. Standing with you beneath the Trinità dei Monti. Riding Fernie singletrack covered with golden pine needles on a luminous autumn afternoon. Having you show me through the telescope the cascade of stars they named after you. Beholding your surprise that I too love your favorite book. Hiking the Alberta Rockies with you. Reminiscing about our adventures. Realizing during a reading group on Plato and Aristotle that friendship is the most important thing worth considering.

I have had the privilege of presenting my thoughts on friendship and politics to the following venues and groups: American Political Science Association, Catholic University of America (Department of Political Science), Center for Ethics and Culture – University of Notre Dame, Chester Ronning Center at Augustana Campus of University of Alberta, Civitas, Eranos Society, Eric Voegelin Society, Groupe de Recherche Interuniversitaire en Philosophie Politique (GRIPP) at McGill University, Institute of Faith and Learning at Baylor University, Newman Center at McGill University, Pacific Northwest Renaissance Society, Princeton University, Redeemer Pacific College, St Mary's College (Calgary), Symposium on Religion and Politics at Calvin College, Trinity Western University, University of Calgary (Department of Political Science), University of Lethbridge (Department of Political Science), and the Western Political Science Association.

Over the years, numerous friends and colleagues read and commented upon chapter drafts; several practised "living together and sharing conversation and thinking." I thank: Richard Avramenko, Jan Bagh, Iain Benson, Ken Boessenkool, Charles Blattberg, Leah Bradshaw, Eva Brann, Barry Cooper, Tom Darby, Peter Emberley, Stephen Evans, Bruce

Fingerhut, April Flakne, Lance Grigg, David Goa, Edward Goerner, Grant Havers, Thomas Heilke, Michael Henkel, Agnes Horvath, Vern Kimball, Preston King, Paul Kirkland, David Klassen, Rainer Knopff, Wolfgang Leidhold, Rebecca LeMoine, Jacob Levy, Brad Lewis, Collin May, Steve McGuire, Stephen Miller, Rob Miner, Christopher Morrissey, Marco Navarro-Genie, Philip Ney, James Old, Anthony Parel, Zdravko Planinc, Jeff Polet, Fr Brendan Purcell, James Rhodes, Derval Ryan, Joe Sachs, Tilo Schabert, David Lewis Schaefer, Fr James Schall, Roger Scruton, Travis D. Smith, Sean Steel, Peter Stockland, Arpad Szakolczai, Lee Trepanier, Fred Wall, David Walsh, Ronald Weed, Jonathan Wensveen, and Jen Whiting.

Parts of chapter 2 were originally published as "'Sunaisthetic' Friendship and the Foundations of Political Anthropology," in *International Political Anthropology* 1, no. 2 (2008), and parts of chapter 4 were originally published as "Hermes as Eros in Plato's *Lysis*," in *History of the Human Sciences* 26, no. 5 (2013). The discussion of the Calgary Stampede was originally published as "Tolerance in Festivity: The Case of the Calgary Stampede," in *Convivium* (October/November 2014). I thank these journals for permission to publish those parts.

I also thank the people at McGill-Queen's University Press, including Jacqueline Mason for her splendid shepherding skills, and the two anonymous reviewers for their comments and suggestions. Scott Howard provided splendid copy-editing.

Merle Christe provided secretarial assistance, Philip Ney performed research for chapter 3, and Rachel Tams provided editorial work. Jonathan played the Athenian Stranger and Lance played Megillus. I would also like to thank the University of Lethbridge for providing me with two sabbaticals during the lengthy time I took to write this book.

This book has been published with the help of a grant from the Federation for the Humanities and Social Sciences, through the Awards to Scholarly Publications Program, using funds provided by the Social Sciences and Humanities Research Council of Canada.

This book is dedicated to my best friend: Sonya.

THE FORM OF POLITICS

1

Introduction: Friendship Is the Form of Politics

FRIENDS WITH THE "HIGHEST OUTLOOK"

Winston Churchill makes an astonishing claim in his biography of his great ancestor, John Churchill, Duke of Marlborough. As competent and strategically minded that King William was, he lacked Marlborough's capacity to develop a broad-based network of friends to assist him with his plans:

> These incomplete relationships were the King's own fault, and a misfortune to his reign. If in 1689 and 1690 William, with two kingdoms to govern and the diplomacy of half Europe in his hands, had treated Marlborough fairly and had not denied him his rightful opportunity upon the battlefields, he might have found that talisman of victory without which all his painstaking, adroit combinations and noble exertions could but achieve a mediocre result. He might have found across the differences of rank that same comradeship, never disturbed by doubt or jealousy, true to the supreme tests of war and fortune, which later shone between Marlborough and Eugene [of Savoy].[1]

Churchill notes that Marlborough had "close friendly relations" with such figures as the future Queen Anne, the future treasurer Lord Godolphin, and Robert Harley, the speaker of the House of Commons whose friendship Marlborough could use to influence that institution.

But Churchill criticizes King William for failing to cultivate friendship with an international ally, as Marlborough did with Prince Eugene during the War of Spanish Succession. Marlborough marched the British Army, the "red caterpillar," down country to the Danube to

1 Churchill, *Marlborough: His Life and Times*, vol. 1, 441.

escape the "obstinate" Dutch meddling in his command and to meet up with Eugene. There they each found salvation in one another as friends and allies.

Both, moreover, possessed the highest outlook on the war; for Eugene, though in the field, was still head of the Imperial War Council, and Marlborough was not only Commander-in-Chief of the English and Dutch armies, but very largely a Prime Minister as well. They could therefore feel toward the whole problem a responsibility different from that of the leaders of individual armies, however large … Each felt the relief which comes from the shadows of a great rock in a thirsty land. In the midst of the intrigues, cross-purposes, and half-measures of a vast, unwieldy coalition trying to make war, here was the spirit of concord, design, and action.[2]

Alluding to Isaiah 32:2, Churchill compares the solace the two men found in each other to the relief of finding shade in the desert. The alliance against King Louis XIV required a deep sense of commonality and friendship between Marlborough and Eugene, whose friendship was undoubtedly based, at least in part, on sharing the "highest outlook on the war" for each country. As presidents of the United States claim of their friendships with past presidents, only those who have experienced it have any idea of the moral, political, and spiritual demands that such power and responsibility place on an individual.[3] Moreover, both Marlborough and Eugene possessed that Clausewitzian *coup d'oeil* that enabled them to discern the motions and patterns of battle that only military genius can discern:

Nothing but genius, the daemon in man, can answer the riddles of war, and genius, though it may be armed, cannot be acquired, either by reading or experience. In default of genius nations have to make war as best they can, and since that quality is much rarer than the largest and purest diamonds, most wars are mainly tales of muddle. But when from time to time it flashes upon the scene, order and design with a sense almost of infallibility draw out from hazard and confusion. "The mere aspirant after a type of character only shows his hopeless inferiority when the natural orator or fighter or lover comes along."[4]

2 Churchill, *Marlborough*, vol. 1, 774.

3 Nancy Gibbs and Michael Duffy, *The Presidents Club: Inside the World's Most Exclusive Fraternity*.

4 Churchill, *Marlborough*, vol. 1, 569–70, citing William James, *The Varieties of Religious Experience*, Lectures 11–13.

From each man's paramount position, "both thought and spoke about war in the same way, measured the vast forces at work by the same standards, and above all alike looked to a great battle with its awful risks as the means by which their problems would be solved."[5] They were "two bodies with one soul" "working like two lobes of the same brain," and in their respective genius shared a daemon.[6]

Churchill cites William James when referring to "the daemon in man," but his point is essentially Platonic. In the *Symposium,* Plato has Socrates claim that a "daimonic man" is someone who is wise in "the whole intercourse and conversation of gods with human beings" "for it is in the middle of both and fills up the interval so that the whole itself has been bound together by it" (203a). Referring to the *Symposium,* Eric Voegelin describes the "spiritual man, *daimonios aner,* who lives in the tension between needy and full being," as erotic: Eros is "the symbol of the tension experienced between the poles of temporal and eternal being," where the divine and human partake in one another.[7] He is also the measure of right and possesses the "power of influence on others – and the reciprocal experience of gratitude" in others.[8] In beholding the "bloom" of each other's well-being (see *NE* 1174b34), Marlborough and Eugene enjoyed what Aristotle called virtue-friendship, or joint perception of the good (*sunaisthesis*). This is the theme upon which the argument of this book pivots; I will explain Aristotle's understanding of it in chapter 2. Their shared daimonism points beyond Aristotle's horizon of practical wisdom toward a Platonic notion of friendship, considered in chapters 4 through 7.

Churchill's biography of Marlborough is a chronicle of his political and military career, judged by how well Marlborough conducted his friendships, which were crucial for his political success. One of the main lessons of the work is that a statesman must cultivate not simply alliances and networks, but lifelong friendships based upon the moral and intellectual virtue that inspire undying loyalty, and that can sustain those statesmen through tumultuous times and fortunes. The biography is also Churchill's own personal and historical anamnesis of the fundamental principles of political order. It is very much his statement of his own political philosophy, written as political history, and its fundamental

5 Churchill, *Marlborough,* vol. 1, 774.

6 Ibid., 775 and 825. Churchill compares the "comradeship" of Generals Robert Lee and Stonewall Jackson to that of Marlborough and Eugene (vol. 4 of *History of the English Speaking Peoples,* 171).

7 Voegelin, *Anamnesis,* 325–6.

8 Richard J. Bishirjian, "Daimonic Men," 159.

category is friendship: both Aristotelian virtue-friendship and political friendship, because the former seems to create possibilities for the latter. Pivotal were the so-called "Cockpit" friendships between Marlborough, his wife Sarah, Lord Godolphin, and Princess Anne (the future queen whose residence in the Royal Cockpit gave them their name). "The Cockpit friendships," Churchill wrote, "were the crucible from which the power and glory of England were soon to rise gleaming among nations."[9]

So much of politics and life in general is a history of loyalties and betrayals, and the subsequent telling of stories about them. Friendships and personal relationships are frequently the subtexts of political controversies. Indeed, politics is conducted by persons with distinct personalities, moral aims, and motivations. One thinks of Churchill's own friendship with Franklin Roosevelt that sustained the alliance against Hitler; Margaret Thatcher and Ronald Reagan's friendship that continued the "special relationship"; the friendship of Washington and James Madison; the monumental correspondence between John Adams and Thomas Jefferson, whose reconciliation had a profound impact on the course of American history in wake of the revolution; Abraham Lincoln's "team of rivals," whose modus operandi was turning rivals for power (especially William Seward) into friends; the friendship between Louis-Hippolyte LaFontaine and Robert Baldwin, the two founders of responsible government in Canada before Confederation; and the friendship between John A. MacDonald and Étienne Cartier, the "Siamese twins" who were Confederation's guides.[10] Jean Yarbrough explains the political significance of the Adams-Jefferson friendship:

> The Adams-Jefferson correspondence illuminates some of the most fundamental issues in American politics: the connection between first principles and constitutional forms, the origin of political parties, progress and human nature, the place of aristocracy in republican government, the best regime, the significance of the French Revolution, the Missouri Compromise, and slavery. But it is also

9 Churchill, *Marlborough*, vol. 1, 349.

10 Jon Meacham, *Franklin and Winston: An Intimate Portrait of an Epic Friendship*; Doris Kearns Goodwin, *Team of Rivals: The Political Genius of Abraham Lincoln*; Richard Aldous, *Reagan and Thatcher: The Difficult Relationship* (Aldous's general argument challenges claims that the two were good friends, but his evidence does more to support the other side); Stuart Leibiger, *Founding Friendship: George Washington, James Madison, and the Creation of the American Republic*; Merrill D. Peterson, *Adams and Jefferson: A Revolutionary Dialogue*; John Ralston Saul, *Louis-Hippolyte LaFontaine and Robert Baldwin*, and Yolanda Stewart (ed.), *My Dearest Friend: The Letters of Louis Hippolyte LaFontaine and Robert Baldwin*; and Alastair Sweeny, *George-Étienne Cartier*.

true that, having reached a certain level of understanding about these questions, the two drifted away from politics and began to cultivate the kind of philosophic friendship for which their education and inclinations had long prepared them.[11]

Or consider how the friendship of Moses with Aaron shaped the Israelite nation in its exodus from Egypt. This friendship in particular was one that moved Churchill, who wrote about it during the so-called "wilderness years" in the 1930s when he was out of office.[12] Aaron was the voice of Moses, as Churchill once characterized himself as the voice of Britain.[13] The "modern" friendships discussed above stand in a long line of paradigmatic ancient friendships, including those of Gilgamesh and Enkidu, Achilles and Patroclus, Heracles and Iolaus, Harmodius and Aristogeiton, Jonathan and David, and Cicero and Pompey, that captured the imaginations of statesmen, poets, and philosophers throughout the ages.[14]

When considering the grand sweep of historical movements and the great ideas of political philosophy, it is easy to overlook the interplay of *personal* relationships as the crucible of political and moral decision-making. I shall argue that friendships are the highest kinds of personal relationships, and they play an important part in shaping our political world.[15] Indeed, incapacity to practise friendship seems to be a key factor in political failure, for friendship plays a central role in the construction of networks and coalition. The isolated politician is the failed politician.[16] The extreme of the isolated politician is, of course, the tyrant,

11 Jean M. Yarbrough, "Politics and Friendship in the Adams-Jefferson Correspondence," in *Friends and Citizens: Essays in Honor of Wilson Carey McWilliams*, 76–7.

12 Churchill, "Moses as Political Leader."

13 Gertrude Himmelfarb, *The Moral Imagination*, 265n.

14 Jonathan Y. Rowe, *Sons Or Lovers: An Interpretation of David and Jonathan's Friendship*; Beryl Rawson, *The Politics of Friendship: Pompey and Cicero*; Quintus Tullius Cicero, *How to Win an Election: An Ancient Guide for Modern Politicians* (a manual on elections by Cicero's brother Quintus, which positions friendship as the key to creating networks of clients and allies to secure victory); John von Heyking, "Befriending Those No Decent Person Would Talk To," *C2C Journal*, 25 June 2012, http://c2cjournal.ca/2012/06/befriending-those-no-decent-person-would-talk-to-2/.

15 I elsewhere discuss the importance of friendship within the practices of statecraft ("Friendship as Precondition and Consequence of Creativity in Politics"; *"Comprehensive Judgment" and "Absolute Selflessness": Winston Churchill on Politics as Friendship*). See also Tilo Schabert, *How World Politics Is Made: France and the Reunification of Germany*.

16 For examples, see David Rothkopf on Barack Obama: "This Man is an Island," *Foreign Policy* 5, 5 November 2014, http://foreignpolicy.com/2014/11/05/this-man-is-an-island-2. On Lyndon Johnson and on Richard Nixon, see Gibbs and Duffy, *The Presidents Club*, 167 and 269.

whom Plato and Aristotle regarded as incapable of friendship and thus of achieving life's greatest goods. Creative statesmanship, then, involves the capacity to practise genuine friendship as well as introspective solitude, as exemplified by a Lincoln or a Churchill.

Conversely, the incapacity to practise friendship might explain why one finds lonely individuals looking to politics, in the form of utopianism, solidarity, and other romantic adventures, as a way of experiencing the erotic intensity they lack in virtue-friendships. Utopianism that demands too much from political friendship seems to be a misplaced or misdirected form of longing for personal friendship. This might help explain why utopian thinkers regularly overlook friendship in their analyses of human life, and, frequently, in their personal lives. Like Swift's Laputians, the importance they place upon the cosmic or trans-historic, as well as the microscopic, leads them to overlook the intermediate.

For all the talk about ambition, fame, honour, and legacy, more reflective statesmen come to recognize that, like the rest of us, all we have left under the light of being are the things we know and what we are, and the people we love. They come to recognize, as Marlborough and Eugene may have when they reflected upon their position at the "highest outlook on war," that each is alone with the other, with the only other person who could understand him. This is perhaps why there are so many lonely people in politics. Seeking satisfaction in power, they forget about friendship. Thus many stay in politics too long, mistakenly thinking that they would be even lonelier if they left, when in fact, by staying, they are digging even deeper holes into their souls.[17]

FRIENDSHIP AND POLITICS: PLATO AND ARISTOTLE, OR ARISTOTLE AND PLATO

It is perhaps for the reasons listed above that, in his common sense approach that constantly strives to "maintain the phenomena,"[18] Aristotle

17 I am thankful for Ian Brodie for pointing this out to me. For a recent illustration of how this dynamic plays out among the political class in Washington, DC, where "Washington friendship" is an ironic term for those craving deeper connections, see Mark Leibovitch, *This Town: Two Parties and a Funeral in America's Gilded Capital.*

18 "To speak, then, of friendship in the primary sense only is to do violence to the phenomena, and makes one assert paradoxes; but it is impossible for all friendships to come under one definition. The only alternative left is that in a sense there is only one friendship, the primary; but in a sense all kinds are friendship, not as possessing a common name accidentally without being specially related to one another nor yet as falling under one species, but rather as in relation to one and the same thing" (*Eudemian Ethics* 1236b21–6 in *The Complete Works of Aristotle*; see Stephen Salkever, "Taking Friendship Seriously," 77n.10).

famously claims that the legislator is more concerned with friendship than justice: "friendship seems to hold cities together, and lawmakers seem to take it more seriously than justice" (*NE* 1155a23). The same holds true for Plato, as indicated by the importance of *philia* and *eros* in his discussions of justice and the virtues in various dialogues. Indeed, despite Aristotle's criticism that the *Republic* identifies political friendship too closely with virtue-friendship (*Politics* II.1–4), he agrees with his teacher that virtue-friendship – specifically considered as *sunaisthesis* in this study – is the standard or perhaps regulative ideal of a polity. For both, friendship is the form of politics. This does not mean that political friendship is as high or as noble as virtue-friendship. Indeed, political friendship includes a wider but lower array of the human goods that we normally associate with things that are necessary for life, including material well-being and physical security. But the goods that make life worth living are found in those virtue-friendships whose moral horizon reaches higher than that found even in political friendship. Virtue-friendship is the measure of political friendship, a point this book elaborates in detail.

Political friendship is the condition of legislation, and it also is the expression of citizens practising civic virtue together. Political friendship, of course, is not so high as virtue-friendship. A polity whose citizens are inexperienced in that higher friendship will also fail to enjoy political friendship: they will locate that higher virtue-friendship within politics, thus distorting both virtue-friendship and political friendship. This is Aristotle's basic criticism of Plato's *Republic*. Even so, Plato's consideration of political friendship in the *Laws* is closer to Aristotle than the *Republic*, and scholars have noticed the affinities between the *Politics* and the *Laws*.[19]

The practice of justice seems to depend in large part on affective relations. This is not to say that we must necessarily like the person to whom we have an obligation. Rather, our readiness to discharge our obligation toward the other is enhanced by our habits of affection and love generally – especially the habits we practise in our closer relationships. If justice involves owing a good to another, then friendship, in which I make your good *my* good, aims higher. This higher aim assists with the intellectual and affective acts of sympathy involved in discerning just what the good of another is.[20] Being habituated in friendship helps us see the person to

19 For sources, see citations in chapter 3. I shall elaborate the differences between Plato and Aristotle below, as well as explain why I focus on the texts I do.

20 On this distinction between justice and friendship, see Robert Sokolowski, "Phenomenology of Friendship."

whom we are obliged as just, which renders justice a relation between persons, instead of an abstraction expressing relations among things.

Thus, for Aristotle, legislators need to be more concerned with friendship than with justice, just as a football coach ensures that practice is more rigorous than the game. Political friendship involves like-mindedness (*homonoia*) regarding the most important things that ought to be done (see *NE* 1155a20–30; 1167a25–30). Of course, even the best regime is characterized by different factions with different opinions regarding the just and the advantageous. Yet their like-mindedness is characterized by their willingness to seek the just and the advantageous together with *these* particular other citizens. This is why Aristotle's examples of like-mindedness pertain to the constitutional or involve foreign policy: "cities are likeminded whenever it seems good to everyone for the offices to be elected, or to make an alliance with the Spartans, or for Pittacus to rule, when he too was willing" (*NE* 1167a30–35).

Like-mindedness is proximately about the rules of the game, and about directing the force of the polity against a foreign enemy. As such, it is infrequently a topic of special concern for the partisan factions of a political society, because their everyday political activity is predicated upon like-mindedness. Like-mindedness is not the object of legislation or political action, but their condition. One of the remarkable aspects of Aristotle's treatment of political friendship is how rarely he analyzes it.[21] He explains that "like-mindedness seems to be something similar to friendship" (*NE* 1155a25), and, elsewhere, "something involved in friendship" (*NE* 1167a23). But he does not actually show it in action and it is rarely a direct topic of analysis. One might also notice that he does not provide his readers with a portrayal of virtue-friendship, for similar reasons.

The reason for this omission is that political friendship rarely speaks in its own name. Political friendship resides in the backdrop of "regular" political deliberations and activities, which are the stuff of factions whose extremes are restrained not only by constitutional forms, but by the like-mindedness upon which those forms rest. It is the condition of politics. As backdrop, it is usually only seen when the entirety of political society comes together, as in the examples of war and constitutionalism Aristotle lists, or in times of festivity. Like-mindedness might be seen in what Walter Bagehot called the "dignified" elements of our liberal democratic constitutions – the rituals and ceremonies that are distinct from the "efficient" elements that have a direct bearing on our lives as citizens. For

21 As noticed by Suzanne Stern-Gillet, "Souls Great and Small: Aristotle on Self-Knowledge, Friendship, and Civic Engagement," 59–60.

this reason, we tend to dismiss the "dignified" aspects as merely decorative and not constitutive. Thus political friendship, as a condition or form of politics, is analogous to the way in which virtue-friendship is a condition of inferior friendships – which Aristotle questions whether to call friendships at all (*NE* 1156a6–20).

This hiddenness of political friendship is a major reason why liberal democrats skeptical of the importance of political friendship (and Plato and Aristotle, by extension) are mistaken. They forget that political pluralism is embedded within a like-mindedness expressed in terms of constitutionalism, which itself expresses social friendship and hence agreement concerning the highest things humans ought to do. Ambition counteracting ambition is constrained by agreement on constitutional fundamentals, expressed as a social friendship that prevents such conflict from degenerating into fratricidal war.[22] Political strategists in a liberal demoracy who boast that it is their job to "destroy the opponent" really ought to read about politics in Renaissance Florence, where that really meant something.

In October 2014, Canadians witnessed a paramount instance of the dignified element of our constitution taking on a supremely efficient role when the sergeant-at-arms of the House of Commons, 58-year-old Kevin Vickers, performed a spinning dive in his ceremonial gown to kill an attacker in the corridors of the House.[23] Like a corybantic dancer protecting baby Zeus from predatory Kronos, he showed how the symbols of like-mindedness assert themselves to protect the main institutions of parliamentary democracy – the regime of persuasion (*peitho*), where Nous rules.[24] The relationship between Nous and friendship will be considered more fully in chapters 5 to 7 on Plato's *Laws*, the dialogue that, in refiguring the primordial myth of the birth of Zeus and his rulership, portrays three elderly gentlemen considering the rule of Nous as a problem of learning how to dance together like Corybantes.

Aristotle famously claims the polis comes into being "for the sake of living, it exists for the sake of living well" (*Politics* 1252b28–9). The logic of political action is directed toward the self-sufficiency of the polis as an

22 On "social friendship," see Bertrand de Jouvenal, *On Sovereignty*, chapter 8, and George Carey, "Social Friendship in the Founding Era."

23 "Kevin Vickers took out gunman Michael Zehaf-Bibeau with spinning dive straight out of an action movie," *National Post*, 27 October 2014 (http://news.nationalpost.com/news/canada/kevin-vickers-took-out-gunman-michael-zehaf-bibeau-with-spinning-dive-straight-out-of-an-action-movie).

24 For details on how the House of Commons is the house of political reason and persuasion (Nous/*phronesis* and *peitho* to the Greeks), see my "Liberal Education Embedded in Civic Education for Responsible Government: The Case of John George Bourinot."

aspiration. In its highest form – what Aristotle in Books VII and VIII of the *Politics* calls the regime for which we can only pray – self-sufficiency includes like-mindedness, meaning agreement about the best things humans ought to do. Democracies, oligarchies, tyrannies, and other deficient regimes may have a degree of like-mindedness concerning civic virtue, though these regimes can better be characterized as factional alliances whose unity comes not through genuine like-mindedness but through domination. Only the best regime is genuinely political. Only its version of civic virtue is predicated upon a self-sufficient good in which living together is for the sake of "noble actions, not [merely] for the sake of living together" (*Politics* 1281a2–3).

But what is this self-sufficient good for which the best regime aims, and which somehow expresses itself as political friendship? Of course it is the completion of civic virtue. But what does that look like? What is the characteristic action of civic virtue? I address this question directly in chapter 3 on Aristotle's *Politics* and *Poetics*, and in chapters 5 to 7 on Plato's *Laws*. I argue that the common good of the best regime is to be found in festivity, the civic version of virtue-friendship. These philosophers' respective accounts of festivity show us the fullness of civic virtue and how citizens exercise it. That the character of the best regime is "dreamlike," or something for which one prays, is a reminder that political friendship normally does not appear so directly to us because it operates in the background of our inferior regimes, whose characteristic virtues seem to be lesser than those expected here. But by bringing to the fore what normally operates in the background, Plato and Aristotle reveal what our inferior regimes, at their best, aspire to. I apply these insights to a contemporary example of what I take to be not just a cultural but *political* festival, in my discussion of the Calgary Stampede in the conclusion of this book.

The advantage of considering festivity as political friendship is that it illuminates the characteristic action of political friendship, or like-mindedness, that many considerations of the common good omit. Many considerations state only *that* the common good involves like-mindedness and friendship; rarely do they move beyond that by considering what the common good looks like. Some versions consider further the meaning of common good by arguing that like-mindedness concerning the self-sufficient good of the good regime can only be secured when philosophy, the most genuine self-sufficient good, rules over society. These versions sometimes focus upon the philosophical treatment of musical education in the *Politics*, but they do not complete their own trajectory because they do not adequately consider the mediated or mimetic manner in which musical education is to be experienced by the citizens themselves, or what characteristic action that education is to produce. Conversely, scholars of festivity – including Josef Pieper and Karl Kérenyi, upon whom this study draws – generally treat festivity in isolation from broader political considerations. This study bridges their cultural and religious work with the scholarship of political theorists on Plato and Aristotle.[25]

My discussion of festivity as political friendship takes as one of its bearings a passage from Homer's *Odyssey*. Odysseus is in the palace of the Phaikians, and has just listened to Demodocus sing of his, Odysseus's, travails. Before Odysseus proceeds to tell his own tale, he declares:

Alcinous, majesty, shining among your island people,
What a fine thing it is to listen to such a bard
As we have here – the man sings like a god.
The crown of life, I'd say. There's nothing better
Than when deep joy holds sway throughout the realm
And banqueters up and down the palace sit in ranks,
Enthralled to hear the bard, and before them all, the tables
Heaped with bread and meats, and drawing wine from a mixing-bowl
The steward makes his rounds and keeps the winecups flowing.
This, to my mind, is the best that life can offer.[26]

Aristotle cites part of Odysseus's statement as evidence that "those of earlier times," the Homeric heroes, regarded banqueting and listening to the bard as the "pastime [*diagoge*] of free persons" (*Politics* 1338a14, 23–4). I will show in chapter 3 that Aristotle does not fully agree with the view of "those of earlier times." However, Aristotle sees enough truth in the statement to use it to advance his own view of political friendship, and the characteristic action of the good regime. In order to discern why we can view this statement as pointing toward the characteristic action of political friendship, we need first to return to virtue-friendship, which provides its basis. So too with Plato. In the *Republic*, Plato has Socrates cite part of Odysseus's proclamation to suggest that Homer's "wisest man" thinks that the most beautiful thing is indulging in food and wine, which helps motivate Socrates's claim that Homer corrupts (*Republic* 390b, citing *Odyssey* IX.8–10). Later, in Book X, Socrates proclaims Homer the greatest of the poets, but holds that, as a poet, he corrupts. Even so, defenders of poetry, referring to poetry as a personified woman,

25 See the sources cited in each of the subsequent chapters.
26 Homer, *Odyssey*, IX.1–12.

may "make an argument in her defense without meter, to the effect that she's not only pleasant but also beneficial to polities and to human life, and we'll listen in a favorable spirit, because assuredly we'll be the ones to gain if she's shown to be not only pleasant but beneficial as well" (*Republic* 607d–e). For both Aristotle and Plato, the truth of Odysseus's statement can only be shown when philosophy wins the "ancient" quarrel with poetry. Chapter 3 shows Aristotle's *Poetics* is such a defense, and chapters 5 to 7 show this of Plato's *Laws* as well.[27]

SUNAISTHESIS

The Pythagorean proverb states that "friends share all things in common" [*koina ta philon*].[28] Friendship is the pinnacle of the moral life, the regulative ideal by which all acts are judged and to which, perhaps, all acts aspire. This is agreed upon by the ancient Greek tradition, and the Biblical one as well. "Greater love hath no man than this, that a man lay down his life for his friends," Jesus tells his disciples, whom he christens his friends moments later.[29] Likewise, Aristotle's discussion of battlefield courage points to, and is refined by, his famous discussion of friendship in the *Nicomachean Ethics,* though the basic structure of the moral act remains similar. As Robert Spaemann explains: "Friendship as the exemplary and most intensive form of benevolence lies beyond all standards of justice in its origin. It is a free gift and a free choice. It is the center of all ethics, since in it that benevolence, which is the basis of all demands of justice, becomes visible in its pure form."[30] One might say, in a manner consistent with St. Thomas Aquinas' claim that charity is the form of virtue, that friendship is the form of virtue too: "It is charity which directs the acts of all other virtues to the last end, and which, consequently, also gives the form to all other acts of virtue: and it is precisely in this sense that charity is called the form of the virtues."[31] More extensive elaboration

27 In a footnote to line 607e of his translation of the *Republic,* Joe Sachs suggests that the *Poetics* "might be regarded as an acceptance of this invitation" (308n187). The citizens of Magnesia will sing their own song, which will be a better tragedy than anything a poet can produce (*Laws* 817b).

28 See Edwin L. Minar, "Pythagorean Communism," *Transactions and Proceedings of the American Philological Association,* 34–46; *Republic* 424a and 449c; *Laws* 739c; *Phaedrus* 279c. See also Euripides, *Orestes,* 725, and Kathy Eden, *Friends Share All Things in Common: Tradition, Intellectual Property, and the Adages of Erasmus.*

29 John 15:13 and 15:15.

30 Robert Spaemann, *Happiness and Benevolence,* 109.

31 Aquinas, *Summa Theologiæ,* II–II.23.8. In Article One of that same Question, Aquinas refers to John 15:15 when arguing that charity is in fact friendship.

on the degree to which philosophic notions of *philia* are compatible with Christian *caritas* is outside the scope of this volume.[32]

In dying for you, my friend, I offer my life to you as a gift that recognizes the emblematic moral excellence that I experience preeminently in you, and which I acknowledge in my outpouring of love to you. You and I behold the good and the beautiful together, and our beholding it is unthinkable without also beholding it together and in each other. Like sculptors, we place and receive each other's "impress" upon one another, under the light of the good (see *NE* 1172a17). Below I shall briefly describe this mutual self-giving, which Aristotle refers to as *sunaisthesis* or "joint perception" of the good (*NE* 1170b10–12), and which Churchill described as the joint *coup d'oeil* of Marlborough and Eugene, and then examine it in greater detail in chapter 2 on Aristotle's *Nicomachean Ethics*, and again in chapter 4 on Plato's *Lysis*. Chapters 3 and 5 to 7 consider how political friendship is predicated upon *sunaisthesis*.

A scholarly book on politics and friendship must respond to a common objection to the project largely motivated by the cynicism of our times toward politics, namely that no such book is possible. Or, that it would have to be an extremely short book. My response to this objection is to start by writing a fairly long book on the topic, in large part because it has become very difficult to discern the type of friendship that I discuss, virtue-friendship, from other forms of association. Friendship has been lost as a category of political analysis for numerous reasons, not the least of which is that we have difficulty even discussing what friendship is. Our popular vocabulary of intimate relations draws almost exclusively from romanticism, which prevents us from even conceiving of such relations other than in erotic and bodily terms. It is hard for us to think of what a union of intellects is. With Lord Byron, many regard friendship as "love without wings."[33] Retrieving a vocabulary about the moral good of friendship, and considering its significance for the realities of politics, is the fundamental aim of this book.

This book focuses on the importance of what Aristotle called virtue-friendship for political life. He famously distinguished three types of friendship: (1) utility, (2) pleasure, and (3) virtue. Friendships of utility are present among individuals who trade goods with one another;

32 But see my "The Luminous Path of Friendship: Augustine's Account of Friendship and Political Order," and "Aquinas's Mediated Cosmopolitanism and the Impasse of Ancient Political Philosophy," in *Cosmopolitanism in the Age of Globalization: Citizens Without States*, 70–96.

33 Lord Byron, "L'amitié est L'Amour Sans Ailes."

economic exchange is a paradigmatic example. You do not need to love the friend in order to conduct the exchange. Or, as Adam Smith put it in *The Wealth of Nations*: "It is not from the benevolence of the butcher, the brewer, or the baker, that we can expect our dinner, but from their regard to their own interest."[34] Friendships of pleasure are present among individuals who share bodily enjoyment of various kinds, such as drinking buddies. Again, friends of pleasure do not necessarily love one another, but rather the pleasure each provides the other. Without anything more, pleasure friendships end when friends cease to amuse each other. That "more" is a regard for the friend's well-being and character, which points to virtue-friendship. Virtue-friendship is present when friends love one another for their characters. People serious about their own moral character conduct such friendships. They either practise the virtues – like courage, moderation, justice, generosity, etc. – or are fully committed to the life of attaining virtue. Stephen Salkever calls this dedication the "prohairetic life" because friends encourage each other to make good choices (*prohairesis*) regarding virtue. They continually have "their rough edges knocked off" (*NE* 1172a17), as Aristotle says.[35]

The peak of the prohairetic life among friends is the sharing of their lives. Virtue-friendship is higher than political friendship insofar as it involves the sharing of the intellect, the highest part of us. Friends love each other while contemplating the good. Our joint perception of the good, *sunaisthesis*, constitutes the very flowering of our intellects:

> But one's being is choiceworthy on account of the awareness of oneself as being good, and such an awareness is pleasant in itself. Therefore one also ought to share in a friend's awareness that he *is* [or share his friend's consciousness of his existence – *sunaisthanesthai hoti estin*], and this would come through living together and sharing conversation and thinking; for this would seem to be what living together means in the case of human beings. (*NE* 1170b10–12)

Our intellect is structured to seek knowledge, and that also includes seeking to be known. Being known here does not mean being honoured or having fame. Rather, it means knowing oneself and one's relationship with the world one inhabits – not only through one's own eyes, but also

34 Smith, *An Inquiry into the Nature and Causes of the Wealth of Nations*, book I, chap. 2, para. 2. Smith thought commercial society better distinguished friendships of utility from virtue-friendships, which premodern societies had conflated in nepotistic practices of economic exchange.

35 Salkever, "Taking Friendship Seriously: Aristotle on the Place(s) of Philia in Human Life," 59–70.

through the eyes of another. It is an act of intellectual triangulation, as it were, but one familiar to just about all of us. We behold a beautiful scene when accompanied by our friend. Our understanding and appreciation of that scene is enhanced because we share the act of beholding it with our friend, and our understanding and love of that beauty redoubles in our understanding and love of our friend. Furthermore, "were it not for an underlying liking and sympathy for one's companion, one would not care what he saw, but feeling this, we simultaneously are pleased by his activity and being, and find that it augments our perception of our activity and being and so is good for us ... In such shared perception and shared thought, the experiences of two people can most closely approach a perfect unity, by converging upon a single object."[36] Put more simply, two sets of eyes are better than one, and we love to talk about the experience of seeing the beauty with our friend long afterward. One might say that our act of beholding that beauty is not complete *unless* we talk about it long afterward. Or perhaps a shared silence is all that is needed.

Of course the beauty of a friend's moral and intellectual excellence is far greater than any beautiful mountain scene or painting. And that beauty is far more difficult to discern. It might be glimpsed in those moments when our moral character is tested and we act in a beautiful manner that sacrifices our good for that of our friend. Yet we also know that we are conflicted beings and that motives are not always pure. Discerning our friend's character, and our own, is a lifelong project. Our capacity to behold the moral character of our friend is based upon a life shared together, with all its ups and downs, "through living together and sharing conversation and thinking." Paradoxically, we are most complete, most alive, when we live for another, and when we tell each other stories about our lives lived together.

Thinking is a shared activity. My insight does not preclude you from having that insight. The sum of our shared insights is probably greater than their parts. In this spirit, Christopher Nelson writes:

> My love doesn't grow less because you love too. And of course, if we should actually love one another, that love is surely greater and stronger for it being reciprocated and reinforced over and over. So it is with the intellect. When I learn something you have shared with me, it does not pass from you to me like milk

36 Lorraine Pangle, *Aristotle and the Philosophy of Friendship*, 190. For other efforts to anchor Aristotelian virtue-friendship in *sunaisthesis*, see Ronna Burger, *Aristotle's Dialogue With Socrates: On the* Nicomachean Ethics, 176–83; Giorgio Agamben, "Friendship"; April Flakne, "Embodied and Embedded: Friendship and the Sunaisthetic Self"; Aryeh Kosman, "Aristotle on the Desirability of Friends"; and chapter 2 of this study.

from a pitcher; you have lost nothing, and yet I have gained something that is now common to us both. The sum of what is common to us has just grown; it has not been redistributed. And should we together go about learning something new, we will each be richer for what we come to have in common.[37]

Hannah Arendt makes a similar observation when she states: "Each time we talk about things that can be experienced only in privacy or intimacy, we bring them out into a sphere where they will assume a kind of reality which, their intensity notwithstanding, they never could have before. The presence of others who see what we see and hear what we hear assures us of the reality of the world and ourselves."[38] The greatest goods are those that are shared together, and the greatest acts of friendship are those performed by friends seeking the common good together, which includes seeking to understand the common good.

Contemplative or sunaisthetic friendship is no mere exercise in abstraction, but a practice of the greatest existential import. We take great risks in putting ourselves before the judgment of truth and of our friends, for everything we know and are could be based upon a radical mistake. We are most vulnerable because we are naked, "clothed in virtue instead of a cloak" (Plato, *Republic* 457a). Or as Søren Kierkegaard observes: "To go swimming one takes off one's clothes; to pursue the truth one must take one's time in a much more inward sense, divesting oneself of a much more inward attire of thoughts, ideas, selfishness and the like, before one is naked enough."[39] Even so, one cannot rule out that friendship must involve sharing goods that are *not* eminently shareable, as sharing these goods still involves immense self-sacrifice (Aristotle, *Politics* II.5). For this reason we cannot rule out the possibility of friendship in politics.

For this reason as well, a full theory of friendship must account not just for its intellectual or sunaisthetic component, but also for our emotions and our bodies. The varieties of friendship include a wide range of *philia*, and our capacity to love and live together depends on our bodily existence. Thus, marriage is a form of friendship, and sports, as shown by Plato in the *Laws*, plays an important role in constituting our political friendships. Even so, this study focuses on the intellectual component of friendship, *sunaisthesis* in personal virtue-friendships, and choral festivity – instead of on sports and war-games, as political friendship. That

37 Nelson, "The Things of Friends Are Common." Asked how he manages to love each of his seven children so well, my friend's response is that his soul opens further and his love for each and all grows. Socrates may have had this experience of parenthood in mind when he compared himself to a midwife, and ideas to children.

38 Arendt, *The Human Condition*, 50.

39 Kierkegaard, *Papers and Journals: A Selection*, 633.

intellectual component plays the biggest role in determining the unity behind the various phenomena of friendship.[40] One might say that the emotions and our bodies have lives of their own, but the reality is that our intellects are always there to ask us whom we are loving and for what purpose. Our intellects help our emotions and our bodies guide our love to its proper targets.

Moments of shared insights are perhaps the purest form of *sunaisthesis.* Our discoveries of fundamental truths coincide with discoveries about ourselves and each other, done together. This, in essence, is what liberal education is about. It is for this reason that Xenophon's description of Socrates and his friends is so compelling: "Just as others are pleased by a good horse or dog or bird, I myself am pleased to an even higher degree by good friends … and the treasures of the wise humans of old which they left behind by writing them in books, I unfold and go through them together with my friends, and if we see something good, we pick it out and regard it as a great gain if we thus become useful to one another."[41]

The intensity of *sunaisthesis* is illuminated by the example of John Keats and his friend Charles Cowden Clarke's reading of Chapman's translation of Homer. Clarke describes how the two of them sat in Clarke's house, "turning to some of the 'famousest' passages, as we had scrappily known them in Pope's version."[42] Adam Nicholson describes how they "were hunched together over pages that were drenched in antiquity. Ghosts must have been seeping out of them. Something that had seemed quaint to the eighteenth century now seemed true to the two young men. They pored over Chapman together."[43] Clarke writes: "I had the reward of one of his delighted stares" after the two of them read Chapman's rendition of Odysseus emerging from the sea on the island of the Phaikians:

Then forth he came, his both knees falt'ring, both
His strong hands hanging down, and all with froth
His cheeks and nostrils flowing, voice and breath
Spent to all use, and down he sank to death.
The sea had soak'd his heart through.[44]

40 On friendship in marriage and family, see Pangle, *Aristotle and the Philosophy of Friendship*, ch. 4. On sports as civic friendship, see Michael Novak, *The Joy of Sports: End Zones, Bases, Baskets, Balls, and the Consecration Of The American Spirit.* For a comparison of contemporary sports spectatorship and ancient Greek *theoria*, see Fr James V. Schall, "On the Seriousness of Sports, Watchers All."

41 Xenophon, *Memorabilia*, I, vi, 14.

42 Clarke, "Recollections of Keats."

43 Nicholson, *The Mighty Dead: Why Homer Matters*, 20.

44 Homer, *Odyssey*, 5.500–5 (the translation is Chapman's as quoted by Nicholson, but the line numbers are from Fagles' edition).

Both were moved by this rendering of Homer's Odysseus, whose "sea-soaked heart is a heart with the heart drained out of it."[45] As Nicholson explains, this is the most famous meeting of Homer and an English poet and his friend: "Keats had read and stared in delight, shocked into a moment of recognition, of what the Greeks called *anagnorisis*, when a clogging surface is stripped away and the essence for which you have been hungering is revealed."[46] Their moment of recognition was a moment of Homer's revelation as well as of themselves with one another.

According to Nicholson, "Clarke and Keats read Chapman together all night, and at six in the morning Keats returned to his Dean Street lodgings ... with Chapman looming in his mind. On the journey home across London he had begun to frame the sonnet which on arrival he wrote down. The manuscript, which he paid a boy to take over to Cowden Clarke that morning, so that it was on his breakfast table by ten o'clock, survives."[47] The title of Keats' "On First Looking into Chapman's Poem" reveals its meaning. He looks not at it but *into* it, submerging with his friend into its depths as for the first time, as Odysseus had been submerged in the ocean. Or as Keats writes: "Yet did I never breathe its pure serene / Till I heard Chapman speak out loud and bold: / Then felt I like some watcher of the skies / When a new planet swims into his ken."[48] He and Clarke were submerged into a new revelation, a new sense of "pure serene," comparable to an astronomer discovering a new planet. The revelation penetrated their souls together: each "had the reward of one of his delighted stares."

Music is an instructive analogue of *sunaisthesis*, and an example from popular culture illustrates its intellectual and emotional triangulation. In a recent interview with Peter Mansbridge of the Canadian Broadcasting Corporation, Geddy Lee, lead singer of the rock band Rush, explains the crowning experience of musicianship and friendship he and his band members share on stage:

> Sometimes it is just you've pushed yourself into this moment musically and you're clicking and you all know you're clicking and you make eye contact and I'll look at Al and Al will look at Pratt and we all look at each other and we start smiling ... everybody disappears at that moment, there is like no audience. There is nothing on stage but the three of us and we still feel like we're that band that

45 Nicholson, *The Mighty Dead*, 22.

46 Ibid., 20.

47 Ibid., 22.

48 Keats, "On First Looking into Chapman's Homer."

started like 38 years ago in a rehearsal room and it is just that kind of inside joke that requires no dialogue. We'll just look at each other and yeah this feels good.[49]

What Lee describes is a musical version of *sunaisthesis* that he shares with his bandmates, who are also his closest friends. Indeed, we must remain cognizant of Aristotle's own use of aesthetic and musical categories to describe that moral experience, which suggests that music and morals are not so far apart. In Lee's terms, when he and his bandmates recognize that they are in "the groove," the three of them behold the good, which in this example is the excellence of their music and their musicianship; and they also behold each other as individuals in that act of beholding, which includes the love and admiration they have for one another, and the recollection of their years of living, working, and playing together. Recalling their humble beginnings and their struggles to build their careers together, they must be astonished and grateful at what they have achieved. This musical analogy, which displays a momentary step outside the rhythm of playing music while remaining within that rhythm, helps illustrate the moral and intellectual phenomenon that thinkers such as Aristotle see in virtue-friendship. There is the excellence of moral action performed together, which is thought about together. Action and contemplation dance together, separate but conjoined.

Bertrand Russell speaks of *sunaisthesis* when he describes his friendship with Joseph Conrad and the immediate sense of connection he felt with him: "At our very first meeting, we talked with continually increasing intimacy. We seemed to sink through layer after layer of what was superficial, till gradually both reached the central fire. It was an experience unlike any other that I have known. We looked into each other's eyes half appalled and half intoxicated to find ourselves together in such a region."[50] Joseph Epstein comments that this "central fire" operated in spite of (or because of) the vastly different political views each men held. Russell thought that human evil could be eradicated by proper social organization (he admired the Soviet Union), and Conrad thought, at bottom, that human beings were alone in the world (despite his own longing for friendship). "The central fire, then, is something beyond and deeper than mere agreement. It is a place where one can receive kindness, understanding, solace, patient attention, and respect for one's

49 Interview with Geddy Lee, *The National*, CBC, 11 June 2012, http://www.cbc.ca/thenational/blog/2012/06/interview-with-geddy-lee.html. I elaborate the musical analogy in chapter 6 of this book, on Plato's *Laws*. See also Alfred Schütz, "Making Music Together."

50 Quoted in Epstein, *Friendship: An Exposé*, 162–3.

point of view, and all this because of an underlying but never spoken sense that everyone around that central fire, or in the community, knows that he and she are all in the same struggle together."[51]

One is reminded here of Aristotle's comparison of the way that goodwill arises in friendship and the way that the spark of beauty arouses erotic longing: "Goodwill seems to be a beginning of friendship, in the same way the pleasure of seeing is the beginning of falling in love, for no one falls in love without first being pleased by someone's looks … Goodwill arises on account of virtue or some sort of fitness [*areten kai epieikeian*], when someone appears to one as beautiful or courageous or some such thing" (*NE* 1167a3–5, 19–21). Falling into friendship involves an element of being captivated, not so much by physical beauty but by the beauty of one's character. Seeing the character of another "hang together" seems an apt way of describing the moral-aesthetic act of beholding the ethos of the friend.[52]

Epstein's description of the "central fire" helps explain the presence of intellectual and emotional attachment, and it explains why the moral practice of friendship is a matter of beholding both the good and the friend in a moment outside the rhythms of friendship. Yet it also explains the absence of these attachments. The ethos of our friend, and ourself, is both present and absent to one another. Friends are and remain an enigma. Beholding the friend's "central fire" in an act of *sunaisthesis* is a way of expressing those momentary glimpses in which we and our friend are present to each other and to the good we share. Spending a life "sharing conversation and thinking" is a way of acknowledging that our selves, our individual ethos, can never be fully contained in any given moment, perhaps not even in a lifetime. But it is only by living together and conversing that our friend's ethos, and ours, becomes available to us.

C.S. Lewis's famous description of friends standing side by side, "their eyes look[ing] ahead," in contrast with lovers who stand face-to-face, seems contrary to the image of *sunaisthesis* being drawn here.[53] However, Lewis's description of friends standing side by side actually concludes an evocative account of friends discovering each other and their mutual love of a good wherein they behold each other, face-to-face as it were: "The typical expression of opening Friendship would be something like, 'What? You too? I thought I was the only one'… It is only when two such persons discover one another, when, whether with immense difficulties and semi-articulate fumblings or with what would seem to us amazing

51 Epstein, *Friendship*, 163. See Yi-Fu Tuan, "Community, Society, and the Individual."

52 Elizabeth Telfer, "Friendship," in *Philosophers on Friendship*, 243–53.

53 C.S. Lewis, *The Four Loves*, 80.

and elliptical speed, they share their vision – it is then that Friendship is born. And instantly they stand together in immense solitude."[54] For Lewis, as for Aristotle, friends behold the good and each other while beholding the good. Friendship love and erotic love are not mutually exclusive, then, although they do differ. Part of the modern prejudice against friendship love is that it is not as intoxicating or enchanting as romance (it is, to recall Byron, "love without wings"). Part of the advantage of considering friendship in light of *sunaisthesis* is to see how friendship love operates, intellectually and emotionally, in a similar way to erotic love, while also pointing to the co-penetration of intellects instead of bodies.

WONDROUS STORIES

In another echo of Aristotle's insight that friends spend their lives together sharing conversation and thinking, Lewis wrote of his lifelong friendship with Tolkien (and other Inklings): "My happiest hours are spent with three or four old friends in old clothes tramping together and putting up in small pubs – or else sitting up till the small hours in someone's college rooms talking nonsense, poetry, theology, metaphysics over beer, tea, and pipes."[55] If Lewis's description of life together with Tolkien and the other Inklings conjures up too much of an old boys' club, then Gail Caldwell's description of her friendship with Caroline Knapp may sing the female part of this drama: "According to the old rule book, men had sports and women had talking; Caroline and I cultivated both, finding that our logging of miles on river or land enhanced the internal ground we covered. And yet I find now that writing about a friendship that flourished within the realm of connection and routine has all the components of trying to capture air. The dailiness of our alliance was both muted and essential: We were the lattice that made room for the rose."[56] Elena Ferrante's presentation of two female Neapolitan friends also displays the kind of *sunaisthesis* Aristotle describes friends as having:

> I sometimes imagined what my life and Lila's would have been if we had both taken the test for admission to middle school and then high school, if together we had studied to get our degree, elbow to elbow, allied, a perfect couple, the

54 Lewis, *The Four Loves*, 78–9.

55 Quoted in Colin Duriez, *Tolkien and C.S. Lewis: The Gift of Friendship*, 127.

56 Gail Caldwell, *Let's Take the Long Way Home: A Memoir of Friendship*, 88–9. It would take a separate study to detail the variety of ways that males and females each conduct their friendships. However, I suspect that such detailing would all come back to the fundamental experiences of virtue-friendship.

> sum of intellectual energies, of the pleasures of understanding and the imagination. We would have written together, we would have been authors together, we would have drawn power from each other, we would have fought shoulder to shoulder because what was ours was inimitably ours.[57]

Ferrante's friends studying "elbow to elbow" and "shoulder to shoulder" look a lot like Lewis's friends.

Lewis, Caldwell, and Ferrante point to a crucial aspect of friendship: storytelling. Friends act together and contemplate together, and together they pursue and discover what they regard as the good and the beautiful. But they also reflect upon their adventures. "Did you see that?" is a common utterance among friends. It is as if one's own perception, observation, or insight not only needs confirmation but is incomplete without having one's friend also participate in it. Eva Brann points to this when she writes: "We save up the events of our days to tell our friends, feeling that until our affairs have been told they haven't quite happened: Thus do our friends confirm our lives."[58]

Storytelling is a major component of the prohairetic life that friends share. Indeed, one can, with Alasdair MacIntyre, claim even more strongly that storytelling is the *form* of the prohairetic life with friends: "A central thesis then begins to emerge: man is in his actions and practice, as well as in his fictions, essentially a story-telling animal. He is not essentially, but becomes through his history, a teller of stories that aspire to truth."[59] Even though MacIntyre does not fully integrate this "central thesis" into any consideration of friendship as the peak of the moral life, one can agree with his general point that storytelling (or narrative or myth) is the form of the prohairetic life because moral choices involve taking actions, and actions are defined by intentions that are based on morally practical ideas about how we ought to live. The moral life takes place within a web of moral meanings that form our relations with others, and society more generally. We draw upon this web of meaning to understand our actions, and to explain them, both prospectively and retrospectively, in the form of stories we share with our friends, who too compose that web of meaning: "Thus do our friends confirm our lives."

As we shall see below, storytelling is also the form that political friendship takes. But for now it is worth noting the reason why thinking more

57 Ferrante, *Those Who Leave and Those Who Stay*, 354. In living out their difficult friendship, Ferrante's characters display the Platonic tripartite structure of the soul, which suggests these psychological insights are common to both sexes (see 193 as well).

58 Brann, *Open Secrets/Inward Prospects: Reflections on World and Soul*, 51.

59 MacIntyre, *After Virtue*, 216.

generally completes action. One finds an analogy here with the way in which philosophical contemplation is linked to political action. Philosophical contemplation done together is superior to political action because political action is impossible without some opinion of the good and beautiful: all action intends to reveal some truth. As statesmen like Lincoln, Churchill, Reagan, and Thatcher believe, politics is a battle of ideas because ideas represent the way one aspires to live, and thus guide one's actions.[60] Churchill explained this early in his career, in his *River War*, when describing the good reasons the Sudanese had for defending themselves against the British imperialists:

> The desire, which most men and all communities manifest at all times, to associate with their actions at least the appearance of moral right ... No community embarks on a great enterprise without fortifying itself with the belief that from some points of view its motives are lofty and disinterested ... The sufferings of a people or a class may be intolerable, but before they will take up arms and risk their lives some unselfish and impersonal spirit must animate them.[61]

Political action is impossible without a fortifying ideology or story that sustains and justifies the deeds that are performed in its name. Churchill suggests that such ideologies and stories aim to be "unselfish and impersonal" because only then can "most men and all communities" believe themselves in the "moral right." Yet, the difficulty is distinguishing those that have the "appearance" of being morally right from those that truly are morally right. The ideologies and stories that guide political action lie beneath the search for truth or political philosophy.

In the words of political philosopher Leo Strauss, "All political action has then in itself a directedness towards knowledge of the good: of the good life, or the good society."[62] What Strauss means here is that all political action is conducted according to some opinion or argument regarding the good. For example, a conservative argues that lower taxes are good, while a liberal argues that higher taxes to pay for more government services are good. The liberal and the conservative each makes a claim about what is good in politics. As Strauss argues, political philosophy aims at replacing opinion about the good with knowledge of the good. Opinion is rarely completely wrong. More often it is incomplete. Knowledge is sought but may be impossible to achieve, except by the gods. Knowledge is also incomplete because political philosophers are

60 On Thatcher, see Richard Aldous, *Reagan and Thatcher*, 24.

61 Churchill, *The River War*, vol. 1, 31–6.

62 Leo Strauss, *What is Political Philosophy?* 10.

also citizens of their own regimes, so they must account for their own place in the rhythm of their polity's political friendship – between their love of truth, and love of their own.[63] Socrates captures this tension when he tells the Athenian jury: "I will do this [engage in philosophic questioning] to whomever, younger or older, I happen to meet, both foreigner and townsman, but more so to the townsmen, inasmuch as you are closer to me in kin."[64] Socrates loved truth more than Athens, but not enough to make him leave, and he loved philosophizing "more so" with his fellow Athenians.

Storytelling is not philosophizing but it shares a similar relationship to action that contemplation does, as described by Strauss. In the context of friendship, storytelling with friends "completes" the "events of our days" by capturing or illuminating the meaning of those events. Without that meaning, the events would not register in the choice-making activity that constitutes our ethical lives. Moreover, as Caldwell notes when she writes that the "dailiness of our alliance was both muted and essential," our friendships and lives are not regularly punctuated by a Dantean perception of our friends' "inner fire." More often than not, it is the "dailiness" that characterizes our "living together and conversation." Storytelling is the narration of a life lived together, created by that life and by friends' reflection upon it.

As I explain in greater detail in chapter 3, which examines Aristotle's *Politics* and *Poetics*, storytelling or myth resides between philosophy and history, between universals and particulars. It occupies this liminal position because friends share the prohairetic life in which they seek universal goods within particular relations that are of paramount importance to them. Storytelling is participatory – it is where friends participate as "characters." I not only reveal myself and my history to you, and you not only reveal yourself and your history to me, but together we intertwine those two stories in our shared adventure through life, and together we can look back on that adventure and discern lines of meaning in it. This is included in Aristotle's observation that the essential work of friends is "living together and conversing." Thomas Mann explains the intertwining function of storytelling in his novel, *Joseph and His Brothers*, where Joseph explains to his Egyptian master and friend: "Literature is a great thing. But greater still, to be sure, is when the life one lives is a story – and that we are in a story together, a most excellent one at that, I am more and more convinced with time. You, however, are part of it because

63 For elaboration, see Thomas Heilke and John von Heyking, "Editors' Introduction," *Hunting and Weaving, Empiricism and Political Philosophy*.

64 Plato, *Apology*, 30a.

I took you into my story."[65] The life of friends *is* a story, and gets expressed *as* a story.

It is for this reason that Hannah Arendt argues that politics, if it "produces" anything at all (as distinguished from endeavours like labour and fabrication), produces stories:

> The realm of human affairs, strictly speaking, consists of the web of human relationships which exists wherever men live together. The disclosure of the "who" through speech, and the setting of a new beginning through action, always fall into an already existing web where their immediate consequences can be felt. Together they start a new process which eventually emerges as the unique life story of the newcomer, affecting uniquely the life stories of all those with whom he comes into contact. It is because of this already existing web of human relationships, with its innumerable, conflicting wills and intentions, that action almost never achieves its purpose; but it is also because of this medium, in which action alone is real, that it "produces" stories with or without intention as naturally as fabrication produces tangible things.[66]

Arendt continues by noting rightly that, since everybody enters life in a world in which the human story has already begun, nobody is an author, but instead an "actor and sufferer." Similarly, Eric Voegelin introduces his magnum opus, *Order and History*, with a similar observation: "Man is not a self-contained spectator. He is an actor, playing a part in the drama of being and, through the brute fact of his existence, committed to play it without knowing what it is ... The role of existence must be played in uncertainty of its meaning, as an adventure of decision on the edge of freedom and necessity."[67] For Voegelin as for Arendt, storytelling or myth is the appropriate mode for reflecting upon the human condition and politics because it is participatory. We contribute our stories with others, embedded within the preexisting webs of relations established by others who have gone before us.

Statesmen seem to be natural-born storytellers. Indeed, their very mode of being seems to be storytelling. For instance, Tilo Schabert recalls that in interviews with governmental officials or politicians during his research, he would often receive as the first response to his question

65 Mann, *Joseph and His Brothers*, 1233.

66 Arendt, *The Human Condition*, 183–4. For Arendt's personal practice of friendship along the lines outlined in this chapter, see Kathleen B. Jones, "Hannah Arendt's Female Friends," *LA Review of Books*, 12 November 2013, http://lareviewofbooks.org/essay/hannah-arendts-female-friends.

67 Voegelin, *Israel and Revelation*, 1.

a reply that began with: "Let me tell you a story!" Analyzing a person involves delving into the flow of a person's existence in order to find there an event, recounted in a story, that reveals something about that person.[68] Storytelling is the primary way of discerning the character, ethos, or "central fire" of another.

This is the truth Aristotle saw in Odysseus's proclamation to the Phaikians that listening to the bard while banqueting is "the best life can offer."[69] Odysseus's statement is an instance of storytelling completing action, and also of storytelling *being* the action. This is the good life that civic friends enjoy with one another and it is an image of the highest friendship, which Aristotle calls *sunaisthesis.*

HOW TO THINK ABOUT FRIENDSHIP AND POLITICS

Shifting our attention back from political friendship and again to virtue-friendship, these examples of *sunaisthesis* help explain the emotional and even erotic intensity of such intellectual and moral sharing: "and so the loving and the friendship among these people is the most intense and best" (*NE* 1156b25). It is ecstatic in the sense that it draws us out of our individual spaces, but, as described by Aristotle, Lewis, Lee, Churchill, Plato, and others, it is not irrational. It is an experience of "enhanced aliveness" that comes only in the company of the friend, not necessarily in a single epiphany, but, precisely because that moment cannot contain *sunaisthesis*, virtue-friendship occurs "through living together and sharing conversation and thinking; for this would seem to be what living together means in the case of human beings" (*NE* 1170b12–13).[70] Virtue-friendship is prohairetic; it involves making choices that form our characters. It requires the full activation of the moral and intellectual virtues in order to sustain the mature life of "living together and sharing conversation and thinking" over the course of one's life and one's life with others. It is this prohairetic character of virtue-friendship that makes theoretical treatments of friendship seem so elusive.

Friendship seems to transcend the boundaries of our theoretical categories precisely because it *is* what our lives revolve around. The best theoretical treatments of friendship tend to burst out of their own

68 Personal communication to author. For details, see Schabert, *How World Politics Is Made.* For elaboration, see von Heyking and Heilke, "Editors' Introduction" in *The Primacy of Persons in Politics*, xv.

69 Homer, *Odyssey*, IX.1–12.

70 "Enhanced aliveness" is Lorraine Pangle's term to summarize all that is packed into the term *sunaisthesis* (*Aristotle and the Philosophy of Friendship*, 191).

conceptual modes of analysis and demand a more participatory mode of knowing about friendship, which better reflects the priority of practice over theory. Voegelin captures this priority of practice, or of what can be called pretheoretical experiences, in his description of the theophany that made philosophy possible. Insight, he writes, is "itself rooted in the real movements of the human spiritual soul toward divine being experienced as transcendent. In the experiences of love for the world-transcendent origin of being, in *philia* toward the *sophon* (the wise), in *eros* toward the *agathon* (the good) and the *kalon* (the beautiful), man became philosopher."[71] The paradox of loving wisdom is that before one can love wisdom, one must be capable of love. But the capacity to love involves wisdom. This capacity, which includes the recognition of the paradox, is an essential difference between the philosopher and the sophist or ideologue.

David Burrell provides a helpful explanation of the mode of knowing required to understand friendship, which turns out to be a practical form of knowing:

> I am suggesting that the reason we will be asked to undertake the requisite [spiritual] exercises lies with the very character of language used to probe such dimensions of existence: we cannot grasp it in its proper semantic mode without realizing that it is inherently analogous. And analogous terms need to be anchored to a primary analogate, so that other uses can be related proportionally to that central use. Otherwise they will appear and be employed in a merely "abstract" manner, and prove unable to lead us on to an understanding beyond that connatural to us. It is that "leading" function of language, dubbed *manuductio* ["taking by the hand and leading"] by Aquinas, which analogous terms exhibit so powerfully when they are properly used. But again, their proper use will require a mode of inquiry and of life which privileges certain paradigm instances over others: "spiritual exercises," if you will.[72]

For Burrell, theoretical understanding of friendship demands a knowledge of its practice. It requires practical reason because knowledge of it occurs within a specific mode of existence, which he, referring to Pierre Hadot's work on ancient philosophy, calls "spiritual exercises." As Aristotle intimates, friendship spills over our theoretical categories because those categories are discovered within the practice of friendship. Necessarily, those categories cannot contain the experience of

71 Voegelin, *Science, Politics, and Gnosticism*, 259.
72 David Burrell, *Friendship and the Ways to Truth*, 27.

friendship. The challenge for understanding friendship theoretically is recognizing this, and in preserving the connection between the analogue and its analogate. Failure to preserve this connection leads to abstraction.

The connection, Burrell notes, is the spiritual exercises in which friends take by the hand and lead. One thinks of the form that the works on friendship considered in this book take. Aristotle's *Nicomachean Ethics* "takes by the hand and leads" because it consists of the lecture notes taken by his students. The treatise is not a textbook, but a protreptic that draws readers and students to higher possibilities in the ethical and theoretical life. Plato's dialogues, including *Lysis* and *Laws* (considered in chapters 4 to 7 of this book), also "take by the hand and lead." Each of these thinkers was keenly aware of the analogy-analogate relationship Burrell describes (though he is drawing upon their writings, and those of Augustine and Aquinas, for his insights). Examples include: philosophers seeking the Good, neighbours loving each other as images of God, Plato's imagery of human beings as idols and divine puppets that reflect God. These thinkers developed ways of symbolizing how persons, as analogues, orient themselves to the primary analogate. Therefore it is important to remember the priority they place upon practical reason over theoretical reason in understanding friendship. Theory serves practice because friendship love encompasses life, according to these thinkers.

It is for this reason that I have placed the chapters on Aristotle before those on Plato. Instead of treating these thinkers chronologically, I order them according to the intellectual, moral, and spiritual horizon in which their writings operate. Aristotle's writings operate within the common sense sphere of practical reason because the topic, politics, is inherently practical. As Carnes Lord explains: "His philosophy may on occasion involve or require 'political philosophy'; it is not identical with political philosophy. Rather, it is 'political science' in its original form – the knowledge or art proper to the statesman or legislator."[73] The purpose of Aristotle's political writings is to effect the rule of right reason, in harmony with the passions, and to effect friendship and political friendship.

Aristotelian sobriety concerning statesmanship contrasts with the philosophic mania that characterizes most Platonic dialogues.[74] If Aristotle's perspective is that of the polis, then Plato's perspective is of the polis and beyond. This is especially true of dialogues dealing with love and friendship, including the *Republic, Phaedrus, Symposium,* and the *Lysis.* Plato's

73 Lord, *Education and Culture in the Political Thought of Aristotle,* 30.

74 On this distinction, see Stanley Rosen, *The Quarrel Between Philosophy and Poetry: Studies in Ancient Thought,* xiii.

extra-political perspective still revolves around the concerns of practical reason in these dialogues, but it is not the same as Aristotle's. For where Aristotle's practical reason serves the political art of the statesman, Plato's serves the political art as it stands under the light of being, foremost where the philosopher resides. Thus we focus on the *Lysis* to consider friendship as it takes place just outside the walls of the city – as the *Republic* takes place at night during a festival for a foreign goddess, as the *Symposium* takes place in the wake of the purported destruction of the Hermes statues by Alcibiades and his friends, and as the *Phaedrus* takes place well away from the city's walls. The *Lysis* raises important questions about the nature of friendship as well as the perplexities involved in determining just what a friend and a person is. Plato's allusions to Hermes are his means of dealing with complex questions of personhood and of loving persons which, it seems, only his skilful use and refiguring of myth can address.

The Hermetic problem of reconciling things that are dissimilar, considered in chapter 4, leads us to the same problem of founding a political regime in the *Laws*, considered in chapters 5 to 7. Having lifted the veil of Platonic philosophic mania in the *Lysis*, there we move on to the effort of three elderly gentlemen, the Athenian Stranger, Kleinias, and Megillus, to constitute a city based upon reason or Nous and whose purpose is political friendship. Like Aristotle, Plato does not simply describe their effort: the performance of the dialogue is itself an effort to effect the rule of reason. In walking us to the cave where Zeus was born and guarded by corybantic dancers, the dialogue details the birth pangs of Nous, whose rule is the precondition for both political justice and political friendship. It is a Hermetic song (*nomos*) that echoes the *Lysis*.

Thus the argument of this book moves from our common sense experience of friendship to more fundamental considerations concerning the nature of the world that makes friendship even a possibility.

Churchill's best friend, F.E. Smith (Lord Birkenhead) gave him a copy of the *Nicomachean Ethics*, "the greatest book" ever written. Churchill appreciated it but remarked that "it is extraordinary how much of it I had already thought out for myself."[75] Harry Jaffa remarks that this is the very point of Aristotle's practical political science: "it is the very genius of Aristotle – as it is of every great teacher – to make you think he is uncovering your own thought in his."[76] Given Churchill's recognition of the

75 Lord Birkenhead, *Contemporary Personalities*, 115.

76 Harry Jaffa, "Aristotle and the Higher Good," *New York Times*, 1 July 2011, http://www.nytimes.com/2011/07/03/books/review/book-review-aristotles-nicomachean-ethics.html?pagewanted=all&_r=0.

shared daimonism of Marlborough and Eugene, perhaps he also would have said the same thing had he read Plato's *Lysis* and *Laws*.[77] Indeed he seemed to have lived that daimonism. Whether it is the horizon of practical reason in Aristotle, or the more daimonic horizon of Plato, their reflections on friendship foreground the phenomena of virtue-friendship and political friendship among reflective statesmen and citizens. For both, that horizon constitutes, and is constituted by, friendship. Friendship is the form of politics.

77 He read the *Republic* during his youthful anti-religious phase. He explains that it represented the succinct "crystallization of much that I have for some time reluctantly believed" (*My Early Life*, 115).

PART ONE

Aristotle and the Horizon of Common Sense

2

Sunaisthetic Friendship: The "Most Intense and Best" Love

VIRTUE-FRIENDSHIP AND THE PRIORITY OF PRACTICE OVER THEORY

Aristotle described political science (*politike episteme*) as the most architectonic (*magista architektonikos*) of the human sciences because he thought human beings achieve the full activation of their moral faculties by living in the polis (*NE* 1094a30). Yet politics depends on pre-political human relationships: not only to sustain it, but also to restrain the claims politics places on individuals, and perhaps ultimately to define, indirectly, the very purpose of politics. Curiously, Aristotle seems to simultaneously claim that politics and the *polis* form the horizon of our moral lives, and point to moral practices that transcend politics, including friendship. In the concluding books of the *Nicomachean Ethics,* he holds friendship to be superior to political justice, and contemplation or *theoria* to be the highest and "most divine [*theiotatōn*]" human activity. In the practice of complete friendship, one sees the fruition of Aristotle's claim in the *Metaphysics* that thought "seems to be the most divine [*theiotatōn*] of phenomena."[1] This chapter examines why virtue-friendship has this character, or, as he puts the matter elsewhere: "the loving and the friendship among these [good] people is the most intense and best [*màlista kaì arı́ste*]" (*NE* 1156b25). For Aristotle, the sharing of intellects in both speculative and practical concerns, for the purpose of striving for the most complete wisdom and virtue, is the highest expression of friendship as well as human possibility. It also seems to be the most satisfying. We can see this in the way that Aristotle constructs the argument of the *Nicomachean Ethics,* in which his treatment of the virtues ascends to a

1 *The Complete Works of Aristotle,* 1074b16–17.

heightened sense of unity with friendship at its crest. Indeed, one might speak of *sunaisthesis* as the "crest of the crest" because it expresses the fully functioning life dedicated to virtue, completed in friendship with others.[2]

The practice of virtue-friendship in society serves as the anchor for moral life within a polis. This does not mean that friendship of this excellence and intensity characterizes the basic bonds of political friendship. For Aristotle, this was Plato's apparent mistake in equating virtue-friendship with the polis (*Politics* 1261a10–1262a25). However, a more considered view suggests that Aristotle, like Plato, models political friendship upon virtue-friendship (*Politics* 1280b38–9). Their primary difference seems to be one of emphasis, with Aristotle giving greater weight to political friendship as a composite good that includes concerns for necessary and useful goods, as well as the beautiful ones to which virtue-friendship aspires.

Even so, citizens lacking experience in virtue-friendship have stunted moral characters, and thereby fall short in their capacity to leaven their lower-order friendships, including their civic ties, with the higher goods of virtue-friendship. Citizens and statesmen require habituation in virtue-friendship to leaven their other relations – including lower-order friendships of utility and pleasure – thereby humanizing and "perfecting" them. This is the import of Aristotle's claim that only virtue-friendship can consistently lay claim to being called friendship. Virtue-friendships leaven those other friendships because the former are more satisfying, though more difficult to create and sustain. Our experience in higher things, those more humanly rewarding goods, helps us put more energy into seeking those goods and to remember them when dealing with lower-order goods. For instance, it is good to recall the deep sense of another's loving presence when we engage in an economic transaction, even when we are not seeking the loving presence of the particular person in that transaction. It is important to remember that the clerk selling us groceries is a person endowed with a soul, with a host of longings and desires not unlike our own. The circumstances of the economic transaction perhaps do not oblige us or give us the opportunity to befriend the person, except in a utilitarian manner. But our experience and memory of what virtue-friendship consists in reminds us that we engage that person in a manner that is not simply utilitarian, even when the purpose of

2 In "Phenomenology of Friendship," Robert Sokolowski demonstrates that the *Nicomachean Ethics* should be read as a series of three ascending "crests" of virtue, including magnanimity, justice, and then friendship. April Flakne demonstrates why his *sunaisthesis* teaching should be placed at the "crest of the crest" ("Embodied and Embedded" 38).

our transaction is utilitarian. We seek our advantage from that person, but our desire for both of us to obtain what is advantageous depends upon the respect we have for their personhood and dignity.

This chapter focuses on *sunaisthesis,* the intellectual dimension of virtue friendship. Without ruling out the emotions and the life of the passions, this focus enables us to see most clearly the manner in which one human psyche is conjoined with another in the most complete and intimate manner. By examining the intellectual act at the root of virtue-friendship, we are able to see the practice of friendship from the "inside," as it were – just as in the next chapter we shall see political friendship, understood as festivity, from the inside, that is, from the perspective of the citizen. Sunaisthetic friendship seems to be the precondition as well as the culmination of the process by which humans join together in love and conversation. It is the precondition because, without intellectual communion, the passions lack any guidance toward their fulfillment. It is the culmination because Aristotle argues that the most fully formed souls are those who most fully engage their intellects as well as their passions in the love of friendship; though they are never so fully formed as to be self-sufficient, they are most dedicated to the life of virtue. Friendship is not only a specific virtue (*NE* 1126b10–1127a10); it is the entirety of virtue (*NE* 1155a1–5).

The intellectual and emotional habits that get cultivated in sunaisthetic friendship have an effect on our experience of political friendship, which will be elaborated in the next chapter. And, as the purest exercise of the intellect with another, sunaisthetic friendship helps cultivate practical reason in our lives as citizens, as shown in the next chapter on the *Politics* and the *Poetics,* as well as in chapters 5 to 7 on Plato's *Laws.*

Sunaisthetic friendship informs political friendship in numerous ways. The most common formulation is that a good political society is based upon the rule of law, and dedicates itself to seeking the common good through active deliberation about the good life.[3] V. Bradley Lewis contends that Aristotle has in mind a threefold definition of the common good: "first, it is a common good in that it is the good for all human beings qua human beings; second, it is common in that it is the good of all of the citizens in an aggregative sense; third, it is a common good because *eudaimonia* cannot be achieved in isolation. The city is the community

3 See Aristotle, *Politics,* 1253a7–18. Thomas W. Smith provides a helpful explanation of the relationship between friendship practices and the common good ("Aristotle on the Limits for and Conditions of the Common Good"). He demonstrates how, for Aristotle, the common good is enhanced by emphasizing "noetic goods and activities that do not diminish in the sharing" (633). This chapter clarifies how this can be done.

that provides all it requires."[4] More specifically, the common good can only be achieved in a good regime, the topic of Aristotle's analysis in *Politics* VII and VIII, which I shall discuss in the next chapter.

Deliberation over the just and the advantageous, an act of practical wisdom, is frequently seen as the characteristic activity of political friendship. It is a function of our natural "*logos*-sociality," whose exercise conduces to the full (or nearly full) activation of our intellectual and moral capacities.[5] Even so, I think there is a deeper – though perhaps more "idealistic" – form in which political society expresses political friendship. Indeed, as we saw in chapter 1, deliberation over the just and advantageous presupposes a prior *homonoia* concerning the ends of life upon which the common good is predicated. Those ends of life are contested in factional debate and deliberation, but a shared dedication to their contestation is prior.

Festivity is the political or civic version of sunaisthetic friendship, and the clearest expression of the common good.[6] This view of the common good is deeper than those that characterize it as common deliberation, because it assumes a higher form of political prudence on the part of citizens than when they are deliberating with one another. Citizens typically deliberate as partisans of a faction, which is why the rule of law is necessary; it reminds them of the presence of the common good by defeating factional claims, primarily those of the wealthy and of the many.[7] While

4 Lewis, "Aristotle, the Common Good, and Us," 76. However, the centrality of speech to the common good does not necessarily equate with "civic republicanism" or "participatory democracy": "this does not mean that political activity as such is necessary for the *eudaimonia* of particular persons" (76). Lewis's article is especially helpful in suggesting the ways Plato's *Laws* informs Aristotle's understanding of the common good. However, I (and Lewis) would agree with Carnes Lord's caution regarding reading Aristotle through Plato: "Interpreting Platonic dialogues is no less hazardous than interpreting Aristotelian treatises, and is arguably much more so if one takes into account their literary character and purpose. Any interpretation of an Aristotelian text that presupposes a specific interpretation of Plato – or prejudges Aristotle's relationship to Plato – must therefore remain radically hypothetical" (*Education and Culture in the Political Thought of Aristotle*, 28).

5 On "logos-sociality," see Kevin Cherry and E.A. Goerner, "Does Aristotle's Polis Exist by Nature?," 581. On active deliberation and the common good, see Aristotle, *Politics*, 1253a2, and Mary Keys, *Aquinas, Aristotle, and the Promise of the Common Good*, 77 and 85. As Lewis argues: "It is thus no accident that philosophy arose around the same time that the city arose as a political form" ("Aristotle, the Common Good, and Us," 72).

6 See also Josef Pieper, *In Tune With the World: A Theory of Festivity*, and Johannes Huizinga, *Homo Ludens: A Study of the Play Element in Culture*.

7 Lewis demonstrates that this is most true for the regime called "polity" or the "generic regime." He explains that rule of law "is a kind of negation in which the exclusive claims of the few rich and the many poor are defeated by being opposed to one another" ("Aristotle, the Common Good, and Us," 81–2).

deliberation takes place in "normal" time, festivity takes place in special time, the time when the regime comes together with and before itself, and where citizens express the essential character of the regime, over and above its factions. Festivity is political friendship appearing in its own name, the normally silent precondition of deliberation. Festivity also takes place with a higher degree of freedom because it is a form of play, and as such it transcends (however momentarily) the realm of necessity in which politics is normally so deeply embedded. The unity and free play of festivity can be seen as the highest and rarest form of political friendship in a good regime, and one that mimics sunaisthetic friendship.

Sunaisthetic friendship is the purest form of friendship among individuals. It seems to be what other forms of friendship aspire to. Although it is rare, its rarity is evidence for the standard it sets for other forms of friendship. So too do festivals serve as the standard of political friendship, for festivals are when the polis comes together to itself, and rises above its factions. This is why Aristotle quotes Odysseus's remark about how free people understand the good life: "And elsewhere Odysseus says that this is the best pastime, when human beings are enjoying good cheer and 'the banqueters seated in order throughout the hall listen to a singer'" (*Politics* 1338a28–30, quoting *Odyssey* 9.5–6). Political societies rarely achieve this level of unity in play, but that is not a compelling reason to reject festivity as the form and standard of political friendship. Rather, it prompts us to consider the ways in which political societies aspire to that standard in rare moments, including celebrations of their foundings and other key holidays.

Finally, virtue-friendship is a practice that seems to be the standard of the good life. Understanding that practice is difficult because our intellectual categories will always fall short of capturing its complexity. Practice is prior to theory in this case, and theory needs to recognize its own limitations. We shall see the ways that Aristotle's own exposition of virtue-friendship in the *Nicomachean Ethics* and the *Eudemian Ethics* falls short of its subject-matter. Even so, in recognizing the priority of practice to theory, we bear in mind that our theoretical exposition of friendship comes from within the practice of friendship. We paradoxically need the experience of friendship in order to understand it, just as for Aristotle we need experience of the good in order to seek it. Virtue-friendship therefore forms our intellectual and moral horizon, which means that we cannot stand outside of it to understand it. Because our understanding is predicated on our practice, our practice is predicated on our understanding. The exposition of virtue-friendship, especially this sunaisthetic friendship, will necessarily be paradoxical and incomplete. Reality is perceived by insight, and insight is itself rooted in real movements of the human soul, as we saw earlier in Voegelin's description of the theophanies that made philosophy possible.[8] *Philia* is an existential virtue that both precedes philosophical inquiry, and, as we shall see, expresses the *telos* of human agency. Friendship both enables and is the end of human action.

SUNAISTHETIC FRIENDSHIP

Aristotle discusses the sunaisthetic nature of the intellect near the end of his discussion of friendship in Book IX of the *Nicomachean Ethics.* It must be emphasized that though his focus (and ours) is on the intellectual act, included within this act is the full engagement of the emotions and the activation of their corresponding moral virtues that orient the soul toward friendship. Nothing in his discussion rules out the characteristic emotional or bodily modes of friendship, including love, of course, but also care, patience, solicitude, and self-sacrifice. His discussion of virtue-friendship is the apex of his teaching on virtue, and contains the discussion of virtue that precedes it. Thus virtue-friendship presupposes the presence of such virtues as moderation, courage, justice, and practical wisdom, along with the others Aristotle discusses. His account of *sunaisthesis* describes the "most intense and best" form of love under the light of reason, as well as – though he would not use this term – the most intimate (*NE* 1156b25). Indeed, for Aristotle it is the light of reason that makes it more intense than even the most intense erotic love. This point is perhaps difficult for we moderns to understand, for we prize bodily intimacy over psychological intimacy, and romance over friendship, which inhibits our receptivity to Aristotle's teaching on virtue-friendship. Indeed, this inability helps explain a good amount of modern isolation and related pathologies, and it is related to the view, common among moderns, that reason is reflective only: instrumental, discursive, or constructive, and thus privative. An example from Jean-Jacques Rousseau illustrates the modern perspective:

> Reason is what engenders egocentrism and reflection strengthens it. Reason is what turns man in upon himself. Reason is what separates him from all that troubles him and afflicts him. Philosophy is what isolates him and what moves him to say in secret, at the sight of a suffering man, "Perish if you will; I am safe and sound." No longer can anything but danger to the entire society trouble the tranquil slumber of the philosopher and yank him from his bed. His fellow man

8 Eric Voegelin, *Science, Politics, and Gnosticism,* 259.

can be killed with impunity underneath his window. He has merely to place his hands over his ears and argue with himself a little in order to prevent nature, which rebels within him, from identifying him with the man being assassinated.[9]

Conversely, Aristotle explains that human existence also involves being conscious of our existence and finding it pleasant. Moreover, "living in its governing sense appears to be perceiving and thinking" (*NE* 1170a20, 1170b1). Our existence, then, necessarily incorporates self-consciousness, and our self-consciousness also comes from the consciousness we have of others and their consciousness of us. It follows that we would practise friendship:

> But one's being is choiceworthy on account of the awareness of oneself as being good, and such an awareness is pleasant in itself. Therefore one also ought to share in a friend's awareness that he *is* [or, share his friend's consciousness of his existence – *sunaisthanesthai hoti estin*], and this would come through living together and sharing conversation and thinking; for this would seem to be what living together means in the case of human beings. (*NE* 1170b10–12)

Aristotle's statement concludes a series of observations about human being-at-work (*energeia*) which forms his general argument that the exercise of reason is also the exercise of friendship, since the intellect is the means by which one soul expands and joins with another.

Aristotle frequently pairs perceiving and thinking as the constituent elements of human action, including in the argument leading up to the key passage on friendship quoted above.[10] Living among things that are good and pleasant in themselves fosters the full activation of the human soul. Being alive is pleasant in itself, and it follows that we are aware of our being alive. Moreover, we are also aware that we are aware of being alive. It follows from our being aware of our awareness that we wish to share in awareness, or joint perception (which is a more literal translation of *sunaisthesis*), with our friend. Our being aware of our own existence implies a desire to share that consciousness with another, because it is the very nature of the intellect to seek identity with its object. As Aristotle claims in the *Metaphysics*, "thought thinks itself because it shares the nature of the object of thought; for it becomes an object of thought in coming into contact with and thinking its objects, so that thought and

9 Jean-Jacques Rousseau, *Discourse on the Origin and Foundations of Inequality Among Men*, 54–5.

10 See *Eudemian Ethics* 1244b24–66 and *Metaphysics* 1072b17 in *The Complete Works of Aristotle*; and *On the Soul* 427a20–427b18.

object of thought are the same" (1072b20–1).[11] In other words, the essential act of one's intellect is to conjoin with that of our friend. Aristotle's description is complex but the phenomenon is well known to us. Our delight in beholding a beautiful painting or mountain scene is enhanced by, indeed inseparable from, our beholding it together with our friend. We seem to understand the vision better when we share it with our friend, for he confirms its beauty for us. Its beauty is also inseparable from the delight we take in seeing it jointly with him. The intellectual vision is triangular, as it were, with two friends beholding the good while beholding one another beholding the good.

So much more beautiful (and complex) is our intellectual vision of the virtues of our friend. April Flakne describes *sunaisthesis,* the peak of Aristotle's teaching on friendship (which itself serves as the peak of his teaching on ethics), as "an experiential event of codetermination of life experienced as a whole."[12] In *sunaisthesis*, the *ēthos* of each friend is beheld as a distinct but inseparable part of the *ēthos* of the other. A note of caution is needed, however. In the highest kind of friendship our intellects are fully activated and determined, which rules out any possibility that one becomes absorbed into the self or soul of one's friend. Thus, Aristotle would probably have dismissed Montaigne's assertion about his friendship with La Boétie that "our souls mingle and blend with each other so completely that they efface the seam that joined them, and cannot find it again."[13] In perfecting our *ēthos*, our *ēthos* becomes determinate and thus individuated, yet still conjoined in friendship. Indeed, the act of "joining" depends on there being a plurality of determinate individuals. One must have a sense of oneself in order to give of oneself (see *Politics* 1263b5).

Central to the way Aristotle links friendship to the exercise of the intellect is that in seeking to know, we also seek to be known. Human beings are incomplete, and knowing reality also means knowing ourselves within reality. Our incompleteness prevents us from fully understanding ourselves because we only see ourselves from the inside, as it were. Friends enable us to see ourselves from the outside. Aristotle describes the link between friendship and thought more directly in the *Eudemian Ethics*, where he states that life, crowned by friendship, is "perception [*sunaisthesis*] and knowledge in common [*sungnosis*]."[14] The full quotation is worth reading:

11 See also Aryeh Kosman, "Metaphysics Λ 9: Divine Thought," 309.

12 Flakne, "Embodied and Embedded," 50.

13 Montaigne, "Of Friendship," 139.

14 Aristotle, *Eudemian Ethics* 1244b25, in *The Complete Works of Aristotle.*

> Since the known and the perceived are [in the class of the desirable], generally speaking, by virtue of participation in a determinate nature, one's desire that one perceive is thus the desire that one should be of a determinate nature. But since we are not each of these things by virtue of ourselves alone, but only by participating in such natures in the acts of perceiving and knowing – for one who perceives becomes what is perceived in respect of and to the degree that he perceives and according to the way and the object he perceives, and so the knower the known – it is therefore because of this that one desires always to live, because one desires always to know, and this is because one desires to be oneself that which is known.[15]

Aristotle, who is usually more lucid, here grapples with the paradoxical nature of *sunaisthesis.* It is simply impossible to describe in a straightforward manner an intellectual act of such complexity, in which the thinking subject simultaneously beholds the good, beholds the friend, and beholds oneself and one's friend beholding the good. Such an intellectual act resists a straightforward description in terms of intentional objects. Trying to give one is comparable to drawing the image of a three-dimensional object on a two-dimensional piece of paper. This passage strains against the treatise and lecture forms of communication and perhaps indicates why Plato chose to write dialogues instead. *Sunaisthesis* bursts open the categories of subject-object for which the philosophical treatise is designed. Even so, Aristotle's point is that the activity of the intellect is to know the object as well as to be known. The intellect necessarily proceeds from itself to know itself. Unlike God who is self-sufficient, the human intellect necessarily proceeds to another, the second self, who, in knowing the first self, completes the act of the first self's intellect.

Aristotle uses the term *sunaisthesis* (as well as *sungnosis*) to describe the common perception and way of knowing that friends undertake. *Sunaisthesis* is an uncommon term. *Aisthesis* means both sensory and intellectual perception, where the latter is further subdivided into the perception of the "ultimate particular" (*eschaton*) in practical judgment, and the perception of noetic insight (*NE* 1142a22–30).[16] Aristotle compares intellectual perception to our perception that a triangle is the last figure

15 Aristotle, *Eudemian Ethics* 1245a1–11, in *The Complete Works of Aristotle,* as translated by Kosman, whose translation of this difficult passage is more lucid than that of Barnes ("Metaphysics Λ 9," 310).

16 "Noetic" is the adjectival form of "Nous," Aristotle's term that usually gets translated as "mind" or "intelligence." He speaks of Nous as (1) one's individual intellect, and (2) the active intelligence that animates all of reality, and in which our individual souls participate.

a polygon can be divided into: we apprehend its essence in a glance, and not by further reflection (*NE* 1142a28–30). The two forms of intellectual perception are normally kept distinct, but Aristotle admits that the same power takes in both ultimate particulars and first principles (*NE* 1143a28–1143b10). Moreover, the meaning of *aisthesis* includes the consciousness of ourselves as perceiving, so that we perceive ourselves perceiving the triangle.[17]

Aristotle claims that a single cognitive faculty, *aisthesis* or intellectual perception, takes in both universal and particular. He does not claim that separate faculties take each in separately (with, for example, speculative reason taking in universals and practical reason taking in ultimate particulars), then somehow get unified afterward. This understanding of *aisthesis* will be important for how he understands the way intellects conjoin in *sunaisthesis*, and the way virtuous friends serve as first principles or universals in action.

In addition to the example of the triangle, Aristotle gives us a way of thinking about the act of perceiving the ultimate particular in relation to the beautiful (which is also good). He shows us how moral seeing (*aisthesis*) operates like "aesthetic" perception.[18] Acting righteously or nobly cannot be reduced to rule-following or to subjectivism. Edward A. Goerner explains the parallel between, and perhaps the identity of, practical reason's perception of the good and of the beautiful (its aesthetic dimension) with an example from art criticism. He cites Michael Brenson's description of a fragment of a jasper head of the Egyptian Queen Tiye: "The head is so complete, so thoroughly thought and worked through, that the fragment seems whole; there is a sense that even if the head were broken further [than just above the mouth] and only the chin remained or a cheek, or even a chunk of lip, the sense of completeness and resolution would not be diminished."[19] Something "fragmentary" and "incomplete," like this jasper head or the Michelangelo torso in the Vatican Museum, is nonetheless complete in its beauty. The artists who made these sculptures worked by the standards of their craft,

17 See *On the Soul*, III.2.425b11 and *Metaphysics* XII.9.1074b34 in *The Complete Works of Aristotle*, where Aristotle states that our noetic activity participates, and is grounded in, divine Nous (see Kosman, "Aristotle on the Desirability of Friends," 141).

18 See Sokolowski's use of "categorical" as a way of explaining moral seeing ("Phenomenology of Friendship," 454).

19 Goerner, "The Political Ethics of the Rule of Law Versus the Political Ethics of the Rule of the Virtuous," 572–4. He quotes Michael Brenson, "The Metropolitan Unveils its Full Egyptian Treasures," *New York Times*, 19 June 1983, http://www.nytimes.com/1983/06/19/arts/the-metropolitan-unveils-its-full-egyptian-treasures.html. A photograph of the Queen Tiye head may be found on the website of the Metropolitan Museum, https://www.metmuseum.org/toah/works-of-art/11.150.26/.

to be sure, but the beauty of their "fair balance or harmony or symmetry or even dynamically balanced asymmetry ... cannot be formulated adequately in any finite set of univocal rules but is nevertheless encompassed in a unity by structures of disciplined analogies". Perceiving a "fair balance" is both an "aesthetic" act and an act of prudent judgment.[20]

Adding the *sun-* prefix to form *sunaisthesis* was rare in antiquity. Plutarch uses it to describe the fellow-feeling Solon created in Athens with his legal reforms. However, its primary meaning in antiquity was self-consciousness without necessarily referring to another, and its meaning in late antiquity shifted to signify the interiorization of the self.[21] Even so, the term "consciousness" (Latin *conscius*) can also mean awareness of something with someone (*alicui conscius*), so that even a modern individualistic thinker like Hobbes could describe consciousness, though not friendship, as "when two or more men know of one and the same fact, they are said to be conscious of it one to another, which is as much as to know it together."[22]

That said, *sunaisthesis*, as the activity of the intellects conjointly knowing and being known, does not simply mean sharing the same opinions. Recall Aristotle's description of friendship in the *Nicomachean Ethics*: "living together and sharing conversation and thinking." Human *energeia* involves the activity of the intellect, which means *sunaisthesis* involves actively thinking with another. Sunaisthetic friendship is active, whereas merely holding the same opinion is inactive – just as friendship is active love, and goodwill is inactive love (*NE* 1157b30). This active sunaisthetic friendship provides the model for Aristotle's "action-based, associational theory" of the polis, which is "constituted not by a shared identity, but rather by a conversation and a sharing in actions and in the goods they instantiate and seek."[23]

The intellect is still in its active condition when it incorporates the form of the object known. Aristotle gives an eloquent description of the active condition of friendship, whereby friends have "their rough edges knocked off" (*apomattontai*) "by the things they like in one another" (*NE* 1172a17). *Apomasso* means "to wipe off" or "wipe clean," as well as "to take an impression of" (as sculptors do) and "to imitate." In this passage,

20 Goerner, "The Political Ethics of the rule of Law Versus the Political Ethics of the Rule of the Virtuous," 573–4.

21 Flakne, "Embodied and Embedded," 42; Kosman, "Aristotle on the Desirability of Friends," 150. Inspired by the Book of Acts, medieval Christian theologians attributed friendship and common perception to the Holy Spirit (see Augustine, *Confessions*, IV.4; for details, see my "The Luminous Path of Friendship: Augustine's Account of Friendship and Political Order," 115–38).

22 Hobbes, *Leviathan*, 48.

23 Mary Keys, *Aquinas, Aristotle, and the Promise of the Common Good*, 77, 85.

which concludes his lengthy discussion of friendship in the *Nicomachean Ethics,* Aristotle points to both meanings. Friends, in dedicating themselves to sharing prohairetic lives together, "wipe clean" each other's faults. In doing so, friends also impress upon each other the form of the other's ethos, as their respective ethos are also informed by the good. *Apomasso,* as something sculptors do, reminds us of the intellectual component of *sunaisthesis,* because joint perception of the good also entails having one's soul formed by the choices friends make with one another. Sunaisthetic friends are, in a sense, sculptors of one another's souls because friends help to determine (that is, actualize) each other's *ēthos.* Friends live together and share conversation and thinking, but they also spiritedly argue (have their rough edges knocked off), as well as imitate one another. The role of sculpting and imitation here is important for Aristotle's account of political friendship in the *Poetics,* as we shall see in chapter 3, as well as for Plato's use of the myth of choral puppets in the *Laws,* discussed in chapter 6.

Sunaisthesis forms the crown of Aristotle's teaching about friendship because it expresses friends' common activity in perception and thought. In *sunaisthesis,* friends behold one another, and themselves, beholding the good. They are fully conscious of themselves as individuals, their "other selves," and the good that informs their activity. Flakne beautifully describes this experience of joint perception:

> I catch myself in the act of perceiving; I *witness* the bloom of your actualization in the face of some object, some end, and simultaneously *feel* my own actualization, which rebounds in your enlivened perception of my perception. *This experience of seeing and feeling, the controvertability of the moment is itself sunaisthetic.* I *am* what I see; I do not have to think myself into this experience, discursively compare or analogize the physical moments of actualization. My eidetic experience is of actualization itself (yours), and I, qua actualized, am part of that *eidos.* In perceiving your *energeia* I experience the pleasure of my own activated intentionality, *energeia,* toward you.[24]

The constituent activities of the intellect are present in Flakne's summary of *sunaisthesis.* In perceiving the "other self" beholding the good as we also behold the good, *sunaisthesis* unites intellectual perception of ultimate particulars (the act of practical judgment) and of first terms (the act of noetic insight). The intellectual and moral virtues are fully activated, meaning the *energeia* (being-at-work) of each partner is fully

24 Flakne, "Embodied and Embedded," 53 (emphasis in original).

determined. Consciousness, as the power of receptivity, is determined by the friend and by each partner's participation in the good.

SUNAISTHESIS AND THOUGHT

So far, our discussion has taken for granted the passive, suffering, or pathetic (all rooted in *pathos*) character of thought, and has thereby kept implicit the manner in which friendship is the moral horizon of our lives. "Pathetic" signifies the identity of the knower and the thing known, which, for Aristotle, is made possible by the nature of the soul as the "place of forms [*topos eidon*]."[25] For Aristotle, "thinking is a way of being acted upon (for it seems to be by virtue of something common that is present in both that one thing acts and another is acted upon)."[26] A few lines later in *On the Soul*, he observes: "Knowledge, in its being-at-work [*energeia*], is the same as the thing it knows, and while knowledge in potency comes first in time in any one knower, in the whole of things it does not take precedence even in time, for all things that come into being have their being from something that is at-work-staying-itself [*entelecheia*]."[27] That which is known acts upon the intellect, which, prior to that, only "knows" potentially, like a tablet "when nothing written is present in it actively."[28] The intellect, like the tablet, is suited to receive the form of the intelligible (indicating that Aristotle's version of the blank slate emphasizes its being a *slate* rather than its blankness, which seems emphasized in modern accounts).

William O'Grady explains that the "*energeia*, the being-at-work, the fullness of being, of that which acts resides in that which is acted upon."[29] This is not to say that, for example, in knowing a tree our mind becomes a tree. Rather, the identity of knower and known is better expressed by Robert Sokolowski: "One might say that a man who knows a lot about trees is 'arboreal but not a tree', and the way he is arboreal is by having taken in 'the tree' and many of its necessities, without having become a tree. He is like *the* tree, but he is not *a* tree."[30] Sokolowski demonstrates the manner in which Aristotle's theory postulates the identity of the

25 Aristotle, *On the Soul* 429a27–8. In calling thinking "pathetic," I do not infer that spoken words are "affections [*pathemata*]" of the soul (see Robert Sokolowski, *Phenomenology of the Human Person*, 277–80).

26 *On the Soul*, 429b26.

27 Ibid., 431a1–3; see also 430a20.

28 Ibid., 429b26.

29 O'Grady, "About Human Knowing," 41.

30 Sokolowski, *Phenomenology of the Human Person*, 279.

knower and the thing known, instead of postulating that representations of the thing known get imaged in the knower's mind. Similarly, in knowing and loving our friend, we become like her, which is to say, we are also unlike her. Both likeness and unlikeness serve to individuate and unite us in a sunaisthetic harmony. Moreover, what unite us are not particular qualities, but the virtues we share and which serve as exemplars for one another. As we become "arboreal but not a tree" by perceiving a tree, so too do we become courageous but not courage by perceiving the courage of our friend: "In my experience of my friend's life as oriented toward 'courage' I will understand, in a flood of pleasurable resonance and as if for the first time, what courage has meant to me, as if 'all along.'"[31]

The final words of Flakne's comment, "as if all along," point to the centrality of recollection in *sunaisthesis*. If we perceive the *ēthos* (or form) of our friend as "courage" or "good", we see her not as an occasion of courage or good, but as courage or good personified. She is a living icon of what is eternal. Because what is eternal cannot be learned as we would learn a particular fact, we become aware of it by recollection. The nature of our friend as a perfect image reminds us of what is, and we are reminded of what courage and the good have been "as if all along" because they are eternal: they have indeed been there all along. For Plato, all knowledge is recollection (or *anamnesis*), and so one may say that "Eros comes to us as anamnesis."[32] Aristotle, more sober than Plato, generally avoids discussing eros, and as a result he restricts himself to dianoetic discourse, unlike Plato who utilizes myth to communicate these realities. Ironically, this makes Aristotle less clear when discussing these points. Even so, knowledge of first things arises when we encounter particular things that awaken the intellectual part of the soul. This is why examples are so important in Aristotle's pedagogy, and it is consistent with his view that knowledge is "pathetic." In the *Physics*, he states "that which is potentially possessed of knowledge becomes possessed by knowledge not by being moved itself but by reason of the presence of something else; for when it meets with a particular object, it knows in a manner the universal in the particular … for we are said to know and to understand when our intellect has reached a state of rest and come to a standstill."[33] The movement from ignorance to knowledge is one of "the soul's settling down out of the restlessness natural to it," which is caused by an agent external to the soul – just as the transition to sobriety, wakefulness, and health is

31 Flakne, "Embodied and Embedded," 58.

32 James M. Rhodes, *Eros, Wisdom, and Silence: Plato's Erotic Dialogues*, 497.

33 Aristotle, *Physics* 247b3–12, in *The Complete Works of Aristotle*

caused by an agent external to the body. Elsewhere, Aristotle speaks of the "whole universal that comes to rest in the soul."[34]

Thought is "pathetic" by taking in everything and identifying with what it knows. Yet, by being passive, thought is the most active of all activities. Joe Sachs refers to this paradox of passivity and activity as "an effortful holding of oneself in readiness": "Like the good reader, the contemplative knower is most active in one way (*energetikos*) just by being least active in another (*poietikos*)."[35] William O'Grady summarizes the moment of noetic insight that crystallizes all thinking:

> Aristotle's analysis singles out a special moment, the highest moment, within our experience of coming to know, what we sometimes speak of as a moment of insight, when we genuinely do come to understand what it is we are facing. It is of *this* moment that he says that we, as would-be knowers, are essentially not working but are being worked upon ... The experience of suffering, of being acted upon by the knowable things, is not said to be characteristic of all moments of our experience as would-be knowers. But I think that Aristotle means that the moment in which to know is to suffer is not merely the highest moment, but also the moment which somehow empowers and guides all the others: as the *telos* (fulfillment) of the would-be knower, it is present from the beginning, not merely as norm or proposed objective, but as effectively moving.[36]

O'Grady focuses on the moment that is accompanied by wonder, and which constitutes other forms of thought, including discursive reasoning. Wonder, of course, is the beginning of philosophy. Most of the ancient and medieval thinkers similarly viewed thinking as pathetic. For example, Plato describes the turn to wisdom, from darkness to light, as a turning around of the soul that the individual suffers (*Republic* 515e), and Aquinas distinguishes discursive reason (*ratio*) from perceptive reason (*intellectus*).[37]

The characterization of reason as pathetic, which for Aristotle is also the most active, is the opposite of the active constructivist view taken by the moderns. Kant, for instance, characterizes reason as "work." Kant criticizes "philosopher[s] of intuition," including Plato and later German romantic philosophers. Intuition produces vanity and self-satisfaction, which are, Kant sarcastically observes, "to be sure, far more inviting and splendid than the law of reason whereby one must work to acquire a

34 Aristotle, *Posterior Analytics* 100a6, in *The Complete Works of Aristotle.*
35 Sachs, "Introduction," *On the Soul and On Memory and Recollection*, 37–8.
36 O'Grady, "About Human Knowing," 41, discussing *On the Soul* III.6.
37 Josef Pieper, *Leisure: The Basis of Culture*, 9–12.

possession." However, while he faults Aristotle's philosophy for being metaphysical, Kant refers to it as work because Aristotle "analyzes all knowledge a priori into its elements, and as an artisan of reason [he] puts these elements back together from reason."[38] This suggests that Kant failed to see or ignored Aristotle's understanding of the noetic or perceptive dimension of thought. According to Joseph Pieper, Kant's (and modernity's) view that knowledge is exclusively discursive, as opposed to receptive and contemplative, is the "most momentous dogmatic assumption of Kantian epistemology."[39] Indeed, Kant's reference to reason acquiring possessions, and to artisans producing artifacts by combining elements, suggests a conflation of *techne* with *noesis,* which is the very essence of technology. As Pieper notes, *techne* is an act conducted by an isolated self, not one performed in friendship.[40]

From the Aristotelian perspective, friendship is impossible for the modern who views reason not as a beholding of the good friend, but as a mode of work to use the friend. There can be no *sunaisthesis,* no virtue-friendship, for the modern in this mode, because in this mode "reason is only what it controls or defines."[41]

The question then shifts from whether we need to "move beyond" Aristotle to make friendship relevant for the modern period. We may indeed need to move beyond him in some sense, and I have indicated some areas where this is necessary. However, before considering what moving beyond looks like (including the progressive assumptions embedded in this kind of language), we would first need to consider whether the modern instrumentalist, discursive, or technological view of reason is the whole story. The limited space of this book prevents even beginning to consider this vast question. However, recent efforts to view modern reason as meditative and "existential" (not "existentialist") shows it to be more in line with Aristotle's concerns about the practice of friendship and *sunaisthesis* explained here.[42]

Thought also wants to be known, and reality is incomplete unless understood. As incomplete beings, we seek to know reality, including the nature of our participation in it. The possibility of our knowing reality, and our place in it, depends on reality having put itself before us (and

38 Kant, "On a Newly Arisen Superior Tone in Philosophy," 56.

39 Pieper, *Leisure,* 8, citing Bernhard Jansen, *Die Geschichte der Erkenntnislehre in der neueren Philosophie,* 235.

40 Pieper, *Leisure,* 16.

41 Rhodes, *Eros, Wisdom, and Silence,* 178. The comment refers to the previously cited essay by Kant. On the "construction" of modern philosophy in general, see David Lachterman, *The Ethics of Geometry: A Genealogy of Modernity.*

42 See David Walsh, *The Modern Philosophical Revolution: The Luminosity of Existence,* and John von Heyking, "'The Sum Total of Our Relationships To Others': Kant on Friendship."

put us in it). This raises the question of foundations. For Aristotle, "thought is moved by the object of thought."[43] The activity of our intellect is predicated on the activity of Nous, the active intelligence animating reality, which Aristotle refers to as god.[44] Even so, this foundation is perceived in the structure of perception and thinking: sense perception and discursive reasoning rest upon a foundation of contemplative thinking, and the activity of the intellect is embedded in sensory experience.[45] O'Grady provides a familiar example when we are affected by the sensible form (*aisthēton eidos*) of an oak tree: "There is an intelligible form residing in the sensible form, and in some wholly mysterious way that sensible form can *give way* to the intelligible form, can allow the intelligible form *to shine through* it, so that we are made to understand not just what it is to be *this* oak tree, but rather what it is to be oak tree simply."[46] O'Grady's observation that the sensory form allows the intelligible form "to shine through it" recalls Aristotle's observation that we behold the "bloom of well-being in people who are at the peak of their powers" (NE 1174b34), and that this is an aspect of *sunaisthesis*.[47] It also recalls the Greek experience of knowledge, which Karl Kerényi calls "radiance," and which I consider further in chapter 6. These statements remind us that an act of intellectual perception, of which *sunaisthesis* is a kind, reveals all the different strata of reality that issue from the divine ground (Nous).

Similarly, a statement at the beginning of the *Nicomachean Ethics* encapsulates Aristotle's understanding of human action as participating in all strata of reality, and of how the ground of reality makes itself known in the course of action. Action can only be intelligible if it is for a purpose. Acting for no purpose, or for a sequence of purposes that goes back *ad infinitum* (which also amounts to no purpose), is unintelligible. Instead, only an act predicated on an ultimate good (*telos*) is intelligible (NE 1094a19). Voegelin's comment on this passage is pertinent:

> One should be aware that we always act as if we had an ultimate purpose in fact, as if our life made some sort of sense. I find students frequently are flabbergasted,

43 Aristotle, *Metaphysics* 1072a20, in *The Complete Works of Aristotle.*

44 Ibid., 1072b31. This also explains the limitations of Aristotle's intentional mode of describing this process, as seen above. Despite these limitations, however, Eric Voegelin demonstrates the exercise of practical wisdom in terms of the revelation of Nous in *Anamnesis: On the Theory of History and Politics*, 140–74. The act of *sunaisthesis* described in this chapter is an instance of what Voegelin describes as "*phronesis*, or political science, [as] an existential virtue; it is the movement of being, in which the divine order of the cosmos attains its truth in the human realm" (156).

45 Sachs, "Introduction," in Aristotle, *On the Soul*, 37.

46 O'Grady, "About Human Knowing," 40.

47 Flakne, "Embodied and Embedded," 53.

especially those who are agnostics, when I tell them that they all act, whether agnostics or not, as if they were immortal! Only under the assumption of immortality, of a fulfillment beyond life, is the seriousness of action intelligible that they actually put into their work and that has a fulfillment nowhere in this life however long they may live ... One shouldn't take their agnosticism too seriously, because in fact they act as if they were not agnostics![48]

Anything else other than such teleological activity is simply a "perpetual and restless desire of power after power that ceaseth only in death."[49] Acting is predicated upon a first cause just as thinking is predicated on Nous: "The object of our search is this – what is the commencement of movement in the soul? The answer is clear: as in the universe, so in the soul, it is god. For in a sense the divine element in us moves everything. The starting-point of reasoning is not reasoning, but something greater. What, then, could be greater than knowledge and intellect but god?"[50]

FRIENDSHIP AND THE PROBLEM OF KNOWING THE *ĒTHOS* OF OUR FRIEND

Friendship is the expression of the human intellect whose nature it is to identify with the known. Sunaisthetic friends sculpt one another and face one another in "an effortful holding of oneself in readiness." For this reason, the perplexity or impasse of the argument that worries numerous scholars – that the virtuous man is self-sufficient and therefore needs no friends – is only apparent.[51] Similarly, Aristotle suggests that love is expressed through gift-giving, and, in demonstrating why love is superior to honour, he describes love in terms of gift-giving, with a benefactor and a beneficiary (*NE* IX.7–9). The logic of his analogy seems to suggest that even virtue-friends end up competing with one another to see who is the superior benefactor. In this light, the political analogy would be the emperor, the prime political example of the self-sufficient human being. Similarly, the prime example of the self-sufficient human being, strictly speaking, would be the wise sage.

48 Voegelin, "In Search of the Ground," 227–8.

49 Hobbes, *Leviathan*, 70. Hobbes seems partially to acknowledge this Aristotelian point when he says, a few lines before the one quoted, that man desires "to assure for ever, the way of his future desire."

50 Aristotle, *Eudemian Ethics* 1248a25–9, in *The Complete Works of Aristotle*.

51 Kosman ("Desirability of Friends") and Flakne ("Embodied and Embedded") begin their analyses by addressing this impasse. My reliance on their work is evident in my citations.

The account of *sunaisthesis* provided in this chapter demonstrates how this picture of friendship misreads Aristotle. As shown in the next chapter, a polity of shared rule by citizens is superior to an empire, according to Aristotle, and the reason has something to do with his account of virtue-friends sharing in each other's "bloom [*akmaiois*] of well-being (*NE* 1174b34). They become like one another – place their "impress" upon one another – because they complement each other. Moreover, their fulfillment as human beings depends upon serving as agents of each other's self-consciousness, which, as demonstrated above, cannot be achieved in isolation. Human beings are always of necessity incomplete. In mirroring one another, friends refract the good through and toward one another.

However, we confront another impasse in our effort to think through politics and foundations by linking friendship with thought and perception. We can perceive the intellectual form of the oak tree in its sensible form, but perceiving the intellectual form or *ēthos* of the human being in *its* sensible form is more problematic. Aristotle raises this problem near the beginning of the *Nicomachean Ethics* when he cites Solon's claim that a human being cannot be said to be happy until he is dead – that is, free from misfortune (1100a10–20). Behind this saying lies a deeper problem for the entirety of Aristotelian ethics: when is a life complete, such that we can say it is happy? At stake is the coherence of the moral life itself. If the soul is said not to have its own characteristic being-at-work (*energeia*), not to have its own inherent and indelible activity, then there can be no genuine moral life, but only customs.[52] The problem with identifying sunaisthetic friendship as the highest human activity is that, at any given time, we have only partial understanding of the human form – that of ourselves and that of our friends. Our intellectual perception of a friend's *ēthos* would seem to resemble a conjecture or guess more than the immediate recognition that, as noted above, a triangle is the last figure a polygon can be divided into (*NE* 1142a28–30). Our practical judgment of a friend's *ēthos* would have to be more tentative and provisional, since human beings lack a facility for knowing how a life will turn out. This is one of the main reasons that Aristotle thinks we can only have a few virtue-friends. As this chapter shows, knowing our friends is extremely difficult and takes a lot of time spent together. As mortals, we only have so much time and energy to practise friendship. We also know that we are unhappy if we lack such friends, as risky as entering

52 Sachs, "Introduction," in Aristotle, *Nicomachean Ethics*, xvi. Alternatively, one can follow the Christian Aristotelian, St Thomas Aquinas, in identifying the completion of human happiness in the vision of God after death.

deep friendships is. We long to be uplifted by the mysterious person who is our friend, and by the human goods that uplift us both in our lives spent together. We are discontent possessing many acquaintances whom we can only know superficially, literally, as their surface masks. We are discontent in activities that fail to call forth moral goods that make our lives worth living.

Fortunately, Aristotle addresses the puzzle of how we can know the *ēthos* of our friends. After mentioning *sunaisthesis* in Book IX of the *Nicomachean Ethics*, Aristotle discusses the number of friends one should have (1170b20–1171b20). That number consists of the number of people whose *ēthos* one can finally know. Given the impasse we just noted, Aristotle here seems to be saying that one can only know the *ēthos* of a few friends over the course of one's life. The *ēthos* of a friend might appear in "an experiential event of codetermination of life experienced as a whole."[53] This would be friendship's equivalent to beholding balance in the fragmentary head of Queen Tiye or torso of David. We seem capable of seeing a whole within a fragment.[54] Alternatively, a friend's *ēthos* could appear serially over the course of her life, and that form is not something static but the development of a moral life in action. Her *ēthos* would take the shape of a narrative, story, or myth, in which the plot (*muthos*) unfolds over the course of time.

Aristotle's observation that we should have only a few friends is rooted in the fact that our perception of our friend's *ēthos* must take place over the course of our lives. The two modes of *sunaisthesis* – a single event of codetermination and a lifetime story or *muthos* – are not mutually exclusive, but most of us are more likely to experience *sunaisthesis* in the latter mode. Characterizing *sunaisthesis* as a lifetime shared together, of sculpting one another or knocking off each other's rough edges, indicates the essentially educative character of friendship (*NE* 1172a17).[55] The exercise of reading and reflecting upon the *Nicomachean Ethics* can assist with this purpose. The treatise not only provides information on virtue and the good life; the structure of the argument dialectically brings the reader into a moral education over the course of reading the treatise. Its

53 Flakne, "Embodied and Embedded," 50. See John 15:13.

54 Elizabeth Telfer compares the intellectual act of "liking" a friend to that of viewing a painting: "Our reaction, like a reaction to a picture, is to a whole personality seen as a unified thing. This is why we often find it very difficult to say what it is we like about a person. Sometimes what we like is partly the way in which everything about the person seems to 'hang together' and be part of a unified style" ("Friendship," 253). For an extensive comparison of how we see the face of the person in image and in a beloved friend, see Roger Scruton, *The Face of God*, chapter 4.

55 See Salkever, "Taking Friendship Seriously."

paradoxes, puzzles, and constant refinements of our common sense understanding of the world draw us into a process of self-reflection and philosophizing that we can conduct together. Similarly, as I argue in the next chapter, Aristotle's *Poetics* demonstrates how tragedy teaches virtue and specifically political friendship through mimesis.[56] Being a spectator to tragedy is a moral education. That work shows us more directly how human life is a story, and politics is about telling stories.

CONCLUDING BY RETURNING TO THE BEGINNING

In concluding this chapter with friendship and education, the reader should not be surprised to have returned to the beginning of our inquiry, which introduced *philia* as an existential virtue that *precedes* inquiry but also concludes it. This circle recapitulates Aristotle's argument that friendship is a particular virtue, as well as, it seems, its entirety. As a particular virtue, friendship has its own set of practices and obligations. As the entirety of virtue, friendship is the moral horizon in which the other virtues operate. I have treated *sunaisthesis* as the expression of that entirety of virtue, with special focus on its intellectual component. As noted above, nothing in this argument rules out the operation of the passions in the act of friendship. However, by focusing on the intellectual component, we can see the point at which the passions and emotions aim, insofar as virtue-friendship consists of the life guided by reason. It also lets us see why virtue-friendship is the "most intense and best" form of love, because it is here that the individual soul finds greatest self-fulfillment and completion: in communion with another individual who too is dedicated to the life of virtue. They face each other in "an effortful holding of oneself in readiness." In our shared moment of insight with another, we bask together in the "bloom of well-being" and enjoy the peak of our powers.

Compared to this experience, all other experiences of ecstasy, and perhaps even transcendence, pale. It takes place in a stratum of reality far above politics, yet our daily lives, including our lives as citizens, depend on it as our bodies depend on oxygen. Our experience of this higher stratum, in freedom and in love, reminds us of that which goes beyond political necessities and obligations, and thereby moderates our expectations of political life. But it also enables us to bring a heightened sense of care to political life, because we realize that the latter creates the spaces

56 On the "protreptic" argumentative structure of the *Nicomachean Ethics*, see Thomas W. Smith, *Revaluing Ethics*.

in which virtue-friendship can flourish. The more we can leaven political life with our experiences of sunaisthetic friendship, the greater chance we have of bringing decency, justice, and political friendship to politics. We turn in the next chapter to the manner in which Aristotle conceives of the civic version of *sunaisthesis*: festivity.

3

Political Friendship as Storytelling, Practical Wisdom through Mimesis

SUNAISTHETIC FRIENDSHIP AND THE COMMON GOOD

Sunaisthetic friendship, the "crest of the crest" of Aristotle's virtue teaching, finds its political friendship counterpart in festivity, which is the focus of this chapter. Sunaisthetic friendship consists of mutual intellectual perception of the good, along with mutual perception of one another perceiving the good. Friends contemplating together in "an effortful holding of oneself in readiness" is the model for this type of friendship. Even so, the common good shared by citizens does not live up to the intensity, intimacy, and moral and intellectual standards of this practice. Political *logos*-sociality is predicated upon greater intellectual and emotional distance between citizens, as it takes the form of common and usually contentious deliberations concerning the just and the advantageous.

Even so, such contentiousness is bounded by recognition of the common good on the part of citizens. Aristotle discusses this question most directly in Books VII and VIII of the *Politics,* but in this chapter I shall argue that the *Poetics* provides a deeper account of the mutual sharing of the common good, in the common education of civic virtue through mimesis: political friendship is best expressed as festivity.[1] That we

1 According to Suzanne Stern-Gillet, "surprisingly enough, the issue of civic friendship is hardly ever broached in the *Politics*" ("Souls Great and Small: Aristotle on Self-Knowledge, Friendship, and Civic Engagement," 59–60). My argument in this chapter draws upon Carnes Lord's demonstration of the connection between the *Politics* and the *Poetics*: "Aristotle regarded music and poetry as essentially educative in a moral sense; that he did not confine their educative role to the music education of the young but extended it to the musical culture of mature men was assigned by him to a cathartic tragedy designed to reinforce moral virtue and prudence" (*Education and Culture in the Political Thought of Aristotle,* 34–5). My argument focuses on the manner in which this civic education in and into "moral virtue and prudence" endeavours to inculcate civic friendship.

should look to the *Poetics* as a text of political philosophy is not so strange.[2] Tragedies, and the civic festivals in which they took place, provide the context for the purest displays of political friendship. Oddone Longo explains the performance of tragedy in general in ancient Athens:

> The theatrical event in ancient Athens was a public event par excellence. The Athenians' dramatic performances were not conceivable as autonomous productions, in some indifferent point in time or space, but were firmly located within the framework of a civic festival, at a time specified according to the community calendar, and in a special place expressly reserved for this function ... These rituals were understood to be celebrations of the *polis* and of its ideology, and they constituted the immediate framework of the plays. The community of the plays' *spectators*, arranged in the auditorium according to tribal order (no different from what happened on the field of battle or in the burial of the war dead), was not distinct from the community of *citizens*. The dramatic spectacle was one of the rituals that deliberately aimed at maintaining social identity and reinforcing the cohesion of the group.[3]

The *Poetics*, when read in conjunction with *Politics* VII and VIII, is Aristotle's attempt to educate us in the form of political friendship characteristic of the best regime. It is here that we see the political counterpart of sunaisthetic friendship, which shows how the latter informs the civic virtues of the good regime, not only indirectly (as when citizens practise sunaisthetic friendship in their private lives), but directly and publicly. Moreover, just as my focus on the intellectual act of sunaisthetic friendship in the previous chapter did not exclude the importance of the appetites and passions in moral virtue, my discussion of civic friendship, rooted in the intellectual act of mimesis, does not undermine the importance of tragedy's education of the passions, including pity, fear, and enthusiasm.

LEISURE AND THE GOOD REGIME

Books VII and VIII of the *Politics* discuss the good regime and how it cultivates civic virtue, as well as the material conditions necessary to

2 On the relationship between *Politics* and *Poetics*, see most recently Thornton Lockwood, "Is There a *Poetics* in Aristotle's *Politics*?" (I thank the author for providing me with a pre-publication copy of this essay); Anne Hewitt, "Aristotle's *Poetics* as an Extension of His Ethical and Political Theory"; and Laurence Berns, "Aristotle's *Poetics*."

3 Longo, "The Theater of the Polis," 15–16. See also Josiah Ober and Barry Strauss, "Drama, Political Rhetoric, and the Discourse of Athenian Democracy," 237–40.

bring it about. It is the regime for which we should pray (1325b37–9, 1331b20) because of the low likelihood of finding citizens capable of achieving the degree of virtue required to dwell there, on top of securing the physical, geographic, economic, and other material factors that its realization requires. Aristotle's inquiry into the good regime is an inquiry into the best one possible given human moral and intellectual capabilities, and the conditions under which it could be achieved. His inquiry is realistic insofar as it is based on what is possible; it is idealistic insofar as it recommends something that is unlikely to happen. The value of his intellectual exercise, however, consists in illuminating how the internal logic of existing regimes points toward the good regime as the model toward which they strive.

The main criterion of the good regime is that it is governed by, and to some extent dedicated to, the search for wisdom, or philosophy. The good regime is not ruled *directly* by philosophy, as it seems to be in Plato's *Republic*. Aristotle's criticisms of the *Republic* in the *Politics* are based on his view that it equates friendship with political justice too closely (although he shares Plato's view that friendship is the form of politics). He argues that philosophy, if it is to rule, must rule *indirectly* through various mediating practices. In Carnes Lord's view, "The best way of life for the city is not the speculative life simply but rather the closest approximation to that life which is possible on the level of politics … The activity in question – the way of life characteristic of the best regime – is the leisured enjoyment of music and poetry."[4] The prime mediating practice is not just any civic education, but the civic education conducted through mimesis in tragedy, in festivity.

Aristotle considers the capacities of regimes to dedicate themselves to leisure: not simply play or relaxation, but active leisure that is conducted for its own sake. As Lord argues, "Noble leisure is the fundamental principle of Aristotle's inquiry because, as we have learned from Book VII [of the *Politics*], it is the end of the best life."[5] One way of seeing how Aristotle viewed leisure (*schole*) as active is by contrasting it with its opposite, occupation (*ascholia*), which literally means the negation of leisure. Mary Nichols explains:

> The words usually translated as occupation and leisure are key words in Aristotle's discussion of education. Leisure is not idleness, as opposed to education; nor is it rest, relaxation, or play (*Politics* 1137b37–38a1). Rather, leisure refers to the

4 Lord, *Education and Culture*, 198.
5 Ibid., 54.

> noble activity or activities that human beings choose for their own sake and that constitute their happiness. Occupation (*ascholia*) is literally the absence of leisure. A person without leisure does not engage in his proper activity ... *Ascholia* is for the sake of leisure, as a means is for the sake of an end. It is more passive than leisure, for it is a reaction to circumstances. Leisure is the truly active human state.[6]

Latin captures the same contrast, as the word for business or occupation (*negotium*) is the negation of leisure (*otium*). Augustine takes advantage of this to ridicule the serious adults who punished him for his youthful leisure, pointing out how perverse it was that their *negotium* was more serious than his *otium*, as if something that is has less value than something that is not.[7]

Aristotle's inquiry is guided by the requirement that philosophy must rule the good regime, yet the very logic of politics requires this too. The purpose of politics is peace, and the regime that does not know what to do with peace will necessarily be warlike. A regime that knows nothing but the pursuit of necessities will only direct its energies into excelling at that pursuit, whose main expression is excellence at war. The good regime, in contrast, must dedicate itself to leisure because only leisure provides the self-sufficiency that characterizes the good regime:

> Since the end is evidently the same for human beings both in common and privately, and there must necessarily be the same defining principle for the best man and the best regime, it is evident that the virtues directed to leisure should be present; for, as has been said repeatedly, peace is the end of war, and leisure of occupation. The virtues useful with a view to leisure and pastime are both those of which the work is in leisure and those of which it is in occupation ... Now courage and endurance are required with a view to occupation; philosophy, with a view to leisure; moderation and [the virtue of] justice, at both times, and particularly when they remain at peace and are at leisure. (*Politics* 1334a12–25)

Aristotle frequently points out that most regimes dedicated to wealth and especially martial courage, because they are enslaved to necessities, are in fact not even political, because they fail to recognize peace as the purpose of politics. They cannot even conceive of what peace is, other than perhaps the cessation of war (see *Politics* 1333b5–40). They understand peace only as a negative. Thus entities normally called "cities" are

6 Nichols, *Citizens and Statesmen: A Study of Aristotle's Politics*, 152–3.

7 "The idling [*nugae*] of men is called business [*negotia*]; the idling of boys, though exactly like, is punished by those same men" (*Confessions*, 1.9).

caught in a tragic cycle of having to expand and thus act as empires because they are unpractised in leisure, and therefore in active peace:

> That the legislator should give serious attention to arranging that legislation, and particularly that connected with matters related to war, is for the sake of being at leisure and of peace, is testified to by events as well as arguments. Most cities of this sort preserve themselves at war, but once having acquired [imperial] rule they come to ruin; they lose their edge, like iron, when they remain at peace. The reason is that the legislator has not educated them to be capable of being at leisure. (*Politics* 1334a1–10)

Most cities simply cannot conceive of what peace is, and therefore do not even qualify as being political in the strict sense of the term. This ignorance leads to imperial expansion conducted as a mindless acquisition of power, either for self-glorification or out of fear or hatred of weaker peoples. Aristotle's criticisms of cities who can see no purpose to politics other than war are not dissimilar to Augustine's criticism that all empires are but large-scale piracies[8]: "For it is disgraceful not to be capable of using good things, it is still more so to be incapable of using them in leisure, but to be seen to be good [men] while occupied at war but servile when remaining at peace and being at leisure" (*Politics* 1334a36–8).

Thus, Aristotle's inquiry into the best regime centres upon how that regime best actualizes the rule of reason over the appetites and the body (*Politics* 1334b25–8): "That the legislator must, therefore, make the education of the young his object above all would be disputed by no one" (*Politics* 1337a10). The regime ruled by reason, the one dedicated to peace and leisure, is the free regime practised in the liberal arts (*Politics* 1337b1–20). It is the regime in which citizens are habituated into performing certain actions for their own sake, for the sake of friends, or for the sake of virtue. Aristotle repeats his insistence on leisure's primacy as the purpose of the good regime:

> Nature itself seeks, as has been said repeatedly, not only to be occupied in correct fashion but also to be capable of being at leisure in noble fashion. For this is the beginning point of everything – if we may speak of this once again [referring to *Politics* VII.14–15, discussed above]. If both are required, but being at leisure is more choiceworthy than occupation and more an end, what must be sought is the activity they should have in leisure. (*Politics* 1337b29–36)

8 Augustine, *City of God*, 4.4; see my *Augustine and Politics as Longing in the World*, 39–40.

The discussion of Books VII and VIII so far leads up to the last sentence of this quotation, which asks what constitutes the characteristic political action of the good regime. How does nature get completed? How is it completed in a political context? For oligarchies, the characteristic political actions are money-making and war. For honour-loving societies like Sparta, the characteristic political action is domination, and therefore, again, war.

But those regimes (meaning all historically existent regimes, including Athens) do not fail to achieve peace simply because they lack dedication to it. Rather, they cannot conceive of a political action that is characteristic of peace because they cannot conceive of an action that is free of occupation and involves, as leisure does, "pleasure, happiness, and living blessedly" (*Politics* 1338a1). Aristotle raises the possibility that play counts as such an activity, since those inferior regimes *can* understand play to some extent, although they understand it to be a form of rest from action. However, Aristotle rejects play for that very reason: play is for the sake of occupation (and war), and is therefore instrumental, while politics must be ruled by the action that is conducted for its own sake, namely leisure. Or, as Lord argues, "play is not the source of happiness because play is inseparable from occupation. Play belongs with occupation because occupation is not in itself satisfying, or because it is always concerned with future happiness or with providing the conditions of happiness and never with the enjoyment of present happiness. Occupation is the 'serious' business of life; play is a necessary and at the same time necessarily unserious refuge from its burdens."[9] Even so, I shall argue that in the contemplative mode of mimesis discussed in the *Poetics*, festive play, it is possible to identify a higher form of play that is closer to the sense of active leisure that Aristotle envisions for citizens of the best possible regime.

Aristotle seems to nominate music and festivity as the pastime (*diagoge*) of those who are free to be leisurely:

> What remains is that it is with a view to the pastime that is in leisure; and it is evidently for just this purpose that [those of earlier times] bring it in. For they arrange to have it in what they suppose to be the pastime of free persons. Hence Homer wrote thus: "but him alone it is needful to invite to the rich banquet," and then goes on to say that there are certain persons "who invite a singer, that he may bring delight to all." And elsewhere Odysseus says that this is the best pastime, when human beings are enjoying good cheer and "the banqueters seated in

9 Lord, *Education and Culture*, 55.

order throughout the hall listen to a singer." (*Politics* 1338a23–9, citing *Odyssey* 17.382–5 and 9.5–6)[10]

In this statement, Aristotle explains that music is one of several components of education promoted by "those of earlier times." The others are letters, drawing, and gymnastics. Aristotle treats all four with some detail in the remainder of Book VIII. Music is the only one of these types of education that is leisurely or free of occupation; the rest are necessary and useful insofar as they serve some economic, military, or political good. Only music transcends this.

It is noteworthy that Aristotle illustrates his point by quoting the words of Odysseus to the Phaikians. Odysseus utters these lines while enjoying the hospitality of the just city, and after hearing the song of their bard, Demodocus, who sings of his deeds. By having Odysseus say these words, Homer creates a moment of recognition between himself, the poet, and the reader/listener of the *Odyssey*. Odysseus's proclamation that there is nothing better than to listen to the singer depicts him as the singer of the deeds of human beings. There are deeds, but better that they be sung about: the deeds find their completion in the song. More than this, Homer's moment of recognition signals how the song becomes the deed itself, and, indeed, Odysseus sings his own song.

Aristotle accomplishes several things by quoting these lines. First, he asserts music as the activity of the good regime when it is at leisure. The good regime sings its deeds. Political rationality takes the form of reflecting musically upon deeds, for deeds necessarily find their completion in being reflected upon. This is not philosophical reflection, but free persons contemplating myths. Philosophy is thus mediated somehow through music, as it must be in order for reason to rule politically. Music is leisurely but it also forms the intellect, as well as the appetites and bodies, according to rational measure. Second, Aristotle does not simply accept the value that "those of earlier times" accorded to music, because they failed to give effect to the rule of reason so that their citizens could truly be leisurely to the best of their ability. Aristotle's effort in the *Politics* (and the rest of his political and ethical treatises) is to effect the rule of reason, which is the project inaugurated by his teacher Plato – a claim I elaborate in the rest of this book.[11] As I suggested in chapter 1,

10 Lord indicates that the first line quoted does not appear in any extant editions of the *Odyssey*, but appears to have followed line 382 in the version used by Aristotle (*Education and Culture*, 269n3).

11 See also Nichols, *Citizens and Statesmen*, 159; and Pangle, *Aristotle's Teaching in the Politics*, 260.

Aristotle's *Poetics* might be regarded as accepting Socrates's invitation in *Republic* X for lovers of poetry to defend poetry as pleasant and beneficial for polities and human life, which can only be done "without meter" and with reason ruling over the passions (*Republic* 607d–e).[12]

Thus it is not just any deed or any song that Aristotle counts as worthy of leisure. Indeed, his criticisms of "those of earlier times" in the earlier parts of Books VII and VIII suggest that the majority of their songs were about deeds of war. Such figures thus would have regarded musical education as unserious.[13] Yet there is an element of truth in Odysseus's comment that Aristotle wishes to tease out. He will elaborate on the musical education that citizens of the good regime should receive in the last three chapters of *Politics* VIII. Notable for our discussion is the education citizens receive specifically through mimesis in music. Music, unlike activities associated with other senses including taste and touch, imparts images of "respectable characters and noble actions":

> For in rhythms and tunes there are likenesses particularly close to the genuine natures of anger and gentleness, and further of courage and moderation and of all the things opposite to these and of the other things pertaining to character … But habituation to feel pain and enjoyment in similar things is close to being in the same condition relative to the truth. For example, if someone enjoys looking at the image of something for no other reason than the form itself, then the very study of the thing the image of which he studies must necessarily be pleasant. (1340a18–27)

Music is meant to bring about proper harmonies in the soul, whose proper perfection is found in the wise (*Politics* 1340b18). Music is a mediated form of philosophy: it is both informed by philosophy and points toward it. Its civic perfection appears to inculcate the virtues of judging not simply good harmonies and rhythms, but the latter's role in the mimesis of "respectable characters and noble actions" (see *Politics* 1340b30–1341a5). Citizens participate in music not so that they may become expert, but so that they may judge it: "Since one should share in the works for the sake of judging, on this account they should practice

12 See Sachs's observation regarding the *Poetics* as a response to this invitation of Socrates (Plato, *Republic* 308n187).

13 Lord, *Education and Culture*, 76, 80–1. Lord argues that Aristotle's treatment of musical education brings out its full "seriousness," which "those of earlier times," namely Homer and the Homeric heroes, overlooked. What they regarded as pastime (*diagoge*) is not genuine pastime, and Aristotle's innovation is to articulate and to some extent effect it – through the education of practical judgment and moral virtue.

the works when they are young, and when they become older leave off the works, and be able to judge the noble things and to enjoy in correct fashion through the learning that occurred in their youth" (*Politics* 1340b36–7). That is, they become the listeners of the bard who judge the adequacy of the bard's evocations of virtue in song. The bard's song completes the deeds of which he sings, but the song and the deeds are now completed by citizens at leisure, who judge the song and therefore their own deeds. One might say that, as the Athenian Stranger teaches in Plato's *Laws* (as described in chapters 5 to 7), Aristotle is teaching the citizens of the good regime to sing and to be their own song, to be their own *nomos*. That is the characteristic action of the good regime with which Aristotle concludes the *Politics*.

We now turn to the *Poetics* to see that characteristic action, and the way it is cultivated, in collective action. The *Poetics*, in argument and in form, displays this collective experience in education, more than it is displayed in the last two books of the *Politics*.[14] The *Poetics* presents an education through mimesis, cultivating insight among citizens and habituating them into "respectable characters and noble actions." It does so by affording citizens the interior perspectives of the characters performing such actions, in addition to the exterior perspectives of outside observers, who can see the consequences and implications of those actions even though they are largely unseen by the tragic characters themselves. This education in sympathetic understanding and objective reflection upon actions, conducted with others and in a participatory mode, is an education in civic friendship at its highest: a civic version of sunaisthetic friendship. It mimics the multi-perspectival knowing perfected in *sunaisthesis*, as analyzed in the previous chapter.

MIMESIS AND LOVING PARTICULAR FRIENDS

In *True Romance*, a 1993 movie by American filmmaker Quentin Tarantino, the character Alabama says to her friend Clarence, "Well, it's just when I see a really good movie I really like to go out and get some pie, and talk about it. It's sort of tradition. Do you like to eat pie after you've seen a good movie?" For Alabama, a movie presents an action that prompts reflection and conversation with friends. In simple terms, this is the essence of Aristotle's view of mimesis and tragedy. He famously claims: "poetry is a more philosophical and more serious thing than

14 See Lord, *Culture and Education*, chapters 3–5. Lord argues that the *Politics* is incomplete, and, crucially, we are left without a complete discussion of poetry there that would accompany Aristotle's more complete discussion of music (148).

history, since poetry speaks more of things that are universal, and history of things that are particular. It is what is universal, the sorts of things that a certain sort of person turns out to say or do as a result of what is likely or necessary, that poetry aims at" (*Poetics* 1451b5–7). This blending of the universal and particular in poetry makes it similar to practical wisdom or prudence (*phronesis*) and thus suitable to teach through mimesis. Lord explains:

> There is a striking congruence between what poetry provides and what prudence requires. Prudence is an intellectual habit or a kind of knowing which encompasses both particulars and universals. It requires both an experience of the world and a correct understanding of that experience. It requires an ability to adapt the universals of moral and political action to particulars, to the contingent circumstances of moral and political life ... On the other hand, mere experience or familiarity with the unique events of "history" is equally insufficient, though it is useful and even in some degree indispensable for political men. Only poetry, as it seems, provides the proper combination of generality and specificity that is necessary for the development of prudence in the full sense of the term.[15]

We saw in the last chapter the mimetic element of Aristotle's virtue teaching and of friendship, whereby friends, as sculptors of souls, put their impress upon one another. Mimesis is what enables poetry to teach practical wisdom or prudence.

In chapter 4 of the *Poetics*, Aristotle describes the genesis as well as the naturalness of the poetic arts for human beings. He argues that poetry has its roots in our desire to know. Specifically, the poetic arts deal with the mimetic form of knowing:

> For imitation is co-natural with human beings from childhood, and in this they differ from the other animals because they are the most imitative and produce their first acts of understanding by means of imitation; also all human beings take delight in imitations. A sign of this is what happens in our actions, for we delight in contemplating the most accurately made images of the very things that are painful for us to see ... What is responsible even for this is that understanding is the most pleasant not only for philosophers but in a similar way for everyone else, though they share in it to a short extent. (1448b3–15)

15 Lord, *Education and Culture*, 178. Lord continues by claiming that the precise way that Aristotle "may have conceived of poetry as the central instrument of an education in prudence must plainly remain a matter for speculation." The purpose of this chapter is to bring some precision, through the education to civic friendship, to Aristotle's conception.

Mimesis is a form of knowing that is especially appropriate for non-philosophers. One might say it is the characteristic form of knowing for citizens. Viewing representations excites our natural desire to know. As Michael Davis observes, "that we imitate … has to do with our uncontrollable urge to see past the surface of things."[16] Indeed, mimesis has the form of thought because, like thought, it puts "this" together with "that" so as to see this as that: "to say 'this is that' one must first think this as independent from that."[17] The gentleness of mimesis, which represents painful things in a pleasurable manner, also makes knowing more appealing for non-philosophical spectators, who would rather know than to go through the painful activity of learning (for who knows what horrors one will find?). However, this appeal is limited because imitations are not real, which suggests that the pain non-philosophers experience at seeing pitiful and fearsome things needs to be leavened by delight in their falsity.

Mimesis can include visual, verbal, and musical images, and in that sense it draws in the entire human person, including reason and emotion. For instance, Aristotle observes that tragedy "came to rest" in its form when Aeschylus made speech dominate rhythm. Its rhythm took the iambic form, which is the natural rhythm of conversation (*Poetics* 1449a10–30). Its mixture of speech and rhythm engages the whole person and helps constitute tragedy as a civic enterprise, which, as noted above, Aristotle signals at the end of the *Politics* with his discussion of musical education that prizes musical knowledge over skill (1340b35, 1341b15).

Mimesis uses images, or particular examples, to communicate universals.[18] While its reliance on images seems to implicate mimesis as an inferior form of knowing (i.e., suitable for non-philosophers), Aristotle's view is more complicated. For instance, the theory of moral action presented in the *Nicomachean Ethics* holds that moral character or ethos is best expressed through action, not speech, and best understood through practical judgment instead of the application of rules: "But at what point and for how much of a deviation one is to be blamed is not easy to determine by a formulation, for no other perceptible thing is either; such things are in the particulars, and the judgment is in the perceiving" (*NE* 1109b21–4; see also *NE* 1126b4 and chapter 2 of this work). Because

16 Davis, *The Poetry of Philosophy*, 3.

17 Davis, *The Poetry of Philosophy*, 27. See Jacob Howland, "Aristotle on Tragedy: Rediscovering the Poetics," 364.

18 Stephen Halliwell, *The Aesthetics of Mimesis: Ancient Texts and Modern Problems*, 195–8; see also Nichols, *Citizens and Statesmen*, 160; and Davis, *The Poetry of Philosophy*.

practice is prior to theory, the truth of moral action cannot be firmly established outside or prior to our experience or encounter with moral truth. Practical wisdom, as a "truth-disclosing condition" (*NE* 1140b2–8), means that we discover or even instantiate moral truth in action.

Aristotle's dialectic account of the virtues, which exercises the practical intellect's ability to make ethical judgments, culminates in examples instead of rules: "An example [*epagoge*] is in fact a source of something universal, while deductive reasoning is from things that are universal. Therefore there are sources from which deductive reasoning proceeds, of which there is no deduction, and therefore what makes them known are examples" (*NE* 1139b39–40).[19] Indeed, elsewhere he argues that being brought face-to-face with the universal in a particular is sufficient for understanding the universal.[20] As we saw in chapter 2, practical judgment is a kind of perception (*aisthesis*) aiming at an "ultimate particular" (*eschaton*) (*NE* 1142a22–30). An example can reveal the universal in a particular because an example can contain the essence of things, which is especially apparent to someone whose intellectual virtues are working together (*NE* 1142a28–9).

While moral science is inherently mimetic because it employs examples, mimesis as the representation of character and story is well suited to teach ethics because it exercises the spectator's practical judgment in a manner that moral science cannot. Michael Davis succinctly explains how the *Poetics* shows how the poetic arts serve this purpose by exercising *phronesis*: "It is the distinctive feature of human action, that whenever we choose what to do, we imagine an action for ourselves as though we were inspecting it from the outside. Intentions are nothing more than imagined actions, internalizations of the external. All action is therefore imitation of action; it is poetic."[21] Philosophers and non-philosophers alike share a reliance on examples or particulars to understand moral action.

Moreover, as Aristotle's account of mimesis shows, it is not simply about servile imitation. That we delight in imitations or representations indicates that we recognize their status as representations. Mimesis has built within it a reflective distance that exercises our practical intellects because we behold a representation of an action, we recognize that the

19 Davis observes that visualizations are to tragedy what examples are to treatises: both show whether such and such is possible (*The Poetry of Philosophy*, 86); see also *NE* 1143a25–30.

20 Aristotle, *Posterior Analytics* 71a7–9 and *Physics* 247b5–7, in *The Complete Works of Aristotle*.

21 Davis, "Introduction," in Aristotle, *On Poetics*, xvii.

characters in a tragedy face difficult choices. In fact, we are more privileged than the characters, because we see their actions from the outside and therefore have a greater sense of the options before them. As spectators we have more leisure than the characters to toy with those possibilities. Even so, we also see their actions as the characters themselves see them, because we follow them in living out their stories. Our pity for them signifies our distance from them, and our fear for them signifies our common perspective. Mimesis enables us to practise making moral choices, and to make them with someone else, including the character and, in some cases, the audience.

For example, Abraham Lincoln frequented the theater, especially to see Shakespeare, as respite from the pressures of office during the Civil War. Probably more so than today, the audiences of nineteenth-century theater were more than audiences; they were, in Lawrence Levine's words, "participants who can enter into the action on that field, who feel a sense of immediacy and at times even of control, who articulate their opinions and feelings vocally and unmistakably." Doris Kearns Goodwin agrees that Lincoln enjoyed the communal experience, "which allowed him to feel the pulse of the people."[22] Our discussion of the role of mimesis in political life suggests that we should not be surprised that the great statesman-storyteller was assassinated by a Shakespearean actor who fancied himself a new Brutus.

Mimesis enables us to befriend characters, and to exercise our abilities to live our lives as stories with others. It exercises *sunaisthesis*, the manner in which the practical intellect beholds the good while also beholding our friend beholding the good. By giving us an external view of lives lived with others, it provides us with a shorthand glance at what a whole life, lived among others, can look like. This is a perspective that individual moral actors enjoy only partially, because we only see our lives with others from within, and because we cannot see the whole of our lives until shortly before our lives end (and perhaps not even then: see *NE* 1100a10).[23] By telling stories about those we can befriend, poetic arts enhance our ability to make the highest kinds of moral judgments, as friendship is the consummation of the moral life.

22 *Team of Rivals*, 610, citing Lawrence Levine, *Highbrow/Lowbrow*, 24–6.

23 The Christian (largely Thomist) critique of Aristotelian eudaimonianism focuses on this impasse. Happiness, philosophically understood, necessitates a synoptic account of a life that for the Christian is offered by faith in eternal life. In other words, the Christian critique is based on the idea that reason leads us toward something that reason cannot itself provide.

WONDER: THE *TELOS* OF THE POETIC ARTS

Wonder is the end of the poetic arts. It not only constitutes the beginning of philosophy, but also makes the soul of the spectator receptive to philosophical wisdom and beholding the individual character of another. Like Aristotle's other treatises (including the *Nicomachean Ethics*), the *Poetics* is a protreptic work that begins with common sense understandings that are refined and qualified as the argument unfolds.[24] This means that the argument has the appearance of repetition if not circularity, as he returns to key terms for reconsideration and refinement; but this concern gives way to deepened understanding as new considerations are added and qualify what has gone on before. For Aristotle, just as science follows the form of its subject matter, mimesis follows the form of its subject matter, the moral life. In analyzing the mimesis of moral life, circularity is meant to deepen practical judgment and improve one's ability to perceive the good instantiated by another human being whom one can call a friend.

The *Poetics* contains several definitions of tragedy, with later ones refining earlier ones as Aristotle elaborates tragedy's parts to illuminate what it is as a whole. In chapter 6, he defines tragedy as "an imitation of an action of serious stature and complete, having magnitude, in language made pleasing in distinct forms in its separate parts, imitating people acting and not using narration, accomplishing by means of pity and fear the cleansing of these states of feeling" (1449b2–28). This definition lists the individual qualities of tragedy that Aristotle will expand upon. It appeals to conventional understandings by calling attention to the emotions tragedy elicits from the audience. The attention contemporary scholarship devotes to the role of *katharsis* at the expense of wonder, which in fact *katharsis* serves, is one indication of how close such scholarship is to conventional understandings, and how little it follows the protreptic treatment of the poetic arts that Aristotle provides. In this first definition Aristotle seems to indicate that *katharsis* is the end of tragedy, but this interpretation is incomplete insofar as *katharsis* merely prepares the soul for a further refinement. *Katharsis* is the means, not the end.

Aristotle's considered definition of tragedy, presented at the end of the treatise, emphasizes the nature of its end: "But this is the right thing to do if one hits the mark that is the end at which the art itself aims (for the end has been stated) that is, if in this way one makes that thing itself or some other part of the poem more awe-striking [*ekplêktikon*]" (*Poetics*

24 On the protreptic nature of the *Nicomachean Ethics*, see Smith, *Revaluing Ethics*.

1460b25). Joe Sachs emphasizes the importance that Aristotle places on *ekplêxis* as the end of the poetic arts.[25] Aristotle mentions this word or its cognates in two other places in the *Poetics*, each time to explain the effect of a discovery that a character makes (1454a4, 1455a19). The second of these instances is especially notable, because there Aristotle states that "the best discovery of all is the kind that arises out of the actions themselves, so that the awe-striking [*ekplêxis*] impact comes about from things that are likely [*to eikos*], as in the *Oedipus* of Sophocles and the *Iphigeneia*."

The "likely" (*to eikos*) and the "necessary" (*to anagkaion*) are the terms Aristotle uses to explain what the tragedy is supposed to mimic (*Poetics* 1451a39). He uses these terms in the *Physics* to explain that a likely result is what follows something else naturally and for the most part.[26] The awe that characters and spectators experience most resembles the awe that we experience when making a discovery about nature: "For tragedy is an imitation not of people but of actions and life" (*Poetics* 1450a18). In this sense, awe-inducing poetic arts are the beginning as well as the result of philosophy. Yet, as Laurence Berns notes, while poetry mimics nature in the sense of good and noble deeds, poetry creates wonder by having "the events inspiring pity and fear come into being in a way that runs counter to accepted opinion and expectation, and yet in such a way that the events come about on account of one another."[27] One might say that poetry inspires wonder by showing the actions of a great individual, and it uplifts us to see reality, especially political reality, from that individual's perspective. His tragic fall, while a natural outcome of his fatal flaw, is bewildering to us, and thereby becomes the object of wonder. It invites us to begin philosophizing: just how did we get to that higher, uplifted perspective, and what made the downfall possible?

Within the context of friendship, it is unsurprising that Aristotle should think wonder is the beginning and end of philosophy, rather than just its beginning. As shown in the previous chapter, the self-sufficient person's self-knowledge necessitates friendship, because knowing necessitates being known. Moreover, we take greater pleasure in knowing when we share that knowledge with friends,[28] which is an exuberant or superabundant, not reactive, pleasure accompanied by the

25 See Joe Sachs, "Introduction," in Aristotle, *Poetics*. See also Laurence Berns, "Aristotle's *Poetics*," 79. Medieval and Renaissance readers considered wonder to be as central to the *Poetics*, and central to their readings of tragedies. See J.V. Cunningham, *Woe or Wonder*.

26 *Physics* 198b34–6, in *The Complete Works of Aristotle*; see *Poetics* 1450b28–30.

27 Berns, "Aristotle's *Poetics*," 81.

28 *Eudemian Ethics* 1245a20, in *The Complete Works of Aristotle*.

halo or "bloom of well-being in people who are at the peak of their powers" (*NE* 1174b35).[29] Aristotle's discussion of wonder, driven by the recognitions and reversals discussed below, seems to be a way of giving citizens a taste of the exuberant good that is enjoyed preeminently by philosophers who participate in sunaisthetic friendships.

Ekplêxis is in fact an excess of wonder.[30] Sachs illustrates the literal meaning of *ekplêxis* by citing the example of Thales, the first philosopher, who fell into a well while looking at the stars: "This is a potent wonder, an experience in which the ground drops away from under one's feet." In choosing the term *ekplêxis,* Aristotle refines a Greek term as part of his protreptic. *Ekplêxis* literally means having the supports knocked out from under you. Thucydides mentions it several times, usually to describe panicked and terrified soldiers in the heat of battle.[31] Similarly, Euripides associates it with the sort of amazement that stuns one into silence.[32] In the *Philebus,* Plato associates it with the amazement resulting from ecstatic pleasure, while in the *Republic,* Socrates refuses to let foolish remarks "knock us off course."[33] These usages conform to its literal meaning, which suggests being stunned and unable to act. This state can be brought about in a multitude of ways: through violence, ecstatic pleasure, stupidity, or, as Aristotle clarifies, nature itself.

As Sachs observes, Aristotle also refines the meaning of *ekplêxis* to refer to being put in the position of "gazing at a human image with our habits of blaming and excusing blocked."[34] It makes the soul receptive to seeing and indeed loving the other, without projecting one's self-love entirely onto the other. It is the counterpart, in political friendship, of the experience of *sunaisthesis* described in the last chapter: "an effortful holding of oneself in readiness." It prepares our practical intellects for friendship. It prepares the ground for what Sokolowski calls friendship's "categorial form," and readies us for the moment, discussed in chapter 2, in which we both actively and passively allow the ethos of the friend to "shine through."

Returning to mimesis as a mode of practical reasoning, Aristotle claims that human beings "delight in seeing images for this reason because understanding and reasoning out [*sullogizesthai*] what each thing is results

29 See also Flakne, "Embodied and Embedded," 51.

30 Aristotle, *Topics* 126b15, in *The Complete Works of Aristotle.*

31 Thucydides, *The Peloponnesian War,* 2.94.1, 4.34.2, 4.55.3, 4.112.1, 4.126.1, 6.46.4, 6.70.1, 6.98.2, 7.42.3, 7.69.2, 7.70.6, 7.71.7, 8.15.1, 8.96.1.

32 Euripides, *Helen,* 548.

33 *Philebus* 47a, *Republic* 436e.

34 Sachs, "Introduction," in Aristotle, *Poetics,* 16.

when they contemplate them, for instance, 'that's who this is,' since if one happens not to have seen him before, the image will not produce pleasure as an imitation" (*Poetics* 1448b17). As Davis observes, the verb *sullogizesthai* literally means "to think together," which suggests shared observation and contemplation, and thus invites a comparison with *sunaisthesis.*[35] *Sullogizesthai* describes how characters, and therefore spectators, think through moral problems during the story. The awe that one experiences when discovering the essence of a character is expressed in the exclamation "That's who this is," and this awe results from having previous familiarity with, but incomplete understanding of, the character in question. We proclaim "That's who this is" when we discover how we have shared our life as a whole with that person, and only now recognize the significance of that person in the unfolding of our life.[36]

Statesmanship is driven by the need for these moments of recognition as well. As Tilo Schabert explains with reference to the world leaders involved in German reunification and the collapse of the Soviet Union, it is imperative for statesmen to discern the moral characters of their colleagues. They do so in mimetic terms, in the form of anecdotes about their colleagues:

> What kind of man (or woman) is he (or she)? ... Who is Reagan? Who is Gorbachev? Of course, one would like to know who they are as men, but one would especially like to know what the man Reagan or the man Gorbachev understands and says about power, abilities, influence, knowledge, ideas of culture, and experience in human things, the inner attitudes that condition his behavior (in Aristotelian terms, "virtues"). Because every human character exerts a political influence in his own way, the question is thus also to know his qualities: Imperious? Peaceful? Tolerant? Fair? Brave? Wise?[37]

Discerning another's moral character through anecdotes furnishes limited understanding compared to the sort of friendship and moral action described in the *Poetics.* However, because of various necessary constraints, the former is usually all that statesmen can afford to do. Even so, an education in Aristotelian mimesis would help cultivate that discernment and enrich the statesman's knowledge of the limitations of such anecdotes.

35 Davis's translation of Aristotle, *On Poetics,* 9n31.

36 The Hebrew Bible also testifies to this moment of recognition when Adam meets Eve: "This one at last, bone of my bones / And flesh of my flesh, / This one shall be called Woman, / For from man this one was taken" (Genesis 2:23, in Alter, *Genesis*).

37 Tilo Schabert, *How World Politics Is Made,* 26. See Heyking, "Friendship as Precondition and Consequence of Creativity in Politics," 93–4.

Aristotle's description of the awe of recognition accords with Dante's description of greeting inhabitants of the afterlife, especially those with whom he shared an earthly tie, such as fellow Florentines. As Erich Auerbach observes, souls in the afterlife exhibit who they truly are, and they are astonished, in reuniting, to discover how their stories turned out.[38] The recognition of "That's who this is" depends on recollection of the story.

Knowledge of the particular, a practical judgment, is the end of the poetic arts. It is both the end and beginning of philosophy. To describe the end of tragedy in contemporary terms (which are somewhat misleading), tragedy silences our "prejudices" at least temporarily, and puts us into the position of seeing the person, who turns out to be the friend, before us as he is. The analysis that follows demonstrates how the parts of tragedy contribute to our awe at the specific human being whose story we discover, as spectators, that we share.

CHARACTER AND *PHILANTHROPIA*

The six parts of tragedy are: story (*muthos*), character (*ethos*), wording, thinking, spectacle, and song-making (*Poetics* 1450a9–10). I will focus on story and character, and begin with character because my analysis has focused on the exercise of practical judgment with its attention to particulars. This approach somewhat reverses Aristotle's priorities insofar as action is manifested less by a particular character than by the story, as highlighted in chapter 14 of the work. The priority of story over character reflects his view that individuals are completed in the polis.[39] Even so, characters are central because their actions represent the polis and the human species.

Tragedy is about imitating men of "serious moral stature" (*Poetics* 1448a2) who are nonetheless not so great as to exhibit decency (*epieikês*) (*Poetics* 1452b34). Davis suggests that decency cannot be adequately imitated on stage.[40] The reason for this is that its attendant virtue, *epieikeia* (equity or the practical wisdom of the *phronimos* who is a law unto himself), is a form of human greatness that includes recognition of one's own moral inadequacy. The tragic protagonist, however, can only aspire to it in the form of the spurious self-understanding that leads to his downfall. But more than that, the individual with *epieikeia* recognizes the ambiguity of the moral life. He has freed himself from the demand that

38 Auerbach, *Dante: Poet of the Secular World*, 141.

39 Hewitt, "Aristotle's *Poetics* as an Extension of His Ethical and Political Theory," 16.

40 Davis, *The Philosophy of Poetry*, 71. See Howland, "Aristotle on Tragedy," 366–7.

justice and virtue will always prevail while endeavouring to have them prevail as much as possible, first in his own soul and then in the actions over which he has some control. There is something tragic to the *phronimos.* He recognizes life's imperfections, for which he must bear his own responsibility; and so he recognizes that action is prospective and subject to innumerable misfortunes, including his own ignorance. Voegelin summarizes Aristotle's insight:

> The truth of the tragedy is action itself, that is, action on the new, differentiated level of a movement in the soul that culminates in the decision [*proairesis*] of a mature, responsible man. The newly discovered humanity of the soul expands into the realm of action. Tragedy as a form is the study of the human soul in the process of making decisions, while the single tragedies construct conditions and experimental situations, in which a fully developed, self-conscious soul is forced into action.[41]

There is something of this tragic idea regarding the *spoudaios* in Leo Strauss's remark about Winston Churchill: "No less enlightening is the lesson conveyed by Churchill's failure, which is too great to be called tragedy. I mean the fact that Churchill's heroic action on behalf of human freedom against Hitler only contributed, through no fault of Churchill's, to increase the threat to freedom which is posed by Stalin or his successors. Churchill did the utmost that a man could do to counter that threat – publicly and most visibly in Greece and in Fulton, Missouri."[42]

In the preface of Lord Charnwood's biography of Abraham Lincoln, Basil Williams makes a similar statement regarding the fleetingness of glory for the statesman, as opposed to other "great" people:

> A warrior, a man of science, an artist or a poet are judged in the main by definite achievements, by the victories they have won over foreign enemies or over ignorance and prejudice, by the joy and enlightenment they have brought to the consciousness of their own and succeeding generations. For the statesman there is no such exact measure of greatness. The greater he is, the less likely is his work to be marked by decisive achievement which can be recalled by anniversaries or signalized by some outstanding event: the chief work of a great statesman rests in a gradual change of direction given to the policy of his people, still more in a change of the spirit within them … He has to do all his work in a society of which a large part cannot see his object and another large part, as far as they do see it,

41 Voegelin, *The World of the Polis*, 247.

42 Leo Strauss, "Churchill's Greatness."

oppose it. Hence his work at the best is often incomplete and he has to be satisfied with a rough average rather than with his ideal.[43]

It is hard to improve upon Williams's statement as a summation of moral action according to Aristotle.

History affords numerous examples of individuals exercising *epieikeia*, of setting aside that which is just in general to establish that which is just in particular, sparking unforeseen and oftentimes horrific consequences that the *phronimos* could not have anticipated or at least could not have prevented. One example might be Augustine's justification of using coercion against heretics, which he regarded as a special circumstance but which later gave him the unjust reputation for being the "first theorist of the Inquisition."[44] Another example might be Harry S. Truman's decision to drop atomic bombs on Hiroshima and Nagasaki. On one hand, that decision ended World War Two, and may have prevented hundreds of thousands of deaths that would have occurred in a conventional offensive against Japan. On the other hand, one can only guess as to what use future political leaders will put atomic weaponry, but we can be reasonably confident that they will use the same justification for their actions that Truman did. Augustine's and Truman's choices, whose consequences they could not foresee or control, demonstrate the fleetingness of achievement and reputation for political actors. History presents them simultaneously as great and disreputable figures.

Moral action depends on foresight, which is necessarily defective. Similarly, tragedy contains a prospective element insofar as spectators live through the protagonists' decisions and their consequences. However, tragedy is also retrospective because spectators are able to see the entirety of the action. In other words, even the *phronimos* must recognize his limitations, which the tragic protagonist, once removed from the *phronimos* and therefore more like us in the audience, learns by suffering the consequences of his ignorance. This, suggests Jacob Howland, is tragedy's point as a project of civic education:

Perhaps tragedy teaches that *phronesis* is, as it were, a regulative ideal of virtue, to which everyone must remain open but which no one can authoritatively claim to possess. Extraordinary excellence is never a sure thing, because every *phronimos* may turn out to be a spurious *phronimos*. Good citizenship would then rest upon humble openness to extraordinary virtue. Political education and philosophical

43 Williams, "Preface," in Lord Charnwood, *Abraham Lincoln*, v–vi.

44 Heyking, *Augustine and Politics as Longing in the World*, chapter 8.

> ambiguity converge in the lessons of tragedy, insofar as genuine moral responsibility paradoxically involves both a refusal to remain satisfied with what is and an acceptance of what is, the former attitude manifesting itself in the habits of individual and communal self-criticism and the latter in a willingness to bear full responsibility for one's own inevitable imperfections.[45]

The characteristic virtue that tragedy teaches, then, is a citizen's *phronesis:* one that is self-critical and communally critical, and one that teaches citizens to bear responsibility together for their choices even when they are mistaken and imperfect. The former is achieved by citizens' reflections on their own tragic flaw (*hamartia*), which they first see in the protagonist; the latter is achieved by reflecting on the way in which that tragic flaw unfolds in the plot (*muthos*). By vicariously becoming part of the plot, citizen-spectators learn the arts of self-rule and moral agency.

The most beautiful tragedies are about a few ruling households, including those of Oedipus and Orestes (*Poetics* 1453a19–20). The political identity of the characters contributes to the political aspect of tragedy. Politics adds tension to the drama, as it places greater demands on characters than private matters do. Tragedies are about decent men suffering bad fortune (*Poetics* 1452b28) and friendships turning to enmity (*Poetics* 1453a19–20). Their characters are noble, but they are not perfectly virtuous, as their bad fortunes are due to their fatal flaw. It is the hero's characteristic virtue, his best part, that undoes him, and we as spectators pity him in a special way because it forces us to recognize that we, too, can be ignorant of our own identity, and of the manner in which our excellences can lead to our downfall.[46]

Characters are to be political and decent, but not excellent or shining in the sense of the *spoudaios* described in the *Nicomachean Ethics.* This enables spectators to pity them and fear the misfortunes they suffer. That they are political reminds spectators that they share community with them (and could be ruled by them, so their actions have an impact on the lives of subjects). That they are decent but not excellent better enables spectators to see themselves in those characters, or at least to consider how they might act if they were in the same situation. The moral

45 Howland, "Aristotle on Tragedy," 397.

46 Amélie Oksenberg Rorty, "The Psychology of Aristotelian Tragedy," 11. Modern biography aspires to capture the *hamartia* of its subjects. For example, one biographer of George W. Bush characterizes his subject's vices as "cousins" of his virtues: his strengths also contribute to his flaws (Peter Grier, "An Insider Look at George W. Bush," review of *Dead Certain: The Presidency of George W. Bush,* by Robert Draper. *Christian Science Monitor,* 18 September 2007, http://www.csmonitor.com/2007/0918/p13s01-bogn.html).

proximity of spectator and character allows spectators to participate in both character and story. This proximity also enables spectators to feel for them while maintaining some reflective distance from them: "By eliciting both pity and fear, tragedy highlights the tension between these two perspectives; on the one hand, we enter into the character's perspective, and on the other hand, we are detached. We are simultaneously practical (concerned with action) and theoretical (concerned with looking or contemplating), and must be so because we are theorizing about practical matters."[47] Politically, this enables spectators to vicariously befriend characters, as one would as a sunaisthetic friend. That is, one can participate in the plot and love the character without being absorbed into either, because the spectator, in order to share, retains a distinctive sense of self. This is the fullest sense of being a spectator, a theorist, as Aristotle describes the point in the *Politics*: "Thus the many are also better judges of the works of music and of the poets; some [appreciate] a certain part, and all of them all the parts" (1281b7).

The decent character who suffers bad fortune arouses love of the human [*philanthropia*] (*Poetics* 1452b35, 1456a21).[48] Aristotle's choice of the word *philanthropia* reveals a complex psychology underlying the political education of the *Poetics*. First, in perceiving and contemplating a character, the audience proclaims, "That's who this is" (1448b18), which expresses knowledge of a specific person. We learn to love that specific character as we learn to love a friend. However, that preferential love is leavened by the recognition that we share a common world with that character, a tragic world where achievements, as noted above, are worthwhile for us to pursue but fleeting. This sharing of a common world explains why tragedy aims at cultivating *philanthropia* and not specific people or Athenians.

Philanthropia for Aristotle is, of course, not love for an abstract "humanity" that reveals itself at the end of history. The awe we experience at *philanthropia* differs in kind from the expansive, bedazzled sentiments about "humanity" that Victor Hugo sings about in his *La Légende des siècles*:

It is joy; it is peace; humanity
Has found its immense voice;
It sails, sacred usurper, blessed conqueror.
Each day backing further into infinity
The somber point where man begins.

47 Davis, *The Poetry of Philosophy*, 41.

48 Davis translates *philanthropia* as "kinship with the human," which has the advantage of signifying the species-love, rooted in reason, that *philanthropia* conveys.

Making with heaven one city for man,
One great immense thought,
It abolishes the old rules;
It abases mountains, sunders towers;

Its divine and chaste task is
To make up above the one and only nation,
Both the last and the first,
To wave the banner in all its radiance
And to make liberty bathe in the light,
High on heaven above.[49]

Hugo holds "humanity" up as a universal and thereby abolishes intermediaries and particular human beings. There is no friend here.

Rather, as William Arrowsmith observes, we witness in Aristotle's notion of *philanthropia* "the great concrete shadow-play of the species itself," as when the Chorus in *Oedipus the King* sings of human transience:

Man after man after man
O mortal generations
Here once
Almost not here
What are we
Dust ghost images a rustling of air …
We are you
We are you Oedipus
Dragging your maimed foot
In agony
And now that I see your life finally revealed
Your life fused with the god.[50]

Aristotle's understanding of *philanthropia* sees that "We are you Oedipus." The universal is in the particular person, to whom we can relate sympathetically, concretely, and even as a friend.

For Aristotle, *philanthropia* involves the kinship toward members of the species that one feels when one has extensive experience of the species. This is the meaning he gives the term in the *Nicomachean Ethics:* "Friendship seems to be present by nature in a parent for a child and in a child for a parent, not only in human beings but also in birds and most

49 As translated in Pierre Manent, *A World Beyond Politics?* 124.

50 Arrowsmith, "Editor's Foreword" in Sophocles, *Oedipus the King*, x; *Oedipus* ll. 1500–20 [1186–1206].

animals, and for animals alike in kind toward one another, and especially among human beings, which is why we praise those who are friends of the human [*philanthropia*]. And one might see among those who travel that every human being is akin and a friend to a human being" (155a18–21). As Hannah Arendt notes, the human love for its particular species in *philanthropia* "manifests itself in a readiness to share the world with other men."[51] The specific way in which we share the world with other human beings – the mode of action, as opposed to labour or fabrication – takes the form of storytelling, which Arendt also notes is the proper way to say "who" one is.[52] While *philanthropia* is prompted by our pity for a specific character, Aristotle's reference to general affection is meant to remind us that, as a species, we share a common manner of participating in the action that tragedy mimics. Our pity and fear for Oedipus elicits love for the human. Because tragedy mimics nature, Aristotle indicates that *philanthropia* is motivated by our awareness of our common human condition. Our love for a specific character is a manifestation of our *philanthropia*, and the latter is possible because our knowledge of character results from its place in the story: the world of signifiers in which human action is made meaningful.

WONDROUS STORIES

While a tragedy is centered on a single character (*Poetics* 1453a12–13), the story or plot (*muthos*) is the "source and like the soul of tragedy" (*Poetics* 1450a35). Tragedy does not depend on music or any of the other accompaniments of tragic performances: "the effect of tragedy is primarily if not entirely the work of its poetry and in particular its plot."[53] Character and action make no sense unless they are embedded into the story of which they are essential parts.[54] As Sachs explains, "story" translates *muthos* better than "plot," which is too static, suggesting a skeletal structure instead of the unrolling and rhythm of a story. The common meaning of *muthos* is "speech" or "something said," but Aristotle's use is his own innovation.[55] He observes that speeches belong to the domain of rhetoric, while tragic mimesis represents actions (*Poetics* 1456a5–6).

51 Arendt, *Men in Dark Times*, 25.

52 Arendt, *The Human Condition*, 181–7; *Men in Dark Times*, 104–5.

53 Lord, *Education and Culture*, 119.

54 Rorty, "The Psychology of Aristotelian Tragedy," 7.

55 According to Davis, before the *Poetics*, *muthos* never means anything like "plot" (see his translation of *Poetics*, n54). As a sign of Aristotle's innovation, he coins the term *mutheuma* ("telling of the story") (*Poetics* 1460a29), and the term does not appear in Greek again for two centuries (n178).

Direct speech about the action – by a narrator, for example – misrepresents the likely and the necessary, for it implies a perspective wholly external to human experience, such as that of a god (*Poetics* 1449b2–28). Conversely, mimesis of action requires the reader and audience to interpret the action for themselves. Story is more fundamental than character to mimesis because it represents events observed from multiple points of view, enabling one to "spot the salient features of a situation."[56] This application of practical wisdom contrasts with narration or a focus on the psychology of a specific character, which has its ethical counterpart in the application of moral rules regardless of the situation. In essence, story encourages *sullogizesthai*, deliberating in common with others.

As the soul of tragedy, the story is known through its unrolling, the most important parts of which are reversals (*peripéteiai*) and discoveries (*anagnoríseis*). These are the revelations about character that induce awe. They are "the greatest means by which tragedy draws the soul [*psuchagôgei*]" (*Poetics* 1450a29). They constitute the point where the action is finally built up and leads to a resolution (*Poetics* 1455b25). In contemporary terminology, this is the climax: "I speak of what is from the beginning up to that part which is the last one [*eschaton*] out of which there is a change into good or bad fortune a building-up, and what is from the beginning of the change up to the end a resolving" (*Poetics* 1455b25–9). As we saw in chapter 2, for Aristotle, the ethical sense of *eschaton* signifies the "ultimate particular" perceived by the practical intellect (*NE* 1142a20, 1143a25–35, 1146a5), as well as the conclusion drawn in the process of deliberation: "they come to the first thing [*proton aiton*] that will be responsible for the end, which is the last thing [*eschaton*] in the process of discovery" (*NE* 1112b20, 1147b15). In the *Politics,* the adjectival form of *eschaton* signifies extremes in political form, such as extreme democracy that dissolves into tyranny (1277b3, 1312b35). It also refers to the ultimate authority in the polis (1281a17).

Eschaton is that point where a thing displays its essence most clearly and authoritatively, and where all the parts are gathered into a unity. In the *Poetics,* it signifies the moment when the essence of a character is unmasked, giving way to the resolution of the story. Davis characterizes this moment of discovery as the crystallization of the story's meaning: "Things which look at first accidental in retrospect become absolutely necessary."[57] Characters suddenly realize that what first appeared as contingency was the culmination of a process that had led to this moment, and henceforth events come to a necessary resolution.

56 Hewitt, "Aristotle's *Poetics,*" 17–18.

57 Davis, "Introduction" to *On Poetics,* xxviii.

Christians would appeal to this sense of *eschaton* to signify the end point of God's providential order.[58] It is a moment of transcendence, insofar as one realizes that what has been going on in the action has been there all along. On one level nothing has changed for the characters, but on another level everything has changed, especially their relationships with others. Christian thinkers, including Augustine, would apply this insight to explain conversion to God, but it also applies to the inculcation of (so-called) natural moral virtue. Recognition and the story in general occur in a human world, so recognition is conditioned by how the character responds to other characters: "Thus, while recognition may be of things, it must ultimately be of people – whether oneself or others. For it is only in one's relationships to other people that the world is significant and so subject to interpretation, reinterpretation, and recognition."[59] Spectators are taught that when they put their friendships to work, they will take on the impress of the other or have "their rough edges knocked off" (*apomattontai*) "by the things they like in one another" (*NE* 1172a17). In moments of recognition, which are filled with shock and exuberant wonder, they will experience their friends' lives as oriented toward the good they share together, as if that good has been there all along (a revelatory process described in chapter 2).

Psuchagôgia carries the religious connotations of leading souls out of Hades, and of enchantment in general. Aristotle uses the adjective *psuchagôgikon* to characterize spectacle (*opsis*), in order to argue that spectacle is the most artless part of the poetic arts (*Poetics* 1450b20). Even so, we have seen the enchantment and ecstasy of *psuchagôgia* with *ekplêxis*, and with reversals (*peripéteiai*) and discoveries (*anagnoríseis*). The association of *psuchogôgia* with spectacle seems to suggest that it implies an enchanting moment of blindness that would hinder rational activity, which is actually a meaning ruled out by his refinements of *ekplêxis*, *peripéteiai*, and *anagnoríseis*.

Closer consideration of Aristotle's understanding of discovery reveals that the *psuchagôgia* he has in mind is the awe we experience at the unexpected, but not necessarily miraculous, sequence of nature's course. In chapter 16 of the *Poetics*, he lists five types of discovery that characters experience; the best are those that arise "out of the actions themselves,

58 See Mark 13:8 and Mathew 24:6–8. The narrative of Augustine's life in the *Confessions* follows this basic principle. For details, see Frederick Crosson, "Structure and Meaning in St Augustine's *Confessions*." For its role in Augustine's treatment of friendship, see my "The Luminous Path of Friendship: Augustine's Account of Friendship and Political Order."

59 Davis, *The Poetry of Philosophy*, 68.

so that the awe-striking impact comes from things that are likely" (1454b20–1455a20). The least artful are those that are the most contrived, including discoveries that take place through signs, such as when Odysseus's nurse discovers him on account of his scar. Slightly better are those "fabricated by the poet" and then "through memory," such as when the Phaikian singer reminds Odysseus of his suffering. Second best are discoveries based upon the reasoning of characters, including when, in the *Libation Bearers,* Electra reasons that Orestes has arrived. Finally, as an example of the best form of discovery which "arises out of the actions themselves," Aristotle lists the *Oedipus* of Sophocles and the *Iphigenia.* His discussion of Oedipus is curious because Aristotle omits mentioning that Oedipus' discovery was the result of his implacable desire to know himself. *Psuchagôgia* like *ekplêxis* signifies awe at events that conduce to naturally occurring sequences. This is not to say that poets do not use fantastic and even "irrational" (*alogon*) devices to astonish spectators. Aristotle cites the example of Achilles chasing Hector around Troy as a "likely but impossible" event that adds delight to the story (*Poetics* 1460a15–25). An epic can better portray this event than a tragedy because it is recited: the same thing would look ridiculous on stage. Yet such delight is appropriate to *muthos* because wonder is pleasant: "a sign of this is the way everybody tells stories by adding things to them, so as to give delight" (*Poetics* 1460a18). Irrational or divine interventions in narrative appear to be more permissible, and perhaps less enchanting, when the *muthos* is spoken than when portrayed visually.

Homer is exemplary at interjecting "likely but impossible things" into the story because he "most of all has taught everyone how they ought to say things that are false [*pseudos*]" (*Poetics* 1460a19). Interjecting such wonders causes wonder, but wonders are steps to the end of the action, which is "likely" (*to eikos*) and "necessary" – that is, in accordance with nature. They ought also to be placed in parts of the story that do not display character or thinking (*Poetics* 1460b5). In this sense, poets' fabrications of divine interventions need to represent natural phenomena. Put more precisely, mimesis, as an art, arranges for one thing to have an effect that properly belongs to another. Its image-making produces effects that otherwise can occur naturally.[60] Mimesis informs the practical

60 Paul Woodruff, "Aristotle on *Mimesis,*" 91. My interpretation of this passage is in some tension with that of Michael Davis, who takes Aristotle's comments about Homer as evidence that poets cannot help but to lie. They do this because their "interventions" appeal to our desire to know the truth, which usually subverts our desire to *learn* the truth. Most humans prefer to have things shown to them, even falsehoods, than to go through the hardships of philosophical inquiry (*Poetry of Philosophy,* 140–1). While the preponderance

intellect by intervention – that is, by providing an image of what a life with others looks like from the outside. It provides an external and an internal image of life, while our general experience is more informed by the internal. Aristotle refers to Homer's divine interventions as examples of *paralogismos*, which can mean "misreasoning," but can also mean "beyond reasoning," a vantage point afforded by the internal and external perspective of mimesis. *Paralogismos* serves the mimicked action, whose story has a beginning, middle, and end (*Poetics* 1450b20–35).

Story should also have the appropriate magnitude, neither too long nor too short. While he allows that a tragedy should last about as long as one circuit of the sun to mimic the course of nature's most divine beings (*Poetics* 1449b13; *NE* 1141a32), Aristotle generally rejects imposing an external limit on its duration.[61] Its magnitude is better governed by the ability of spectators to take in the action in one view and to hold it easily in one's memory (*Poetics* 1451a1–13). Spectators need to be able to remember the story and how it hangs together. By remembering its basic idea they grasp the story, as a mask grasps the essence of a character.[62]

His unwillingness to impose external standards on the size of the tragedy is part of his theory of human action that also operates in his understanding of friendship and the extent of the polis. Unlike anthropologist Robin Dunbar, Aristotle does not derive an algorithm to determine the optimal number of friends because that question depends on the judgment and active exercise of our practical reason.[63] We know we have overreached when our love for our friends is no longer active, but becomes passive, that is, mere goodwill (*NE* 1158a10–15, 1171a1–20).[64]

among the many to avoid learning is no doubt true, Aristotle's comments about "interventions" and *paralogismos* are also directed to the mimetic or participatory dimension of human knowing, and the need to have the "whole" placed before us in some way, which, as noted, Davis elsewhere takes as the contact point between mimesis and *phronesis* ("Introduction" to *On Poetics*, xvii).

61 William Arrowsmith captures this natural sequence in his foreword to Sophocles' *Oedipus the King*: "In his terrible darkness he comes to know the god and even, like Teiresias or the old hero of the Oedipus at Kolonos, to incarnate, even to be, the god. The hero's life is that of all men, rising and shining, then fading and falling. But their life is also the life of the god, daily rising and daily setting. The play's symbolic day – dawn to dusk – is in fact Apollo appearing, as he appears to all, before daily disappearing. The day reveals the man, the hero, the god" (x).

62 Rorty, "The Psychology of Aristotelian Tragedy," 8.

63 See Dunbar, *How Many Friends Does One Person Need?*

64 As Joseph Epstein observes, an excess of friends makes each one even more burdensome. Friendship becomes a duty, which is to say, a matter of justice (*Friendship: An Exposé*, 17). Is it any wonder that early modern political philosophers, including Hobbes, conflate justice with friendship (or try to eliminate political friendship) at the same time

Similarly, Aristotle observes in the *Politics* that a polis needs to be small enough for citizens to be familiar with each other and to be surveyable,[65] yet he avoids identifying an optimal number of citizens (1326a40).[66] A polis, in order for it to be present to itself in the souls of its citizens (1326b5), needs to have its form seen, at some level and in some way, by its citizens, and thus to remain within the realm of human scale. This is the equivalent of the need to recollect the basic story of a tragedy. An overly large city would require a divine power to govern it, just as an overly long tragedy would require a divine mind to remember it. There seems to be a correlation between the size of a regime (limited by the capacity of citizens to know one another somewhat) and the attention span of its citizens to watch a tragedy. Even so, this question of "optics" is not restricted to the size of the polis, or even to the number of friends or citizens who one can hope to exercise fruitful activity. As Janssens points out, there is "no fixed boundary between action and representation, between *praxis, mimesis,* and *poiesis.*"[67] The polis can never be fully present to itself, any more than friends can ever be fully present to each other, and persons can be present to themselves.

Contrast Aristotle's recommendation for tragedies that last from sunrise to sundown, with Alexis de Tocqueville's observation that modern democracy, with its expansive magnitude, breeds art forms that are quickly digested:

> [Democratic people] do not make these pleasures [of literature] the principal charm of their existence; but they consider them as a passing and necessary relaxation in the midst of the serious work of life: such people can never acquire a profound enough knowledge of the literary art to feel its delicacies; the little nuances elude them. Having only a very short time to give to letters, they want to put it wholly to profit. They like books that are procured without trouble, that

that they reject Aristotle's understanding of the internal size limits of a commonwealth? For Hobbes, the size of a commonwealth is a function of how effectively it can gather resources to defeat an enemy (*Leviathan* 17.3). Enmity is prior to friendship. Aristotle's warning about the "divine power" has become Hobbes's and our "mortal god." That our friends have become burdens to us makes us less inclined to rebel.

65 See David Janssens, "Easily, At a Glance: Aristotle's Optics," 388–90.

66 Plato's Athenian Stranger puts the number of citizens for the Magnesian colony at 5,040. Even so, Ernest McClain's observation regarding what Plato is up to in the *Laws* needs to be recalled before one can criticize him: "It is that unflinching control over every detail in the private lives of citizens which has caused the author of the "Laws" to be labeled a fascist. The possibility that he was a musical humorist has never been investigated" (*The Pythagorean Plato: Prelude to the Song Itself,* 99).

67 Janssens, "Easily, At a Glance," 408.

are quickly read, that do not require learned research to be understood. They demand facile beauties that deliver themselves and that one can enjoy at the instant; above all the unexpected and new are necessary to them. Habituated to an existence that is practical, contested, and monotonous, they need lively and rapid motions, sudden clarity, brilliant truths or errors that instantly pull them from themselves and introduce them suddenly, almost violently, into the midst of the subject.[68]

For Tocqueville, the expansive busyness of life in modern democracy leads citizens to seek literature and entertainment that is easily digestible. This contrasts with the significantly less expansive and busy lives of citizens in the polis, whose imaginations and practical intellects are better prepared for more complex forms of tragedy. The possibility of political friendship seems greater in Aristotle's option.

ETHICS AND POLITICS AS STORYTELLING

The *Poetics* teaches spectator-citizens the habits of living their lives as a story, and these habits enable them to share in sunaisthetic friendship. They not only "apply" what they have practised at the theater, they conduct their moral and political lives poetically. In this sense *poesis* and *phronesis* are closer together than may be gleaned from Aristotle's distinction between the two in the *Nicomachean Ethics* (NE 1139b15–1140a22).[69] Aristotle observes that *poesis* produces an object while *phronesis* does not. However, moral action itself is characterized by a conceptual tension between the action itself and the purpose at which the action aims. No moral action is possible without its purpose being intended; but is one still engaged in moral action once that purpose has been achieved? Analogously, is a painter, who defines himself as a producer of paintings, more truly a painter when he is in the midst of painting or when he has completed it (NE 1168a9–10)? Aristotle explains that virtue is a habit and is not completed in any single action, but rather in a life. Yet this causes further problems, because one's life is not yet complete. In life we are like the painter in the midst of painting, but we do not produce any "thing." If action can be said to produce anything, it produces a story, a

68 Tocqueville, *Democracy in America*, 2.1.13.

69 Although Aristotle also indicates that the intellectual virtues are unified in their perfection (NE 1142b28–9).

narrative whole which we piece together.[70] John Wall captures the poetic dimension of moral action:

> Poetic phronesis pursues at once a narrative already told – a narrative whose realism makes it an ongoing end in itself – and a narrative still in the process of being produced – one that is also other than itself. The phronetic capability is for rendering the tensions of one's given moral situation and one's yet unmet larger moral possibilities productive of greater narrative coherency. The narrative end is at once narrated by one's given historical situation and yet, paradoxically, to be narrated anew, to be 'stretched' in as yet unknown directions. The end in itself of an ongoingly coherent ethical narrative is also an end other than itself of a narrative always in the process of being formed.[71]

Yet the *Poetics,* along with the *Nicomachean Ethics* and *Eudemian Ethics,* reminds us that our stories are constructed in conjunction with others. We write our stories with others, as when characters place their "impress" upon us, like the sculptor-like sunaisthetic friends discussed in chapter 2. But in addition, like characters in a story, our stories only make sense when they are shaped and transformed, in moments of recognition, by the mysterious stories of our friends. Some commentators argue that Aristotle misses the mysterious otherness of friends, which leads him finally to regard friendship as the object of our making.[72] However, his attention to wonder, as well as his treatment of friendship in relation to one's ability to judge the ultimate particular, suggests this is not the case. It cannot be the case when *sunaisthesis* involves "an effortful holding of oneself in readiness," a supremely active and passive act of knowing. Wondering at another, at one's friend, is a critical response to the mystery of their personhood, which necessarily eludes our capacity to understand, conceptualize, or frame it. The person's ethos necessarily escapes our grasp. For this reason the subsequent chapters of this study consider Plato's treatment of friendship because his dramatic dialogues are better suited to communicate the limnal mystery of personhood and otherness.

Aristotle's general point, however, is eloquently captured by Thomas Mann's likening of friendship to narrative (discussed in chapter 1): "You, however, are part of [my life] because I took you into my story."[73] The

70 Arendt, *The Human Condition*, 181–7.

71 Wall, "Phronesis as Poetic: Moral Creativity in Contemporary Aristotelianism," 329–30.

72 Ibid., 330.

73 Mann, *Joseph and His Brothers*, 1233.

image of the self as author is qualified by the image of the self that gets written upon, the self that receives the impress of the friend's form – an image that Aristotle's focus on wonder means to instill. Indeed, this language of dramaturgy is the language of politics. Tilo Schabert describes the situation – the "workshop of world politics" – faced by Western leaders and Mikhail Gorbachev during the collapse of the Soviet Union and the reunification of Germany: "Actors found themselves in the middle of the play in which they were acting without any of them having read the script they would have followed or a text they could have recited. The actors were interpreting a play they had to write as they went along and, in giving their performance, were still working on the production they were already staging in public."[74] Statesmen weave their stories together, which is one of the reasons friendship is so important to them.

Aristotle's treatment in the *Poetics* of political friendship as storytelling adds to his discussion in the *Nicomachean Ethics* and the *Politics*. In the *Nicomachean Ethics*, he observes that political life most closely resembles friendships of utility, and that it consists of arguing about the good life. Thinking of political life as storytelling can inform our understanding of both these claims. Concerning the first, Aristotle acknowledges that friendships of utility do not stand alone, and that, in a way, they are not really friendships at all if one compares them to friendships of the good. This means that friendships of utility are in need of virtue and (perhaps diluted) habits of friendships of the good, so that they do not degenerate into crass opportunism. Yet, Aristotle is not completely clear on what it really means for friendships of utility to participate in friendships of the good. The *Nicomachean Ethics* seems to skip this step, as his discussion of friendships of the good quickly becomes a discussion of the happiness of philosophy, which is to say, the idea that friendships of the good are most fully enjoyed by philosophers. Nonetheless, Aristotle does appear to allow for the polis to have a degree of participation in happiness.[75] He certainly emphasizes the utilitarian component of political concord when he observes that the widely known difficulties of achieving the

74 Schabert, *How World Politics Is Made*, 147–8.

75 This lacuna eludes numerous commentators. For example, Lorraine Pangle, one of the most insightful commentators, observes of political friendship: "A political community that seeks to promote the good life for human beings requires something more" than self-interested contracts to hold it together (*Aristotle and the Philosophy of Friendship*, 17). Such sharing is harmony, but Pangle does not elucidate the nature of that political harmony: "Concord, understood as unanimity in upholding good laws and in defending the homeland, is a harmony that is attainable between ordinary people in their common life" (157). Though it is a utilitarian form of friendship, it can be turned to the common advantage by virtuous statesmen who pursue these friendships (158).

virtuous mean motivates human beings to invent money: "and it becomes in a certain way a mean, since it measures all things, and so also their excess and deficiency" (*NE* 1133a19–20).[76] Relationships of trade bind the polis together, at least in part. However, trade is about need, while politics, as shown at the beginning of this chapter, needs the beautiful in the form of leisure for its preservation, and to avoid degenerating into domination. It also needs leisure for its completion, for what it naturally aspires to.

The same point holds for viewing politics as an ongoing deliberation about the good. Deliberation among factions can degenerate into civil war without those factions being committed to a prior common good. Societies frequently symbolize the common good in a mythical manner, as a way of articulating the ends those factions pursue, meaning that those factions offer alternative means of achieving those ends. For instance, both rich and poor live the drama of Athens, as told by the tragic poets and, behind them, Homer. Poets have traditionally created the "great code" – as Northrop Frye called the Bible – of civilizations. As F.W.J. Schelling observed, "Nations do not make myths. Myths make nations."[77] Aristotle's reference in *Politics* VIII to Odysseus's speech to the Phaikians evokes the communion experienced by people held together by the poet's songs about fearsome, pitiful, wondrous, and beautiful deeds. Speech, tone, and rhythm, along with food and drink, engage their entire personalities. It was in this kind of festive communion that tragedies were first improvised, and later "came to rest" (*Poetics* 1448b20–1449a30). Moreover, it is significant that Aristotle quotes Odysseus speaking to a *divine* race, the Phaikians – for it suggests that Odysseus's statement reflects the appropriate activity in the banquet halls of the godly.

MODERN OBSTACLES FOR STORYTELLING AS POLITICAL FRIENDSHIP

The main advantage of considering the *Poetics'* teaching about political friendship is that it provides a way into the manner in which friendship is a matter of practical judgment, and illuminates the storytelling form of political life. Aristotle's treatment, however, leaves the reader with some questions about the adequacy of his account of personhood. Given

76 Tocqueville observes that democracy replaces honour with money as the measure of one's worth (*Democracy in America*, 2.3.17). See Joshua Mitchell, "It is Not Good for Man to Be Alone: Tocqueville on Friendship."

77 Schelling, *Historical-Critical Introduction to the Philosophy of Mythology*, 49, and Lectures 4–6. I thank Steven McGuire for this reference.

Aristotle's concern for mimetic knowledge of "who this is," it is odd that he should display relatively little appreciation for the particular characters of Oedipus, Odysseus, Iphigeneia, and other tragic characters. An exception might be the episode of Achilles chasing Hector around Troy, which Aristotle treats as the paradigmatic example of poetic intervention. But this seeming oversight is related to broader questions regarding the adequacy of both Aristotle's and Plato's attention to particular individuals. Does the individual character have any significance, or is he simply a placeholder for some form of virtue? Chapter 4 takes up this concern in Plato's *Lysis*, but here some consideration can be given to the Aristotelian texts examined in this and the previous chapter.

Regarding the *Poetics*, story is more important than character, just as in the *Politics*, the polis is prior to and greater than the individual. There is no character outside the story, just as there is no citizen outside the polis; apolitical human beings must be either gods or beasts. The reader of the *Poetics* should learn to identify not with characters but with the story itself, which is composed of a beginning, middle, and end, and deals with the likely and the necessary. This makes the reader a better friend to his own and to the human species, rather than to individual characters.[78] Perhaps modern readers see this as an oversight, but Aristotle's brief allusions to those characters would have been sufficiently memorable and powerful for his contemporaries. Aristotle wants to instill *philanthropia* instead of love for specific characters because the latter would fail to promote the distance from one's own required to cultivate such civic virtues as justice and friendship. It might also fit his philosophical protreptic, which is designed to elevate philosophy over popular forms of poetry; Aristotle wants to defend *ratio* over the passions. Mimetic art represents this movement not in the soul of any individual, but in the actions of human beings acting in concert, most notably in sunaisthetic

78 This might be Aristotle's response to Eva Brann's gentle criticism of the ancients, that their "sparely, if weightily stocked minds" are at a disadvantage relative to the "vast store of scenes, styles, works, figures, and auras" that moderns enjoy, and which permit moderns to enjoy a new type of friendship, "friends of the imagination." She writes: "This sturdily delicate friendship, the particular friendship of the soul, is the one in which we open to each other's unintrusive gaze intermittent glimpses of our inner panorama. It is, I think, a manifestation of the imaginative life that is peculiarly modern" (*The World of the Imagination: Sum and Substance*, 789–90). Brann seems to concede Aristotle's point when she notes that human contemplation is active, while the imaginative life "has a musing and even a somewhat passive, cast" (790). The point of difference is over the degree to which the contemplative life can be said to be active, and whether its activity is passive as compared to the imaginative life.

friendships – and part of that mimesis includes involving spectators in that movement.

Aristotle provides a humane vision of political friendship, but it may be difficult to determine what it can teach us today. Our modern or postmodern condition resists a theory of mimesis, and moral action, predicated on a story's having a structured beginning, middle, and end (even allowing for the uncertainties of moral action, which Aristotle recognizes that mimesis simplifies). His theory of human action is a challenge for moderns because it takes place in an intermediate space of action, which is not the modern story of the solitary self or of universal humanity.

However, the modern Laputian perspective of intensive introspection and intensive universalism produces a fragmentation of imagination, politics, society, and selfhood. For Aristotle, this might be our loss. Our fragmentation leads us to confuse *ekplêxis* with sexual ecstasy, *philia* with *eros*, and the "bloom of well-being" with power. Our uncertainty about our ability to share goods of the soul leads us to take the easier path of seeking communion in bodily intimacy.[79] The scientific view of human beings prevents us from articulating our sense of wonder, as Descartes expressed: "We wonder too much … And this may entirely prevent or pervert the use of reason. That is why, although it is good to be born with some inclination towards this passion, because that disposes us for the acquisition of the sciences, we must at the same time afterwards try to free ourselves from it as much as possible."[80] Instead, we seek physical intimacy to compensate for our loneliness. Like the Spartans whose lack of leisure led to empire, we have spare time but lack the knowledge of *how* to spend it with others. Conversation is "too gay," it seems.[81]

At a deeper level, the experience of *ekpêxis*, found in those dramatic moments of recognition and reversal concerning friendships, has, in the modern imagination, been treated as a solitary experience. As Eva Brann notes, the modern imagination seems to know only the "glance of the eye" (*Augenblick*), moments of being, *kairos* time, the historical moment – all signifying a point of culmination "crucial to the coagulation of

79 Kierkegaard's Judge William tries to convince the bachelor to seek married life over single life by arguing that the beauty of a life lived together surpasses that of fleeting erotic love. In other words, erotic love is a sublimated expression of that love for the eternal (*Either/Or: Parts I and II*).

80 René Descartes, *The Passions of the Soul*, Part II, Article LXXVI. See Sachs, "Introduction," *Poetics*, 16.

81 Jennifer Lee, "The Man Date," *New York Times*, 10 April 2005, http://www.nytimes.com/2005/04/10/fashion/the-man-date.html.

consciousness, to the punctuation of life."[82] However, C.S. Lewis regards this as a modern reflection of boredom, a "desire for a desire," comparable to how Augustine describes being in love with the idea of being in love when he frequented the theater.[83] Its political expression consists of rapturous utopianism. Aristotle holds that human consciousness, which includes both knowledge and love of one's own existence, extends outward to include consciousness of one's friend's consciousness of his existence. By comparison, *Augenblick* falls back on itself in self-regarding individualism. As Tocqueville notes, the soul eventually rebels against the confines of its imaginative prison and bursts out in various spiritualist expressions. These sometimes turn into political revolutions that can never heal the self-imposed spiritual ailment.

We moderns, or postmoderns, seem to lack a story (and the capacity to make one) in which our characters are drawn out by one another. If we have anything resembling a story, it seems to be the story of the progress of "humanity." We are tempted to think that humanity is the aggregate of human achievements throughout history, and that we, conveniently, are the culmination of those aggregated achievements. However, our postmodern time is characterized by the collapse of this conception of history.[84] We have rejected the arrogance that contributed to the totalitarian projects that resulted from it, and we also want to reject becoming Last Men, which Nietzsche saw as the result of this humanitarian project. Yet the fact remains that contemporary democratic ideology, driven by technological ambition, prizes the global over the local, and tries to convince us that the digital age enhances our humanity and our possibilities for connection. The result is that political friendship needs to be contrived more and more in order to preserve solidarity within a given space. Communities increasingly rely on propaganda to create stories to maintain these imagined communities.[85] Of course, our day-to-day representations of social communications have more to do with the visual-erotic, a form of mimesis that bears little resemblance to Aristotle's "That's who this is."[86] Finally, as tourists, our perspectives and allegiances become

82 Brann, *The World of the Imagination*, 734.

83 Brann, *The World of the Imagination*, 735, citing Lewis, *Surprised by Joy: The Shape of My Early Life*.

84 David Walsh, *Guarded By Mystery*.

85 Benedict Anderson, *Imagined Communities: Reflection on the Origin and Spread of Nationalism*.

86 See Oliver O'Donovan, *Common Objects of Love: Moral Reflections on the Shaping of Community*, 64–5.

globalized, and our passports become pieces of paper instead of expressions of solidarity with a people.

By listing all the ways that contemporary times conflict with Aristotle's standards, we might be inclined to regard this exercise of retrieving ancient wisdom as fruitless. However, its central purpose has been to resuscitate Aristotle's understanding of sunaisthetic friendship. By recovering this "crest of the crest" of the moral life, we are in a better position to understand its pretenders and to offer a constructive alternative. Consider, in the spirit of Kierkegaard's Judge William, the modern obsession with sexual ecstasy. From Aristotle's perspective, this obsession owes partly to our loss of language for expressing astonishment, awe, erotics, and love in a non-bodily way. Why have "love without wings," as Lord Byron says, when the alternative is so much more exciting and gives us the illusion of communion with the other? We think friendship is diluted *eros*, but Aristotle disagrees (see *NE* 1171a10–12). For Aristotle and for Judge William, we settle for fleeting erotic attachments when we would be more satisfied with sunaisthetic knowledge as "an experiential event of codetermination of life experienced as a whole."[87] This is not to say that all of our erotic yearnings could be replaced with friendships. But our moral lives could be considerably deepened by attending to those moments of recovery and reversal that our culture mistakes for erotic mania.

Finally, it is unclear whether Aristotelian mimesis itself is outdated, or whether the postmodern rejection of Aristotle is more a rejection of Aristotelianism (and Platonism) than of Aristotle's common sense insights.[88] As noted above, Aristotle understands the difficulty and paradox of viewing life as a unity. As a result, his view that the truth of ethics lies in action rather than propositions actually resembles the (so-called) postmodern prioritization of existence over philosophy. This seems to be the impetus behind contemporary efforts, by thinkers such as Paul Ricoeur and less directly David Walsh, to draw on Aristotle's understanding of narrative in order to illustrate the nature of the ethical life.

Aristotle's treatment of poetic mimesis clarifies the storytelling dimension of individual lives and of political life in general. It provides a practical education in sunaisthetic friendship, the "crest of the crest" of his moral teaching, which is especially useful for democratic individualists unfamiliar with experiences of joint perception. Mimesis provides a moral education through the use of examples which contain their essence

87 Flakne, "Embodied and Embedded," 50.

88 Halliwell, *The Aesthetics of Mimesis*, 344–82.

within them. Therefore, his discussion of *philanthropia* simultaneously teaches the love of human beings in general, and the love of a particular individual or people.

CONCLUSION

This chapter, which draws upon the discussion of *sunaisthesis* in chapter 1, demonstrates the importance of mimesis and festivity for Aristotle's understanding of political friendship. Above all else, political friendship is the activity of citizens contemplating together, through mimesis, the moral actions of the decent. Such common contemplation cultivates practical wisdom, and comes closest to the self-sufficient practice of leisure that Aristotle regarded as necessary for living at peace. To interpret this as the characteristic action of the best regime's common good is to give a more complete interpretation of the common good or political friendship than afforded by ones which simply treat these terms as synonymous with *homonoia* or common deliberation. It also clarifies how the contemplative friendships of philosophers inform civic life. Finally, by regarding political friendship as a story (*muthos*) that recollects the shared actions of a political society, this understanding of political friendship shows how it constitutes an intermediate space for citizens' action, between the solitary individual and the universal. In the last section of this chapter, I indicated numerous obstacles to imagining this intermediate space from the vantage point of the modern world. However, in the conclusion of this book I consider a contemporary example of political friendship, in festivity, that goes some way toward exemplifying that intermediate space: the Calgary Stampede, the annual rodeo and exhibition in Calgary, Alberta, Canada. From Aristotle and his horizon of common sense, we now turn to Plato's daimonic horizon, beginning with his perplexing dialogue dedicated to friendship, *Lysis*.

PART TWO

Plato and the Daimonic Horizon

4

Hermes as Eros in Plato's Lysis

Hermes – escorting men is your greatest joy, you above all the gods, and you listen to the wish of those you favor.[1]

I believed I had had a godsend [*hermaion*] and an amazing piece of good luck.[2]

INTRODUCTION

In Plato's dialogues, we see an image of the practice of friendship instantiated in the form of the dialogue itself. This shows, to varying degrees, the capacity of the characters, along with the reader, to enter into the horizon of their friends – that is, to practise what Aristotle calls *sunaisthesis.* The dialogue form mimics the back-and-forth of friendly conversation, which is the essence of friendship. Form and content are united. As Mark Vernon remarks, "the *Lysis* offers a portrayal of friendship as a way of life in which, at its best, Socratic philosophy and becoming friends are one and the same thing."[3]

Vernon rejects the dominant scholarly view of the *Lysis,* according to which it identifies certain problems about friendship, but is fundamentally flawed and fails to say anything insightful about friendship's essence. He suggests that it actually deals with friendship, and especially *sunaisthesis,* at a deeper level than Aristotle does. Even so, a common criticism of Plato's moral and political philosophy is that it subsumes individuals under metaphysical universals. Individuals are mere placeholders for impersonal ideas. Gregory Vlastos speaks for this perspective when he imputes to Plato the view that "we are to love the persons so far, and only insofar, as they are good and beautiful [that is, useful, so that]

1 Homer, *The Iliad,* 24.396.

2 Alcibiades speaking of Socrates, *Plato's "Symposium,"* 217a.

3 Vernon, "The Ambiguity of Friendship: Is the Western Tradition Friend or Foe to Amity?" 12–13.

the individual, in the uniqueness and integrity of his or her individuality, will never be the object of our love."[4] The question of loving the individual is bound up with how best to assess not just Plato's ethics and politics, but also his so-called metaphysical ideas, and the very nature of Socratic philosophizing.

This chapter examines how Plato uses mythological symbolism in the *Lysis*, specifically that of Hermes, to show how our experience of the good makes possible our capacity to practise *sunaisthesis* and still love our friend as an individual. In so doing, it overturns the static dualities usually associated with Plato's metaphysics, which have hindered appreciation of this strange dialogue. Instead of appealing to allegedly impersonal ideas, Plato refigures Greek mythological understandings of Hermes to signal two things. The first is that friendship is a movement of divine love in which human beings participate and to which they are reoriented so that they may behold their friend as an individual, as a person. The second is that this reorientation is necessary in order to place the dialectical inquiry into friendship upon proper pre-dialectical starting points. Voegelin expresses the importance of these pre-dialectical experiences in a statement from *Science, Politics, and Gnosticism* that we considered in chapter 1: "In the experiences of love for the world-transcendent origin of being, in *philia* toward the *sophon* (the wise), in *eros* toward the *agathon* (the good) and the *kalon* (the beautiful), man became philosopher."[5] Philosophy is an existential movement of the soul in friendship, reaching out in love to the good and the beautiful. Instead of eclipsing the individual in the shadow of impersonal ideas, Plato appeals to Hermes – the most human, most creative, and thus most political of Olympians – to show how we must open ourselves up to the divine in order to fully love our friend as an individual person. The Hermetic setting of the *Lysis* serves as a reminder that friendship expresses the existential condition of making or choosing ourselves when we make ethical decisions. In common sense terms, this is captured by the proverb that one is known by the company one keeps. The notion of choosing ourselves is on display most vividly in *Republic* X, where the souls of the dead choose their lot in their next life. This myth also represents the choice we make at every instant of our lives in forming our character. In hearing about Hermes in the *Lysis*, ancient Greeks would have been reminded that it is Hermes, above all other Olympians, who makes himself in a way that is

4 Vlastos, *Platonic Studies*, 31.

5 Voegelin, *Science, Politics, Gnosticism*, 259.

analogous to humans choosing lots. Aristotle also makes explicit the connection between a person's making of oneself and friendship:

> One's *being* is choiceworthy and loveable for everyone, but we *are* by being-at-work (since it is by living and acting), and the work is, in a certain way, its maker at-work; so he loves the work because he also loves to *be*. And this is natural, for that which something is in potency, its work reveals in its being-at-work. At the same time, for the one doing the favor something beautiful comes from the act, so that he delights in the one in whom this is present, but for the one receiving it there is nothing beautiful in the one doing it, but if anything, something advantageous, and this is less pleasing and loveable. (*NE* 1168a3–13)

Hermes, the transgressor and yet preserver of boundaries, and hence of our individuality, enables us to practise *sunaisthesis*, to enter into the horizon of our friend. He simultaneously unsettles us and our horizons, astonishing us with gifts and even acts of theft, and serves as a divine bridge between the unsettled horizons of each friend. This chapter thus moves the inquiry from Aristotle's horizon of common sense outward toward Plato's daimonic horizon.

For the Greeks, to experience Hermes was to experience a "windfall" or "godsend" (*hermaion*).[6] In the most simple and vulgar sense, the herms statue was a gift on the roadside for the traveller. Socrates would have walked by many herms statues on his "way from the Academy straight to the Lyceum," as he describes his journey at the beginning of the dialogue (*Lysis* 203a). In Greek religion, Hermes represented a liminal (and possibly shamanistic) power that united the underworld with Olympus, which, as he was also the being who simultaneously maintains and disrupts boundaries, enabled him to be the patron of political societies. Of all the Olympians, Hermes was the only one to have created his own roles, to have made himself rather than had his roles given to him. He was creative, and thus the god one might be most likely to regard as a person. In the most sophisticated (though still mythological) sense, to experience Hermes was to participate in the completion of the theological cosmogony of world-creation and unity. Hermes "must once have struck the eye as a brilliant flash out of the depths, that it saw a world in the God, and the God in the whole world. This is the origin of the figure of Hermes, which Homer recognized and which later generations held

6 Socrates uses this term to describe his contrivance of having Glaucon and Adeimantus build a just city in speech (*Republic* 492e–493a).

fast to."[7] Drawing upon Eric Voegelin's theory of compact and differentiated forms of symbolism, where compact myths reflect a cosmos in which gods and humans are blended together in a primordial community, and philosophy and revelation represents a differentiated cosmos where the individual psyche is attuned to divine order, I shall argue that the *Lysis* constitutes a more differentiated account of the compact Hermetic myth.[8] Now, in addition to seeing "a world in the God, and the God in the whole world," Plato's refiguring of Hermetic symbolism enables us to see *the person* in both the world and God, and the world and God in the person. The Hermes symbolism of the *Lysis* reminds the reader that instead of viewing one's friend as a passive placeholder for the impersonal ideas, friendship is best practised by those who also share the characteristics of creativity, personhood, music, and wisdom – that is, the characteristics of Hermes. In beholding our friend, we behold "a brilliant flash out of the depths." Loving the friend means recognizing that he "*is* ... an image of the divine,"[9] where the divine, paradoxically, is the most personable of the gods – and of course, the most divine of persons is Socrates.[10] The creativity of Hermes-Socrates unsettles the metaphysical dualism usually associated with Plato and reminds us that our friend is in fact the intersection of the cosmos, which is to say, a person.

It is necessary to consider the mythological symbolism and dialectical starting point of Hermes because the experience of him, of windfall, illuminates ("answers" would be too strong a term) two key lacunae in the

7 Karl Kerényi, *Hermes: Guide of Souls; The Mythologem of the Masculine Source of Life*, 3; quoting W.F. Otto, *The Homeric Gods*.

8 For a brief summary of the theory, see Voegelin, *Israel and Revelation* (volume 1 of *Order and History*), 1–12. The five volumes of *Order and History* present a fuller account of the theory.

9 James Rhodes, "Platonic *Philia* and Political Order," 46 (emphasis original).

10 My reading of the *Lysis* is most indebted to that of Rhodes, whose dramatic reading demonstrates why the starting points of the dialogue necessitate that the interlocutors draw inadequate and even ridiculous conclusions regarding friendship. This chapter is an attempt to recover the starting points that Rhodes has demonstrated have been lost by the pathologies of the interlocutors, most notably those of Lysis himself. Planinc is a helpful guide for demonstrating how Plato's dialogues refigure compact mythological symbolism (see *Plato's Political Philosophy: Prudence in the Republic and the Laws*; *Plato Through Homer: Poetry and Philosophy in the Cosmological Dialogues*; and "Tracking the Good in Plato's *Republic*: The Literary and Dialogic Form of the Sun, Line, and Cave Imagery"). However, unlike his work on other Platonic dialogues, I have been unable to identify any overarching Homeric symbolisms in the *Lysis*. Finally, by claiming that the *Lysis* constitutes a more differentiated account of Hermes than earlier myths, I am drawing upon Voegelin's theory of compact and differentiated symbolizations (in volumes 1 and 2 of *Order and History: Plato and Aristotle* and *The World of the Polis*).

dialogue: first, what friends are *for*, as opposed to what need they fulfill; and second, whether the philosopher's relationship with the good can in any way be considered friendship – in which, as Paul Friendländer once suggested, "true philo-sophy, i.e., love of sophia … is returned by sophia."[11]

Lysis is a vexing dialogue. The interlocutors – Socrates and the two boys, Lysis and Menexenus – fail to arrive at a coherent understanding of friendship, perhaps because of the limits of their characters as well as the elusive nature of friendship itself. What they do come up with is odd because they frame the discussion in terms of the usefulness of the friend (which preoccupies the arrogant Lysis himself; see 207c–211d). The inadequacy of this dialectical starting point is apparent in some of the absurd conclusions and perplexities Socrates and the boys reach. They first consider whether friends are useful for the good or for the bad, but they determine that friends who are both good or both bad do not benefit each other because good people, by definition, have no need of any benefit, and bad people, by definition, have no benefit to offer to another (211d–216b). The interlocutors lean toward agreeing that friends who are neither good nor bad do provide benefits to one another, but the best they can do to describe the bond that unites such in-between friends is to suggest that they are "akin" (*oikeion*) to one another, which, to say the least, fails to illuminate the manner in which friends are so akin (221d–222e). In benefiting each other, friends are said to help each other escape evils (216c–218c). If friends help friends escape the unease of existence, their good is defined as a negative, which makes it difficult to discern what good friends are for. It is as if Francis Bacon, who famously argued that friends ease each other's bodily humors, wrote this dialogue. However, when Socrates describes friends in terms of the good they serve, they are described in terms of "phantoms" or "idols" (*eidola*) who stand beneath the "first friend" (*proton philia*), a symbol that suggests a metaphysical first principle of friendship (218c–d). Such a principle or idea seems to overshadow individual friends, ostensibly validating Vlastos' critique of Plato. As this survey of the dialogue shows, no matter which way the dialectic cuts, friends seem to be phantoms. Perhaps we have learned what friendship is not, but we have not learned what it is.

READING THE *LYSIS* AS DRAMATIC MYTH

For the reasons canvassed above, the *Lysis* has traditionally been taken to be one of Plato's "aporetic" dialogues. However, more recent scholarship

11 Friedländer, *Plato: The Dialogues, First Period*, vol. 2, 96.

attends to its dramatic setting to show how it supplements the discursive elements in a way that helps explain the more perplexing, and even ridiculous, parts of the dialogue. This chapter builds on these more dramatic interpretations by demonstrating the crucial role of the Hermetic elements in symbolizing the person of the friend. My analysis focuses on the text's references and allusions to Hermes, as well as to the points in the dialogue where the interlocutors draw inadequate or ridiculous conclusions that point us back to the starting points of the argument. I do not provide a comprehensive reading of the dialogue in all of its dialectical turns, which has been done numerous times, and quite capably, by other scholars (discussed below). Rather, my interest resides in the intersection between the starting points of those arguments and the Hermetic symbolism. That intersection is the intersection between the discursive or dianoetic dimension of the dialogue, and the visionary or noetic dimension that concerns the movement of intellect or Nous itself.

Various commentators have noticed the special importance of Hermes to the discursive dimension of the *Lysis*.[12] Of these, Francisco Gonzalez has gone the furthest, arguing that the significance of Hermes consists in his being the preserver and transgressor of boundaries.[13] There is a lot of transgressing and preserving of boundaries in the *Lysis*. Socrates's presence in the palaestra, or wrestling school, on a day when the intermingling of adults and youths is prohibited, is an obvious example of transgression. However, just as his ghostly ability enables him to enter the palaestra, so too does it mean that he will not stay with the boys. In serving as their midwife and ours, Socrates shows that "the one is not indebted to the other for anything, but both are indebted to the god for everything."[14]

According to Gonzalez, Hermes as intermediary helps further the movement of the *Lysis*, mediating the opposites of good and good, bad and bad, and good and bad that characterize the interlocutors' attempts to define friendship. Hermes "transforms love from a two-term relation to a three-term relation: a love triangle, as it were … This characterization of love as a relation between what is neither good nor bad and the ultimate good also makes it a form of mediation between human beings and something more than human: a type of mediation of course

12 F.V. Trivigno, "Philosophy and the Ordinary: On the Setting of the *Lysis*"; Francisco Gonzalez, "How to Read a Platonic Prologue: *Lysis* 203a–207d" and "Plato's *Lysis*: An Enactment of Philosophic Friendship"; C. Planeaux, "Socrates as Unreliable Narrator? The Dramatic Setting of the "Lysis""; and J. Haden, "Friendship in Plato's Lysis."

13 Gonzalez, "How to Read a Platonic Prologue," 39–40.

14 Søren Kierkegaard, *Philosophical Fragments/Johannes Climacus*, 66.

represented by Hermes."[15] One might say that Hermes not only makes love between two (or more) individuals possible, but also makes dialectic possible. Gonzalez shows the profound role that Plato gives Hermes in realizing both friendship and philosophy.

This point is not mere speculation, and is firmly rooted in Socrates's understanding of dialectic, whereby something is known through its look or form – sensory perceptions being unintelligible without intellect (*Republic* 508e). A similar observation may be made of the individual sciences. Each has its first principles, which can be known only by a superior science. Thus, physics, the science of three-dimensional objects and motion, presupposes mathematics, which presupposes logic, and so forth (*Republic* 522a–534d). Finally, Socrates seems to think that an art can only be fully understood by those whom it serves because the advantage and thus completion of each is found in serving its object (*Republic* 341e–342d). To know something is to know its nature, which includes knowing its first principles. In the case of most things, this involves beholding them in their totality, but this is impossible in the case of humans, and perhaps especially in the case of friendship. Humans can never be beheld in the way that we behold objects – a fact which Lysis, who views friends as things to be possessed, does not understand. We cannot simply stand before other human beings in the mode of subject-object – summoning them and demanding their reasons for being the way they are, as an object[16] – because we share the same ontological standing. We must go outside of ourselves to understand what unites us in friendship. Myth provides us with a participatory knowledge that, in the case of friendship, is operationalized through the experience of Hermes.

Most importantly, like Hermes, Socrates is a mediator between gods and humans, claiming that his knowledge of love derives from the god.[17] Indeed, Socrates claims "it has been given [*hermeta*] to me from a god – to be able quickly to recognize both a lover and a beloved" (*Lysis* 204c). This capacity is of divine origin because it requires the ability to perceive and understand what goes on between, and thus above, human beings. Gonzalez outlines the allusions to Hermes but his analysis remains at the textual level, without advancing to the experiential core of Hermes and its relationship to friendship. The experiential core is that of "windfall" (*hermaion*) which, in compact form, is the revelation of existence and the origin of that existence, in which human beings recognize that

15 Gonzalez, "How to Read a Platonic Prologue," 4.
16 See George Grant, "Thinking about Technology," 21.
17 Gonzalez, "How to Read a Platonic Prologue," 42.

everything that they have (and so that can be taken away from them) is from the gods. The gift of the friend is the most vivid expression of this experience.

Plato's use of Hermetic tropes is more than window dressing. It represents his way of recalling mystic, shamanic, daimonic, erotic, and participatory experiences that were previously symbolized in Greek poetry and religious traditions, but which, in Plato's hands, are expressed in noetic and discursive terms. Hermes represents the daimonic horizon in which Plato philosophizes about friendship. As noted in chapter 1, Voegelin draws upon the *Symposium* to identify the meaning of the daimonic when he describes the "spiritual man, *daimonios aner*, who lives in the tension between needy and full being," as supremely erotic: Eros is "the symbol of the tension experienced between the poles of temporal and eternal being," where the divine and human partake in one another.[18] The spiritual man is also the measure of right, and possesses the "power of influence on others – and the reciprocal experience of gratitude" in others.[19] Daimonic Hermetic symbols clarify the experience of being an intermediary, which Socrates refers to when he claims his knowledge of lover and beloved has been given to him (*hermeta*) by a god, and when this god-sent knowledge enables him to perceive the in-between. Philosophy shares the same concern as myth, namely humanity's participation in a divine cosmos, and Plato frequently uses myth to articulate central philosophical, though non- or meta-discursive, experiences.

In the history of Greek religion, the withdrawal of the gods from the cosmos meant that "divine meaning is no longer experienced as part of the world, in its ceaseless and complete change of living and dying, and ascends to a realm beyond the world of immutable perfection, [an event which] is accompanied by the experience of the discovery of an individual soul, a little atom of immortality that must alone make the difficult passage to being, truth, plentitude, of meaning, the gods, however the *terminus ad quem* is symbolized."[20] The discovery of Nous gave Plato a new way to symbolize the order of human existence, in which the individual soul is the center, instead of as a cosmos full of gods where beings melted together in a compact (and diffuse) manner.[21] However, the discovery of Nous also makes friendship among individuals challenging to understand and symbolize. After all, if the individual soul is an "atom", no

18 Voegelin, *Anamnesis*, 325–6.

19 Richard J. Bishirjian, "Daimonic Men," 159.

20 Barry Cooper, "'A Lump Bred Up in Darknesse': Two Tellurian Themes in the *Republic*," 104.

21 Eric Voegelin, "Reason: The Classic Experience."

longer straightforwardly consubstantial with the cosmos (as was the case in compact myth), then how does one explain what unites individual atoms to one another? And how best to conceive of that relationship, when the very act of understanding it is part of the relationship itself? Plato utilized myth to symbolize the participatory or daimonic whole in which human beings live. His use of Hermes symbolism in the *Lysis* serves as a reminder of the mysterious ground that suddenly appears in a moment of silent recognition, binding human beings in the relationship called friendship.

RETHINKING THE STARTING POINTS OF THE ARGUMENT

The *Lysis* takes place during the festival of Hermes. This is indicated at the beginning of the dialogue, when we find Lysis and Menexenus sacrificing to Hermes, and at the end, when the boys' attendants return from making sacrifices of their own.[22] Socrates takes advantage of the departure of the attendants, who go to observe the Hermaea, to converse with Lysis and Menexenus (206d). Indeed, Menexenus seems more observant of Hermes than Lysis; he leaves to worship him during the conversation between Socrates and Lysis that reveals the latter's *libido dominandi* as well as humiliates him (207d and 211a). Perhaps Menexenus' piety towards Hermes makes him a better learner and gives him a greater capacity for friendship, as evidenced by his presence at Socrates's death in *Phaedo* and his role in the dialogue named after him. At the conclusion of the *Lysis*, the attendants, "like some daemons," call the boys away from Socrates and back to their tasks (223a–b). The attendants had been drinking at the Hermaea, which would have been the third day of the Anthesteria festival.[23] This three-day festival, which Jane Harrison and others have compared to All Soul's, was dedicated to the dead.[24] During the festival, ghosts were permitted to wander the earth among the living. Socrates refers to the attendants as daemons, which reminds the reader of another mention of ghosts earlier in the dialogue when he compares individual friends, who are mere "phantoms" (*eidola*) (*Lysis* 219d), to the ontological "first friend" (*proton philia*) whom all friendships apparently serve.

The dialogue is rife with ghosts and the dead because the action takes place in the realm of Hermes. Indeed, Socrates's appearance at the

22 Gonzalez, "How to Read a Platonic Prologue," 36–7.

23 Planeaux, "Socrates as Unreliable Narrator?"

24 Harrison, *Epilegomena to the Study of Greek Religion and Themis*, 36.

palaestra refigures this ghostly wandering, which makes its mark on the dialogue as a whole. As Planeaux observes:

> Plato subtly paints a most intricate and elaborate image through the use of a single word: "Hermaea." During a Dionysian celebration, when strangers were in Athens in large numbers, when revelers dressed up as satyrs frolicked about town in almost uncontrolled wantonness, Plato displays his own Silenus/Marsyas entering the wrestling school near Panops on one of the few days out of the year when he could do so unimpeded. Celebrating youths were initiated into the community on this day, while dangerous ghosts and demons coursed through the streets of Athens, and Plato's own musical satyr engages these assembled young men in discussions of *philia* – a virtue that can turn excessive, intense, and even violent – in an attempt to initiate them into philosophy.[25]

As is appropriate for Hermes, "this was a day of turmoil, of being 'topsy-turvy'",[26] and this must be remembered when reading the dialectic. For example, if the friend is to be referred to as the first friend (*proton philia*), we need to ask whether it is indeed a metaphysical first principle, or whether Plato, through Hermes, actually intends us to overturn this Platonist metaphysic, especially right here in a dialogue dedicated to the friend. Metaphorically speaking, if we are to refer to the "first friend," do we look up or down – to the heavens or under the earth (Hermes's origin)?[27]

Additionally, the dramatic setting of the Anthesteria festival reminds the reader that festivals in general are civic gatherings in which friendships, both civic and personal, are renewed.[28] As discussed in our analysis of Plato's *Laws* in the following chapters, festivals take place outside the rhythms of workaday life because they serve as reminders of the divine order in which the polis is situated: "Taking pity on this suffering that is natural to the human race, the gods have ordained the change of holidays as times of rest from labor. They have given as fellow celebrants the Muses, with their leader Apollo, and Dionysus – in order that these divinities might set humans right again. Thus men are sustained by their holidays in the company of the gods" (*Laws* 653d). As Josef Pieper notes, the realm of festivity is the realm of freedom and play, that is, the serious play human beings engage in, which displays the highest things they

25 Planeaux, "Socrates as Unreliable Narrator?," 66.

26 Ibid., 65.

27 A similar overturning is seen in the *Symposium*, where the ugly Socrates contrasts with the beautiful object of erotic longing.

28 Planeaux, "Socrates as Unreliable Narrator?," 65.

aspire to.[29] Setting the *Lysis* during the Anthesteria festival reminds the reader that friendship is situated in the realm of freedom. The Anthesteria in particular was a festival meant to purify the city of ghosts, as well as an initiation ritual for the young.[30] Ghostly Socrates comes to the palaestra both to purify and to initiate, during a festival when the youths were ritualistically anticipating such a visitation. We shall return to festivity in chapters 5 to 7 when considering Plato's *Laws.*

As noted above, the arguments of the interlocutors run into perplexities. Indeed, the very form of argumentation, in which pairs of likes and opposites are presented as if there were no other mode of understanding their relationship, is a form of sophistry, as shown in the *Euthydemus* (a dialogue whose dramatic date might immediately precede that of the *Lysis*).[31] Framing the argument in terms of opposites (i.e., good and good, bad and bad, good and bad) makes it difficult to find the middle term (i.e., neither good nor bad) for which the interlocutors strive near the end of the dialogue. For this reason, Socrates points us to Hermes: "I say through divination that whatever is neither good nor bad is a friend of the beautiful and good" (*Lysis* 216d). The attempt to find the middle term, which will be important when the interlocutors refer to the bond that friends share as "akin" (*oikeion*), is an attempt to discern the substance of friendship in a participatory or Hermetic mode, for the middle term participates in both of the terms between which it is said to be. But, as James Rhodes has shown, the search for this participatory mode is not a mere intellectual exercise, but must also involve the taming of Lysis's *libido dominandi.*

Socrates attempts to purge Lysis's libido using a maze of arguments and sophistries. His libido is most clearly on display in the series of exchanges between him and Socrates that begins with Socrates asking whether his parents love him (207d), and concludes with Lysis making it clear that he views rulers as the happiest people because they are most free to do what they want (210a–c). Rhodes explains: "Lysis is not wise or just. He wants to enslave and use other human beings for his own

29 Pieper, *In Tune With the World: A Theory of Festivity.*

30 Planeaux, "Socrates as Unreliable Narrator?," 65n22. On initiation festivals, see A. van Gennep, *The Rites of Passage.*

31 The dramatic date of the *Lysis* is difficult, if not impossible, to determine. As a result, my comparisons of the *Lysis* to the argument and action of other dialogues are based on thematic similarities, and draw upon attempts at dating the dialogue as suggestive, but nothing more definitive than that. The best that can be said is that, on the basis of Lysis's age as a boy (born in 422, according to Debra Nails, *The People of Plato,* 195–6), the dialogue likely falls somewhere between 409 (Nails, 363) and 406 (Catherine Zuckert, *Plato's Philosophers,* 9). Zuckert dates the *Euthydemus* as taking place in 407, and the *Lysis* in 406.

advantage, profit, and pleasure. This is strong evidence that his friendships fizzle because he is the selfish type of utilitarian who alienates people by trying to exploit them."[32] Socrates's ironic questioning of Lysis is an attempt to bring him to perplexity, to neediness, because that is the opening of the soul to otherness and to love and friendship,[33] although Socrates is probably aware that the boy's soul is too proud to be opened. Socrates's mode of questioning is why either Plato or a later editor added a subtitle to the *Lysis*: "On *Philia*: Obstetric." Socrates practises the art of the midwife with the boys, trying to initiate them into the love of wisdom. Because Lysis never appears in any other Platonic dialogue, one may assume that Socrates's attempt with Lysis yielded nothing. Conversely, Menexenus and Ctessipus are both present at Socrates's death in the *Phaedo*, while Ctessipus is Socrates's ally against the sophists in the *Euthydemus*. Menexenus gets his own dialogue, whose dramatic date is strangely later than that of the *Phaedo*. As a reminder of Socrates's entrance to the palaestra at Anthesteria – the day of ghosts wandering the earth – Socrates appears to Menexenus in his eponymous dialogue as a god-send to bring order to Athens. Thus, the dialogue is meant to clear away misunderstandings, and it points to the importance of purging *libido dominandi* as a prelude to understanding and practising friendship. Socrates suggests as much at the end of the dialogue when he "already had in mind to set in motion someone else among the older fellows" who would presumably be a more mature interlocutor (*Lysis* 223a).[34] However, the entrance of the attendants, the daimons, prevents this conversation from occurring, so we are left to wonder what character this might have been. It is up to the reader to rethink the starting points of the conversation.

A closer examination of the Hermetic setting of the dialogue reveals the alternative starting point represented by Lysis, who, because or in spite of the fact that he is "beautiful and good" (207a), is libidinous. Gonzalez argues that Hermes helps illuminate "in-between" features of friendship that the speeches fail to grasp. As the god of boundaries, Hermes is the god of intermediaries. He is also the god to whom Socrates refers when he tells his interlocutors that "this has somehow been given to me [*hermeta*] from a god – to be able quickly to recognize both a lover and a beloved." As the god who oversees the dialogue and its setting, Hermes also oversees the practical choices the interlocutors make.

32 Rhodes, "Platonic *Philia* and Political Order," 31.

33 Mary P. Nichols, *Socrates on Friendship and Community: Reflections on Plato's "Symposium," "Phaedrus," and "Lysis,"* 160.

34 Rhodes, "Platonic *Philia* and Political Order," 42.

Among these practical choices is their insistence that friendship is reciprocal and that friends are somehow between good and bad. Indeed, Socrates asserts, without explaining why, that he and the boys are "in the middle of the bad and the good" (220d), and so the strange category of being "akin" (*oikeion*) appears to make some sense for them. The middle or "akin" is a function of the god's gift to Socrates: "that whatever is neither good nor bad is a friend of the beautiful and good" (216d).

THE EXPERIENCE OF HERMES IN GREEK RELIGION

In order to understand the significance of Plato's references to Hermes, it is necessary to consider the nature of the god, and thus the experience of Hermes, according to the Greeks. Hermes undergoes a remarkable transformation in the history of Greek religion, which is evident in an examination of how he appears in Greek folk religion and in the Homeric *Hymn to Hermes*, sung during the Anthesteria festival.[35] Using Voegelin's terminology, his meaning is distinguished from that of a compactly symbolized chthonic fertility god, to a more differentiated Olympian spokesman for the justice of Zeus. The latter is exemplified in Aeschylus' *Prometheus Bound*, where, indeed, Hermes recognizes personal responsibility to a greater extent than Zeus does.[36] As mediator between gods and men, and as the guide of the souls of the dead, Hermes represents a shamanistic power that unites the two realms and, in Plato's dialogues, is refigured as erotic.[37] Hermes is a god of boundaries who also transgresses those boundaries; but in transgressing those boundaries he also maintains them. Thus, he is also the patron of those who found political societies. One can see this Hermetic aspect of political creativity in Tilo Schabert's observation that the paradox of maintaining and disrupting boundaries is the central political, and indeed human, activity: "Governing is creativity, an encompassing and incessant process of creation. It is the process of creativity that appears as government … The paradigm of

35 Hermes also performs an important functions in Homer's epics, Plato's other dialogues (discussed later in this chapter), and in Athenian tragedy (Aeschylus' *Oresteia* in particular). For example, in *Eumenides* he silently accompanies Orestes from Delphi, where he is purified by Apollo, to Athens, where he receives judgment from Athena. His role there can be compared in part to that of Orestes' friend, Pylades in *Libation Bearers* (M. Griffith, "Brilliant Dynasts: Power and Politics in the 'Oresteia,'" *Classical Antiquity*, 62–129, 91; M. McMenomy, "Roles of Hermes in Athenian Drama").

36 See Aeschylus, *Prometheus Bound*, 1443–1640; Voegelin, *The World of the Polis*, 259; and Swanson, "The Political Philosophy of Aeschylus' *Prometheus Bound*," 236.

37 E.A.S. Butterworth, *Some Traces of the Pre-Olympian World in Greek Literature and Myth*, 154; and *The Tree at the Navel of the Earth*, 64.

governing … is a fluid state between chaos and form."[38] Hermes is the condition of human relations. He is also the "companion to the feast," which makes him the aim or the crown of political life.[39] His importance in the *Lysis*, and in Plato's refiguring of him in the person of Socrates, is that, as godsend or windfall, he is the precondition of friendship. By accompanying Hermes-Socrates in this journey, we go outside of ourselves and thus glimpse, through myth and symbol, the ground of friendship.

Hermes was the god of herdsman, thieves, graves, and heralds.[40] He was also associated with fertility, as the famous phallic statues of the herms indicate. Hermes was "the patron god of the fundamental anthropological and sociological principle of reciprocity."[41] His humble yet dubious beginnings as a fertility deity, along with his being the patron god of herdsmen and thieves, prove auspicious. Implicit in these meanings is his role as the god of boundaries, indeed, of origins and becoming, as well as an erotic power.[42] As R.B. Onians notes of the herms statues, whose heads and genital organs were their outward essentials, the Greeks regarded the human head as the vessel of the generative power and the psyche: "Hermes was the generative power in the world at large, as it were the universal fertilizing psyche … so giver of increase, wealth."[43]

The transformation of Hermes from a cultic deity to an Olympian god has been noticed with some astonishment, but never fully understood.[44] James Haden summarizes the evolution of Hermes in the Greek mind:

> He begins as an indistinct chthonic fertility deity, protector of flocks and herds, and ends as brother and virtual equal of Apollo, the deity most beloved by Socrates and Plato. Thus while by the fourth century he has important connections with logos, in his earliest, Arcadian chthonic manifestation he was symbolized merely by heaps of stones contributed by wayfarers, of whom he was the guardian. That particular aspect of Hermes develops into his role as conductor of souls to the Underworld, and he is a special link between the Olympian world

38 Schabert, "A Classical Prince: The Style of Francois Mitterand," 235.

39 Jenny Strauss Clay, *The Politics of Olympus: Form and Meaning in the Major Homeric Hymns*, 140, citing "Hymn to Hermes," 436.

40 Walter Burkert, *The Greek Religion*, 158.

41 C. Watkins, "Studies in Indo-European Legal Language, Institutions, and Mythology," 345.

42 See especially: Kerényi, *Hermes;* Butterworth, *Some Traces of the Pre-Olympian World in Greek Literature and Myth*, 154; and Watkins, "Studies in Indo-European Legal Language, Institutions, and Mythology," 64.

43 Onians, *The Origins of European Thought: About the Body, the Mind, the Soul, the World, Time and Fate*, 122.

44 Burkert, *The Greek Religion*, 156.

> of light and the chthonian darkness, moving with ease in either direction. His appearance alters radically, as shown by iconographic evidence; originally a strong, virile bearded man, his representation gradually melts into that of a supple youth, and eventually even into an androgynous form. He becomes the patron of commerce as well as of thieves.[45]

With his chthonic origins and as spokesman of Zeus, Hermes becomes Eros, who binds together the upper and the lower. As Kerényi notes, it is the common origin between Hermes and men that enables Hermes to "so convincingly hover before us, lead us on our ways, show us golden treasures in everyone through the split-second timing which is the spirit of finding and thieving."[46]

Kerényi argues that the meaning of Hermes for the Greeks was stable since at least the time of Homer.[47] He claims that Hermes was the most existential of the gods because the experience of him encompassed that of all others: "Hermes too, therefore, is more than merely the luminous idea of a world … he is its source, through whom that world originated and through whom it becomes intelligible."[48] Hermes is the in-between of existence who not only points to existence's divine source, but, as god of commerce and communication, acts as the medium through which our knowledge of the human condition is conveyed. Hermes was the "basic image of living reality."[49] No wonder, then, that he oversees so many disparate human activities: he is the condition for all of them.

Kerényi notes that there is no contradiction between Hermes as giver of "windfall" and Hermes as god of thieves: "These were the windfalls for hungry travellers who stole them from the God in his own spirit, just as he would have done."[50] This dual meaning of theft and grateful receiving is appropriate for Hermes the liminal figure. It is also appropriate for Socrates, whose characteristic act of piety was to set out to prove that the oracle was wrong to regard him as the wisest man in all of Greece.

The experience of Hermes was that of an unexpected arrival. One of the fragments of Heraclitus states, "Hermes has come in," which W.F. Otto compares to the contemporary saying that an angel has entered the room: it is as if the nocturnal mysteries were stirring in daylight in the form of "the remarkable silence that may intervene in the midst of the liveliest

45 Haden, "Friendship in Plato's *Lysis*," 345.
46 Kerényi, *Hermes*, 51.
47 Ibid., 1.
48 Ibid., 55.
49 Ibid., 4.
50 Ibid., 59–60.

conversations; it was said, at such times, that Hermes had entered the room."[51] In greeting Hermes, "we must be prepared not only for what is immediately intelligible, but also for what is strangely uncanny."[52] Instead of viewing this uncanny experience as a disruption to social intercourse, the Greeks tended to view it as its foundation. According to Jenny Strauss Clay, "Hermes' sudden, uncanny, one might also say, demonic, presence attests not only to his patronage of social institutions, but also to his power to mediate between the Olympians and mankind."[53]

It may seem strange that the "windfall" of Hermes should be "quite natural" but produce silence, especially when Hermes is the god of communication and commerce. Yet this is not so strange. Consider the silence that ensues when Hermes enters the room. It is customary to think of miracles and gifts from the gods as astonishing and accompanied by divine signs that reinforce the recipient's awareness that the gift they have received is indeed from the god. However, this view is inadequate and misunderstands the nature of divine communication, as understood by numerous traditions. For instance, in his *Confessions*, Augustine describes the occasion of his conversion to God in almost naturalistic terms: he hears a child's voice telling him to "pick up and read," and he emphasizes that he does not know the origin of the voice. Could it be a child? Could it be a god? Either way, the voice tells him to pick up and read, and he picks up his copy of the Bible and is thunderstruck by the passage that speaks directly to his soul's restlessness. The voice spoke to him. But, again, is it the voice of a natural being or the voice of a god?[54]

Part of the mystery of the divine is that natural causation and divine gifts are difficult to distinguish. Thus, Kerényi observes that the Greeks could describe the experience of Hermes both in terms of science and as something more, as a gift: "impressions that are palpable and manifest, that in no way contradict the observations and conclusions of natural science," and yet extend beyond the attitude of "scientifically evaluated sense impressions."[55] A Christian might see in this discussion a distinction between general providence and special providence, which are simply two separate modes of divine governance.[56] Whatever the equivalences of experience between that of compact Hermes and the differentiated Christian view of providence, it must be recalled that Hermes's origins are chthonic while he brings the upper and lower worlds

51 Otto, *The Homeric Gods*, 118; see also Plutarch, "Of Garrulity, or Talkativeness."

52 Kerényi, *Hermes*, 5.

53 Clay, *The Politics of Olympus*, 126.

54 See Heyking, "The Luminous Path of Friendship," 122–5.

55 Kerényi, *Hermes*, 53.

56 Aquinas, *Summa Theologiæ*, I.105.6.

together. He is in-between while providing the conditions for in-betweenness, just as Socrates claims that the god has given him the ability to identify lovers. As Kerényi shows, Hermes is like Eros (he suggests that Socrates's account of the latter in the *Symposium* refigures the older understanding of Hermes).[57] Eros is between resource and poverty – which is to say, between windfall and death, being and nonbeing. When understood in this way, the silence of Hermes entering the room reflects the perplexity (or what Aristotle calls astonishment or *ekplêxis*) of confronting more than just an ordinary being, but rather, the condition for human communication. Hermes was seen as the patron god of founders of cities. Like them, Hermes has an ambiguous relationship with his beneficiaries. Founders are of the city they found, but, as founders, also beyond it – just like Socrates who transverses the walls of Athens to arrive at the palaestra.

HERMES IN THE *ILIAD* AND THE *ODYSSEY*

The vulnerable traveller needs all the help he can get. Perhaps the clearest example of this experience is Hermes's assistance to Priam in retrieving Hector's body at the end of the *Iliad*, which "stands under the sign of Hermes."[58] In sending Hermes to help Priam, Zeus says to him, "Hermes – escorting men is your greatest joy, you above all the gods, and you listen to the wish of those you favor."[59] It is nothing short of miraculous that Priam successfully makes his way unnoticed through the Achaean ships to meet Achilles, and, further, avoids being killed by Achilles himself. Their meeting is made possible because both have lost what is dearest to each: Priam has lost Hector and Achilles has lost Patroclus. Fraught with the tension of their mutual enmity, their encounter is nonetheless a moment of *sunaisthesis*:

They reached out for the good things that lay at hand
And when they had put aside desire for food and drink,
Priam the son of Dardanus gazed at Achilles, marveling
Now at the man's beauty, his magnificent build –
Face-to-face he seemed a deathless god…
And Achilles gazed and marveled at Dardan Priam,
Beholding his noble looks, listening to his words.
But once they'd had their fill of gazing at each other,
The old majestic Priam broke the silence first.[60]

57 Kerényi, *Hermes*, 56.
58 Ibid., 9.
59 Homer, *Iliad*, 24.396.
60 Ibid., 24.740–6.

Homer's narration is entirely matter-of-fact: "no miracle ensues, but a windfall such as the old man had not even ventured to hope for occurs in a manner apparently quite natural."[61] Indeed, Priam does not even realize his guide has been Hermes until he has returned.

Hermes is more central to the *Odyssey* than the *Iliad.* Odysseus identifies with Hermes. Both share the same epithet, "many turns" (*polutropos*).[62] It is with Hermes that we greet Odysseus for the first time in the epic.[63] Homer emphasizes Hermes's speed when describing his descent from Olympus to Calypso's island, which is fitting for the intermediary who crosses the infinity between immortal and mortal in an instant: "swooping down from Pieria, down the high clear air, plunged to the sea and skimmed the waves like a tern that down the deadly gulfs of the barren salt swells and glides for fish, dipping its beating wings in bursts of spray – so Hermes skimmed the crests on endless crests."[64] The suddenness of this windfall contrasts with Odysseus's immediate recognition of Hermes, which is so ordinary, when he arrives to help Odysseus flee the island of Calypso. They are not only alike, but Odysseus's grandfather, Autolycos, was said to have been a son of Hermes and a master in taking oaths.[65] The Phaikians, to whom Odysseus narrates his story, are a Hermetic people. They sacrifice to Hermes before going to sleep.[66] Hermes hovers over the final book of the *Odyssey* in his role as the dead suitors' *psychopomp.* Hermes also hovers over the prophecy Tiresias bestows upon Odysseus in Hades.[67] Just as Odysseus knew Hermes at once, the Theban prophet recognizes Odysseus right away, and goes on to prophesy the conclusion of Odysseus's liminal journey following his return to Ithaca. Odysseus will carry his paddle to a race of people who have never seen the sea: "When another traveller falls in with you and calls that weight across your shoulder a fan to winnow grain, then plant your bladed, balanced oar in the earth and sacrifice fine beasts to the lord god of the sea, Poseidon."[68] Odysseus's many turns will conclude when he unites heaven and earth, as Hermes unites Olympus and humanity. Tiresias does not identify the other traveller who offers the "unmistakable sign," but

61 Otto, *The Homeric Gods*, 116. David Malouf's novel *Ransom* is a dramatic retelling of the story that skillfully represents the Hermetic reordering and reconciliation of enmity between Priam and Achilles.

62 Clay, *The Politics of Olympus*, 100.

63 Homer, *Odyssey*, 5.1–90.

64 Ibid., 5.52–9.

65 Ibid., 19.450–60.

66 Ibid., 7.160–3.

67 Ibid., 11:100–70.

68 Ibid., 11:146–9.

the Hermetic theme is unmistakable. The Hermetic messenger gains wisdom in his quest to unite the two realms. In the same way that Hermes as *psychopompos* silently hosts Tiresias' prophecy, Odysseus is told that he will die "far from the sea," but "with all your people there in blessed peace around you," upon completing this quest.[69] Hermes necessarily gives way to the order he founds. We shall see in chapters 5 to 7 the Athenian Stranger echoing this Hermetic act of giving way to the order that he founds.

These aspects warrant mention if only to remind us of the general affinities between Socrates and Odysseus, and the manner in which Plato refigures numerous Homeric tropes to characterize philosophizing in other dialogues.[70] Even so, in the *Lysis*, Socrates refers specifically to Odyssean Hermes. As part of his argument that friends are alike to one another, he quotes a line by Melanthios, goatherd of one of Penelope's suitors, to Eumaios and Odysseus, who is disguised as a beggar: "Always a god leads [the one who is] like to [the one who is] like" (214b).[71]

However, Socrates quotes only part of the passage. The full version includes the lines: "Look! … One scum nosing another scum along, dirt finds dirt by the will of god – it never fails!"[72] The scene to which Socrates refers is of course portentous for the death of the suitors, and it contains multiple layers of meaning. The surface significance is Melanthios' contempt for the two similar swineherds. However, Odysseus is disguised as a swineherd when in fact he is the king of Ithaca. The deeper meaning is that these two people, Eumaios and Odysseus, are very much unlike. And yet an even deeper layer of meaning is suggested if we recall the initial greeting of Eumaios and Odysseus, which starts with Eumaios offering hospitality to Odysseus (disguised as a beggar), but ends with them sharing meat with one another in a sacrifice to Hermes.[73] Despite the untruth of Melanthios' insult, it implies a Hermetic truth. Hermes presides over the arrival of Odysseus at Ithaca, the arrival of the souls of the suitors who receive Odysseus's wrath, and the re-establishment of his rule: "[Hermes's] presence softens the effects of Odysseus's fearful revenge, just as the ferocity of Achilles was calmed in the last book of the *Iliad*."[74] Hermes is the condition of friendship and of political society.

69 Ibid., 11:154–5.

70 See Planinc, *Plato's Political Philosophy*; *Plato Through Homer*; and "Tracking the Good in Plato's *Republic*: The Literary and Dialogic Form of the Sun, Line, and Cave Imagery."

71 Quoting, with alteration, Homer, *Odyssey*, 17.236.

72 Homer, *Odyssey*, 17.236.

73 Ibid., 14.494.

74 Kerényi, *Hermes*, 12.

THE *HYMN TO HERMES*

The Homeric *Hymn to Hermes* shows Hermes to be the great cosmic unifier, the shaman.[75] It is also an existential hymn, a theological cosmogony, that shows Hermes creating his role as he discovers it: "As a swift thought darts through the heart of a man when thronging cares haunt him, or as bright glances flash from the eye, so glorious Hermes planned both thought and deed at once."[76] The hymn tells the story of Hermes's struggle to make the transition from a chthonic entity to an Olympian. It tells of Hermes's birth, his invention of the lyre, his theft of Apollo's cattle, and his reconciliation and friendship with Apollo. The hymn would have been chanted at the festival of Hermes.[77] E.A.S. Butterworth notes that its contents and the style of its recitation are both shamanistic.[78] The occasion of the *Lysis* and the ritual function of the hymn reflect the existential character of the hymn itself. Menexenus and the boys' attendants may have chanted it when they departed the palaestra to attend the Hermetic rites.

The struggle to become an Olympian requires that Hermes, unlike his brother Apollo whose Olympian roles are given to him, must discover his proper place and role, which involves nothing less than "consort[ing] with all mortals and immortals."[79] Hermes must wrest and even steal his roles. He makes himself. But instead of undermining the Olympian order with his theft, he solidifies it, for in stealing his roles he also recognizes the Olympian order: "Hermes, then, introduces dynamic movement and vitality into what might otherwise be a beautifully ordered but static cosmos."[80] Unlike Dionysius who overturns order, Hermes passes through boundaries while leaving them intact. He is the model founder of civilization and the basis of human communication.

Hermes is the last born of the Olympians, whereas Apollo, his brother, is the first born. His realm is the in-between, and not any specific cosmic region, whether sky, sea, or underworld. As Clay observes, this gives the hymn its existential tone:

75 On shamanism, see especially Butterworth, *Some Traces of the Pre-Olympian World in Greek Literature and Myth*, 154–9.

76 "Hymn to Hermes," 44–6.

77 S. Iles Johnston, "Myth, Festival, and Poet: The 'Homeric Hymn to Hermes' and Its Performative Context."

78 Butterworth, *Some Traces of the Pre-Olympian World in Greek Literature and Myth*, 418–27.

79 "Hymn to Hermes," 576.

80 Clay, *The Politics of Olympus*, 102.

> The abstract character of Hermes' *timai* poses peculiar problems for the hymn-poet who works in what is essentially a narrative medium … Instead, [the hymn-poet] manifests and incorporates [Hermes's function] into the dramatic movement of the narrative, in which Hermes *becomes* his function by enacting it … Unlike Apollo who can lay claim to his prerogatives moments after his birth, Hermes must invent them and, even before that, he must discover his proper place. For it is by no means immediately clear whether he belongs with the gods or among men.[81]

The most important part of the hymn is the theological cosmogony that Hermes sings while playing the lyre, because it initiates the reconciliation between himself and Apollo, the last born and the first born, signified by Apollo's ordination of Hermes as the keeper of herds.[82] Hermes teaches Apollo the nature of music: "for the sweet throb of the marvelous music went to his heart, and a soft longing took hold of his soul as he listened."[83] Hermes knows how the soul can turn inward through music and thus be more sociable. By turning people inward, music enables friendship among them.[84]

Hermes is the first god to sing a theological cosmogony because none can be sung until the theogonic process has been completed.[85] It is Hermes who brings the Olympian order to completion by tying together the "deathless gods and dark earth."[86] As Clay observes, "Hermes is the first to be able to sing a theogony, because only with his birth is the configuration of the divine cosmos complete. As Hymn poetry is coterminous with, and a continuation of, theogonic poetry, Hermes' performance inevitably ends with a hymn to Hermes."[87] Like Odysseus, who sings of his deeds while acting them out, Hermes's act of singing is the theological cosmogony itself. Necessarily, then, Hermes teaches Apollo to play the lyre in a playfully back and forth or dialogical manner that mimics the reciprocity found in friendship.[88] Hermes is proficient in eros and music.[89] After Hermes teaches Apollo the lyre, the two of them negotiate their respective roles and reach an agreement, sealing it with a pact that

81 Clay, *The Politics of Olympus*, 102.
82 "Hymn to Hermes," 417–35, 497.
83 Ibid., 419–20.
84 See *Republic* 397e, 411c–d, 424d–e, 443d.
85 Clay, *The Politics of Olympus*, 139.
86 "Hymn to Hermes," 427.
87 Clay, *The Politics of Olympus*, 139–40.
88 Ibid., 143.
89 Kerényi, *Hermes*, 53–9.

becomes the paradigm of all agreements and pacts.[90] Apollo and Hermes become the model for friendship. The hymn concludes with their establishment of the pact and, the "existential" character of Hermes notwithstanding, it offers no narrative about the subsequent character of their friendship.[91] This is unsurprising. The theogony of the hymn teaches that those who partake in Hermes can now make themselves, as Hermes made himself. The Myth of Er, at *Republic* X, where souls choose themselves in choosing their lots, is perhaps the clearest expression of this insight. Friendship, as symbolized by Hermes and Apollo, expresses the existential condition of the soul capable of choosing itself.

HERMES IN PLATO'S OTHER DIALOGUES

Plato's dialogues represent the most differentiated stage in the classical Greek understanding of Hermes. Hermes is mentioned or alluded to in several dialogues, as we saw above when Socrates, in the *Republic*, describes the just city in speech as a godsend. In the *Symposium*, Alcibiades refers to Socrates as a "godsend [*hermaion*] and a rare stroke of luck" (*Symposium* 217a), and expresses his shock at seeing Socrates at Agathon's home by evoking Heracles, whom Hermes had guided through the underworld (213b). He compares Socrates to the silenus statues he sees in the shops of the herms sculptors (215b). Calling Socrates a "godsend" (*hermaion*) is mirrored in Alcibiades's own surprising and sudden entrance into Agathon's home. That Hermes arrives as a gift which transforms those who receive it can be seen in many of the examples we have considered: the surprise that the boys in the paleastra would have felt at the sight of Socrates's sudden entrance in the *Lysis*; Hermes's appearance to Odysseus on the island of Calypso; or Socrates's entrance to Agathon's home in the *Symposium*. Just as Alcibiades's subsequent speech about Socrates inadvertently reveals inner truths about the nature of Eros, so too does he reveal the windfall that is Socrates.

The association of Socrates with Hermes is seen most directly in Socrates's famous oath, "by the dog" – a direct reference to the Egyptian dog Anubis whom the Greeks saw as Hermes, and who conducts the souls of the dead. The oath also associates Socrates with Heracles, who, guided by Hermes, brought a monster from Hades into the light of day. In the context of our present discussion, Socrates utters this oath in the *Lysis* before claiming that he would rather have a friend "than the gold

90 "Hymn to Hermes," 575.

91 Ibid., 506–7, 525, 574–5.

of Darius, and rather than Darius himself – that's the kind of lover of companions I am" (211e). Right before this, Socrates claims not that he is a "lover of companions," but that "when it comes to the acquisition of friends I'm quite passionately in love" (211e). It is the hunt for friends and not the possession of friends that Socrates emphasizes.

Eva Brann notes that Socrates's oath is distinctly his own, and that he generally utters it "in passages concerned with the philosopher's part both in true speech and in politics."[92] They are the passages in Platonic dialogues in which the "principle of the Doric harmony between logos and ergon" is especially pronounced.[93] Given the central importance of this Socratic question, his oath in the *Lysis* indicates a close connection between the love of wisdom and the practice of friendship.[94] Hermes reveals the truth of existence. By swearing his oath, Socrates chooses his lot.

Socrates gives the oath twice in the *Republic*. The first time, it is to show Glaucon that, in their discussion of music, "without noticing it, we've been making a city pure again that we just now claimed was living in luxury" (399e). Hermes is here associated with the act of purification, something Socrates-Hermes guides Glaucon to perform, just as he attempts to do with Lysis.

The oath appears again at the end of Book IX, when Socrates and Glaucon agree that the just city is in fact the soul of the just man: "it's a pattern laid up in heaven ... for anyone who wants to see it and for the one who's seen it to establish in himself. It makes no difference whether it is or will be present anywhere, because his actions will be those that belong to this city alone, and to no other" (592a–b). As Heracles brings the monster up into the daylight, Socrates's descent into Hades brings up the saving tale of the just city.

Similarly, Socrates utters his oath in the *Gorgias*, this time identifying the dog as "the god of the Egyptians." He utters his oath while explaining to Callicles that he will remain discordant with himself as long as he follows his two lovers, "the Athenian people and the son of Pyrilampes," in failing to agree that injustice and shirking the penalty for it are "the utmost of all evils" (481d–482c). Callicles (and everyone else) would be better off listening to Socrates's "friend and comrade, philosophy," who tells him that these are indeed the utmost of evils, and that it is better to suffer injustice than to commit injustice. Callicles would be the monster Heracles brings up from Hades. During a discussion in which Callicles

92 Brann, *The Music of the Republic*, 118.

93 Hans-Georg Gadamer, *Dialogue and Dialectic: Eight Hermeneutical Studies on Plato*, 6.

94 Voegelin, *Science, Politics, and Gnosticism*, 259.

refers to Socrates as his friend when attempting to convince him to enter politics (499c), Socrates invokes Hermes to point out the fundamental disorder of the soul that prevents Callicles from even being a friend to himself.

Along the same lines, Socrates swears his oath to the Athenian assembly in his defence speech when he explains – "for it is necessary to speak the truth before you" – how he was serving the god by disproving the Delphic oracle. He even alludes to the famous labours of Heracles, and probably Odysseus's wanderings as well, when he adds, "indeed, I must display my wandering to you as a performing of certain labors" (*Apology* 22a).

More overt references to Hermes in the Platonic dialogues focus on Hermes's bestowal of both language and the arts of politics upon human beings. In the discussion of natural names in the *Cratylus*, Socrates claims that the name "Hermes" has something to do with interpretation and carrying messages, as well as with thieving and deception. Hermes is "he who wrought discoursing [*eirein mêsasthai*]," which reminds the reader of Odysseus and perhaps Socrates (407e–408b). Similarly, Socrates alludes to Hermes the *psychopompos* in the *Phaedrus*, when he claims that the power of speech is the "leading of the soul [*psychagogue*]" (271c). In the *Protagoras*, Protagoras claims that Zeus sent Hermes to save human beings by bringing them the political arts as a way of correcting the damage wrought by Prometheus and Epimetheus. Hermes brought "humans a sense of shame and of a right way, so there could be orderly behavior in cities and bonds of friendship to unite people" (322c–d). It is characteristic of Hermes's traditional hospitality that he distributed shame equally to all human beings.

Socrates utters his oath to Hermes when he reveals the truth of existence, the basic orientation of the soul in its erotic openness to the agathon. Such openness is the precondition for philosophizing. This is why it is important to pay attention to Socrates's appeals to myth, which transpose Heracles's and Odysseus's labours (that is, the descent into the depths to bring up the truth of existence) onto Socrates's attempts to purify Lysis, Glaucon, and his other interlocutors. Socrates is a windfall sent by the gods to perform this task. In the history of Greek religion, he is the event of the divine, departing from the cosmos to the transcendent, and now descending to human beings. When divine Nous has been differentiated, the individual psyche of the spiritual man, Socrates, becomes the order of existence. Put into the compact terms of myth, Socrates fulfills the theological cosmogony described in the *Hymn to Hermes*, and so it is appropriate that before he dies in the *Phaedo*, he tells

Crito that "we owe a cock to Asclepius." As Brann observes, cocks were also sacrificed to Anubis – that is, Hermes.[95]

Viewing Socrates, like Hermes, as the fulfillment of the theological cosmogony returns the inquiry to the *Symposium.* Kerényi sees parallels between Socrates's description of the birth of Eros and Hermes: "the relationship among these realities – Poros and eros to Hermes – is what concerns us."[96] He observes that Poros, Eros's father in Socrates's account, is mentioned by Alkman, a lyric poet of the seventh century, as one of the oldest deities and identical with Hesiod's Chaos. As Kerényi writes: "yet, while this oldest being of the *Theogony* is original formlessness, lacking direction nor movement and taking back into itself everything that has form, Poros, according to his name and his son, seems to be the world's fullness on its path towards free unfolding in eternal movement forward, masculine and active, prepared for ambush and attack and overflowing with every kind of creativity and fruitfulness."[97] Hermes has a close affinity with Poros, and Plato may have had this affinity in mind in his description of Eros, as well. Kerényi stops short of identifying Eros with Hermes, because the former is too limited and lacks Hermes's cunning. However, Diotima certainly ascribes Hermetic qualities to Eros, which she ascribes to her father, Poros: "in accordance with his father he plots to trap the beautiful and the good, and is courageous, stout and keen, a skilled hunter, always weaving devices, desirous of practical wisdom and inventive, philosophizing through all his life, a skilled magician, druggist, sophist" (*Symposium* 203d–e). Hermetic activities here include cattle rustling, sophistic or clever speechmaking, invention, and supplying a drug to Odysseus to protect him from Circe's charms. Eros is like Odysseus and Socrates in being of many turns (*polytropos*).

Even so, the association of Hermes with Poros serves as a reminder of the relationship that Hermes and Eros have with logos and creation.[98] Eros necessarily accompanies creation because Eros is creative and destructive. As Tilo Schabert observes, "Eros, the philosophical, pervades the mythical language of the creation stories and highlights the necessity from which creation is chaos."[99] The reason for this is that the world is

95 Brann, *Music of the Republic*, 32.

96 Kerényi, *Hermes*, 57.

97 Ibid. Indeed, it is doubtful that Hesiod regarded Chaos as formlessness, as all the primordial partners in creation (Chaos, Eros, and Gaia) are generative and thus between form and formlessness (Voegelin, *In Search of Order*, 75).

98 See Francis Cornford, "Hermes, Pan, Logos."

99 Schabert, "Chaos and Eros: On the Order of Human Existence," 117.

perpetually between creation and destruction, between unity and plurality: "[Things] are in-between things, either in chaos in which the creative Eros divides itself, or in creation toward which strives Eros, the unifying force. All things enjoy their 'order' through Eros."[100] Thus, Eros, like Hermes, is necessarily creative. We see this in Plato's reference to Eros as always contriving devices; in Hermes's thievery, such as when he steals his roles in the *Hymn to Hermes;* and in Hermes's narrating his theological cosmogony: "Eros makes happen what things are. It is the history which rests in things. Through the movements of Eros, things come apart and they unite through him. Through Eros they are parts just as they are whole. The world is the world through Eros."[101]

Hermes, therefore, was understood in classical Greek religion as the shamanistic power of cosmic unification and origins. In all of the above examples, Hermes is the god who unites the cosmos, and also who completes it in a shamanistic quest that sees him transcend and then re-enter it, transforming dwellings as he creates them. He is the force of creativity and of being's plenitude. He is the precondition of communication and civilization because he is the precondition of giving. "Hermes has entered the room" is the windfall or godsend that silences us when we unexpectedly turn toward the opening of being. If we understand the Platonic dialogues as recording the experience of divine Nous, and the individual psyche as the locus of that order, then it is possible to see the transformation of Hermes in the classical Greek religious tradition as the differentiation of divine order from the cosmos to the transcendent, as experienced in the individual psyche. The windfall of Hermes then represents the irruption of eternal being in time, as seen in the sudden arrival of Socrates in the *Lysis,* and in the identification of Hermes with Poros/Eros in the *Symposium.* These mythological allusions serve as the proper starting points for the discussion of friendship, including the question of its reciprocity and its grounds.

OPENING SCENE: "I WAS ON MY WAY"

The *Lysis* opens with Socrates narrating to an unnamed interlocutor.[102] As Catherine Zuckert observes, the dialogue mimics actual conversation,

100 Schabert, "Chaos and Eros," 119.

101 Ibid., 118.

102 See also Rhodes, "Platonic *Philia* and Political Order," 25–33, where he considers the opening scene with a reflection upon the dialogue's subtitle, "On *Philia*: Obstetric." The reference to obstetric suggests that Plato, or a later editor who appended the subtitle,

perhaps between friends, with the reader taking the place of this interlocutor.[103] In this way, the *Lysis* is like the *Republic*, which also has Socrates narrate the action to an unnamed interlocutor – a figure who can, as Zdravko Planinc has shown, be understood as Socrates's friend because the reader stays with Socrates's entire voyage.[104] The shorter length of the *Lysis* places fewer demands on the reader, but here too Socrates leads us toward an unspecified port.

He states: "I was on my way from the Academy straight to the Lyceum, along the road outside the wall and close under the wall itself. When I came to the little gate near the spring of Panops" (*Lysis* 203a). Socrates is "on my way" (*eporenomen*). The *Lysis* begins with him in transit, and the Platonic dialogues frequently begin this way.[105] The first word of the *Republic* is *kateben*, "I went down"; in this case, Socrates went down to the Piraeus, which dramatically stands in for Hades.[106] The *Phaedrus* also opens with Socrates asking Phaedrus where he is headed: "Phaedrus, my friend! Where to? And from where?" (227a). Socrates is a wayfarer. This fact alone introduces a perplexity to a dialogue in which the friend is the central theme, for the wayfarer is a loner who never settles in one place. Socrates, while a homebody in the sense that he never liked to leave Athens, is nonetheless a loner. While the dialogues depict his friendship with various individuals (e.g., Crito), it is difficult to say that he was in fact friends with them. Perhaps this is why Socrates claims to be passionately in love with *seeking* a friend, which means that he has yet to find one (*Lysis* 211e). To the Greek mind, his wayfaring would show an affinity with Hermes, who is, among other things, the god of travellers and guide to the dead. As the *Lysis* takes place on the third day of Anthesteria when the ghosts are wandering the earth, Kerényi's description of Hermes the wayfarer is pertinent to the presentation of Socrates in this dialogue: the journeyer "makes himself vanish (volatizes himself) to everyone, also to himself. Everything around him becomes to him ghostly and improbable, and even his own reality appears to him as ghostlike. He is

wants the reader to acknowledge that Socrates is practising the midwife's art: "Socrates will not give us a propositional 'theory of philia.' Rather, the 'pregnant' characters in the play and we ourselves need to be delivered of the virtue of friendly love" (25–6).

103 Zuckert, *Plato's Philosophers*, 512.

104 Planinc, *Plato's Political Philosophy*; *Plato Through Homer*; and "Tracking the Good in Plato's *Republic*."

105 R.M. Dancy, in *Plato's Introduction of Forms*, notes that the most common opening question in the dialogues is, "where are you coming from?" (26n10).

106 See Voegelin, *Plato and Aristotle*, 52–61; Cooper, "'A Lump Bred Up in Darknesse,'" 104–14; and Brann, *The Music of the Republic*, 116–22.

completely absorbed by movement, but never by a human community that would tie him down."[107]

Unlike the *Republic*, in which Socrates explains his reason for being in the Piraeus with Glaucon, the reasons for his visiting the Academy and Lyceum in the *Lysis* are not stated. However, a glance at his route is suggestive. Christopher Planeaux has demonstrated that there is nothing "straight" about the way from the Academy to the Lyceum.[108] The Academy was northwest of Athens, and the Lyceum was likely to the east or southeast. Travelling directly through the city would have afforded a more direct route than the one Socrates actually took, which was around the city's walls. Socrates's interlocutors would have recognized this, and the fact that Socrates repeats his claim that he has come "straight" there (*Lysis* 203b) indicates that Plato wants us, too, to notice that his route was really quite indirect. It is significant that Socrates's route was entirely outside the walls of the city, for in only one other dialogue, the *Phaedrus*, do we see him outside the walls of Athens. In that dialogue on erotic love, Socrates is well beyond the walls. In the *Lysis*, on friendship, we see Socrates in that liminal area immediately outside the walls but not entirely outside of the city, which Nichols takes as a reminder that friendship is neither completely inside nor completely outside the city.[109]

Retracing Socrates's route through modern Athens, Planeaux suggests that Socrates is effectively saying, "I went from the Kerameikos directly to Syntagma Square via Omonia Square."[110] The Kerameikos ("Potters Quarter") happened to be the site of the public cemetery and site of Pericles's Funeral Oration, and it was on the route that the Eleusian procession took from Athens to the Academy. The Academy to which Socrates refers, of course, is not yet Plato's Academy, but the gymnasium that was sacred to Athena, Zeus, Prometheus, Hephaiestos, Hermes, and Heracles, and contained an altar to Eros.[111]

On the day of Anthesteria, when the ghosts were about, Socrates's sudden appearance after a trip originating at the national cemetery would have seemed auspicious. Instead of heading directly through Athens, he would have headed due east to what is today Omonia Square – the likely location in ancient Athens of the Cynosarges gymnasium. Meaning "swift" or even "white dog," Pausanias mentions that the Cynosarges was

107 Kerényi, *Hermes*, 13 (parentheses in original).
108 Planeaux, "Socrates as Unreliable Narrator?"
109 Nichols, *Socrates on Friendship and Community*, 157.
110 Planeaux, "Socrates as Unreliable Narrator?," 60.
111 R.E. Wycherley, *The Stones of Athens*, 219.

known as a sanctuary for Heracles.[112] It is even possible that the wrestling school where the *Lysis* takes place is actually the Cynosarges (though there are reasons, mentioned below, to doubt this). Ctesippus explains to Socrates that Lysis has a family connection to Heracles, as his grandfather on his mother's side was the founder of the deme, Aixone, in which Lysis's family lived.[113] Debra Nails suggests that Lysis's family held the hereditary priesthood of the cult of Heracles in Aixone.[114]

The Heracles connection, and perhaps the Cynosarges itself, is Hermetic. This is reinforced by the proximity of the palaestra to the spring of Panops, which is also associated with Hermes (*Lysis* 203a). As Haden observes, "'Panoptes' is the epithet of Argus, the all-seeing guardian whom Hermes killed in the process of stealing Io. This might seem an arbitrary association, except for the curious fact that the quotation from Homer which plays an important part in the dialogue comes from that episode in the *Odyssey* where Odysseus is at last nearing his home, disguised as a beggar, only to be recognized at the gate by his aged hound, also named Argus."[115] Even so, Socrates does not specify the name of the palaestra he visits, only that he happened upon it on the way to the Lyceum. This particular palaestra is situated somewhere between the Cynosarges and the Lyceum, and between the Lyceum and the Academy, *and* between these locations and the walls of Athens. Socrates, like Hermes, haunts boundaries.

For its part, the Lyceum, somewhere east of the walls, was sacred to Apollo.[116] Taking a cue from Planeaux's geographic reading of Socrates's voyage, we might reread that voyage in a mythical manner. The journey from the Academy, associated with the Eleusian Mysteries and close to the national cemetery, to the Lyceum, home of Apollo, is a refiguration of Hermes's liminal quest from the underworld to the Olympian heights. In keeping with our finding that Socrates is the exemplar of the individual psyche under divine Nous, and the fulfillment of the theological cosmogony, we might say that Socrates comes to the palaestra to solicit from the boys their choice of lots, themselves.

The Lyceum plays an important role in the Platonic dialogues and the treatment of friendship therein. The *Euthydemus* takes place there.

112 Pausanias, *Description of Greece*, I.19.3.

113 *Lysis* 206d; R.S. Stroud, "The Gravestone of Socrates' Friend, Lysis."

114 Nails, *The People of Plato*, 196.

115 Haden, "Friendship in Plato's *Lysis*", 346, referring to Homer, *Odyssey*, 17.290.

116 Pausanias, *Description of Greece*, I.19.3. See also J.P. Lynch, *Aristotle's School: A Study of a Greek Educational Institution*, 16.

It is thematically connected with the *Lysis* because it shares a concern with the nature of wisdom and the possibility of combining with others. Further, Zuckert claims that the *Euthydemus* takes place shortly before the *Lysis.*[117] In *Euthydemus,* Socrates recounts to his friend Crito how he and Ctessipus (who also takes part in *Lysis*) faced off against two sophist brothers, Dionysodorus and Euthydemus. The sophists' style of argumentation is reminiscent of the one used by Socrates and Lysis, in that the two find it difficult to determine how two opposites can share something between them. Socrates expresses his frustration with the brothers: "It's not easy to persuade them that human beings, like everything else that's in the middle ground of any pair of things and manages to have a share in both, in those cases in which the pair consists of a bad thing and a good one, end up being better than the one and worse than the other."[118] The two brothers claim knowledge of everything, which Lysis regards as most beneficial[119] and which he himself also seeks. Dionysodorus and Euthydemus stick together, despite their discordant arguments (and the underlying disharmony between them and within themselves).[120] Even so, Socrates ironically sees something beautiful in their argument that one can have mastery over one's own associates (*oikeion*).[121] Like the *Lysis,* the *Euthydemus* raises the question of the conditions of philosophy and of openness toward another, as displayed in the fragile unity of the brothers that is imperiled by their own corrupt souls. The dramatic setting and the possible date of the *Euthydemus* before the *Lysis* suggest that Socrates had to find out something important at the Academy in order to return to the Lyceum. As a liminal figure, he had to go down before coming up again. The *Gorgias,* which takes place in the agora and concludes with Socrates's myth of divine judgment, comes immediately after the *Lysis,* if indeed the *Gorgias* can be dated.[122] Socrates must have learned something in the *Lysis* to have gone from its liminal setting down to the agora to face those more formidable sophists.

117 Zuckert, *Plato's Philosophers,* 484.

118 Plato, *Euthydemus* 306a.

119 Ibid., 294d.

120 See e.g., Plato, *Euthydemus* 296e–297b.

121 Plato, *Euthydemus* 301e.

122 Zuckert, *Plato's Philosophers,* 9, 509, 531–2. Rhodes argues the *Gorgias* cannot be dated dramatically because it takes place outside time, in mythic time, or in eternity (personal communication with author).

HERMETIC "MARVELS" IN MODERN DEMOCRACY: CONCLUDING REMARKS

A mythological and dramatic reading of Plato's *Lysis*, which focuses on Hermes, illuminates but also deepens the mysteries of the dialogue. The dialogue's perplexities, most notably concerning reciprocity and the foundations of friendship, are illuminated if we refer to the Greek understanding of Hermetic experience. Plato incorporates Hermes into Socratic philosophizing and Eros into his dialogues by identifying "godsend" as the divine movement that prompts philosophizing, and therefore friendship. As the liminal power that traverses and unites the opposite poles of reality, Hermes is also the creative force that creates and sustains human relationships, including friendships and political societies. Travelling with Hermes involves descending to the human depths as well as crossing all boundaries. Hermes gets us outside of ourselves, as it were, which in plainer language means that he opens us up to the gift of otherness in the friend – something that is expressed vividly by Socrates's surprising and unsettling arrival at the wrestling school. The Hermes symbolism provides one with a better sense of the astonishing pretheoretical experiences in which friendship consists. The experiential core of "windfall" (*hermaion*) is human beings' recognition that everything they have, and could lose, is from the gods. The gift of the friend most dramatically expresses this experience. This Hermetic interpretation of the dialogue might also finally enable one to make sense of Paul Friedländer's characterization of "true philo-sophy, i.e., love of sophia that is returned by sophia."[123] Hermes as godsend symbolizes the turning around of the soul that is both a precondition and constituent of friendship in its existential openness and generosity. Instead of seeing one's friend subsumed under a so-called metaphysical idea of friendship, Hermes, who is both above and below us, reminds us that our friend is a cosmos, an image of the divine. Who better to reveal the mystery of the other, than he who traverses boundaries? The Hermetic experience of friendship is a characteristically Platonic way of conceiving of daimonic personhood.

The Hermetic element of friendship seems far removed from our own seemingly disenchanted world dominated by technology. Part of the aim of this chapter has been to show how a utilitarian logic of subject-object, seen in the *libido dominandi* of Lysis, can be transcended. I have also

123 Friedländer, *Plato: The Dialogues, First Period*, vol. 2, 96.

suggested some experiences equivalent to that of Hermes in other religious outlooks, including in the more differentiated Christian view of providence. The windfall of Hermes may indeed be the opening light of being, but it remains to be seen whether Hermes has any meaning in the modern world.

Kerényi, for one, believed that Hermes remained central to the modern world. His wife notes that his lecture on Hermes facilitated "permission to leave Hungary and then later to establish himself definitely in the free world."[124] In a century marked by disposession and the mass migrations of refugees from totalitarian regimes, Hermes, the patron god of travellers, indeed of pilgrims, guides souls and teaches them that their lives and communities are both their own and not their own.

Recall the central experience of Hermes's arrival: "In the remarkable silence that may intervene in the midst of the liveliest conversations; it was said, at such times, that Hermes had entered the room."[125] Plato's appeal to Hermes reminds us that friendship transcends our capacity to fully understand it. Friendship practises us as much as we practise friendship.

One relatively contemporary figure who understood this, though without as much perspicacity as Plato, is Alexis de Tocqueville, a fact which is manifest in both his writings and his personal life. Tocqueville thought that the central problem of democracy was that the individual gets eclipsed by humanity. This leads to the erosion of self-government and freedom, because individuals, sensing they are the same everywhere, find it in their interest to submit to a centralized authority that takes care of their needs. The problem of democracy is not unlike the common interpretation of Plato eclipsing the individual with the impersonal idea.[126]

Tocqueville had a small but close network of friends who regarded themselves as politically isolated and out of step with the revolutionary times. Yet their political activities consisted in forging together elements in an attempt to both moderate and restrain the democratic revolution: "In these friendships, Tocqueville made the comparison, for himself and his friends, to 'the Jews of the Middle Ages, who needed to live together in order to recover a homeland.'"[127] While Tocqueville's reference is to the Jews in the Middle Ages, his point is one that Socrates-Hermes would recognize as his own. In his personal, political, and philosophical life,

124 Kerényi, *Hermes*, v.

125 Otto, *The Homeric Gods*, 115, 118.

126 Tocqueville even describes the problem of homogenization under "humanity" in the Hermetic terms of travelling (*Democracy in America*, 2.3.17, 588).

127 A. Jardin, *Tocqueville: A Biography*, 469 (no citation given).

Tocqueville continually practised the Hermetic art of forging together dissimilars.

In a well-known and key passage of *Democracy in America*, Tocqueville observes of the miracle of political freedom (by which he means the practice of self-government and the art of association) that "sentiments and ideas renew themselves, the heart is enlarged, and the human mind is developed only by the reciprocal action of men upon one another."[128] Because democracy inclines human beings toward individualism, and thus to loneliness, Tocqueville felt that "the science of association is the mother science; the progress of all the others depends on the progress of that one."[129] In democracy, "the notion of intermediate power is obscured and effaced."[130] Democracy corrodes the spirit of association, and so there is something counter-cultural in the activity of association. Democracy demands that the political and social state be democratic, but freedom depends on pluralism in the social state. The moral, intellectual, and spiritual capacity for self-government must draw from a tradition and set of habits beyond the democratic regime itself. In short, saving democracy from itself depends on combining democratic elements with non-democratic elements, combining the goods brought about by equality with the good brought about by the aristocratic desire for greatness. The science of association involves combining dissimilars, within a regime that either resists their combination or inclines us to only combine that which is similar. Tocqueville's own practice of virtue-friendship, upon which he frequently reflected, sustained his insights and also enabled him to sustain his own political isolation.[131]

The "holy enterprise" of political freedom is hard work, and Tocqueville is not shy about characterizing it as divine or alchemic: "There is nothing more prolific in marvels [*merveilles*] than the art of being free; but there is nothing harder than the apprenticeship of freedom."[132] We should take Tocqueville's reference to "marvels" seriously because "the art of being free" entails forging dissimilar elements. The "hand of the legislator"[133] must be proficient in these marvels not only because political institutions must be designed to enlarge the hearts of citizens as they

128 Tocqueville, *Democracy in America*, 2.2.5, 491.

129 Ibid., 2.2.5, 492.

130 Ibid., 2.4.2, 642.

131 See the letters in Roger Boesche, ed., *Alexis de Tocqueville: Selected Letters on Politics and Society*.

132 Tocqueville, *Democracy in America*, 1.2.6, 229.

133 Ibid., 1.1.5, 89–90.

act reciprocally upon one another, but also because Tocqueville, like Plato, understands that no theory can properly capture that insight.

Tocqueville's "holy enterprise," as he called his intellectual and political activities, is Hermetic because it attempts to bring dissimilars together, and because it is predicated on his practice of the highest form thereof, friendship. Democratic citizenship, as well as statesmanship, is predicated on the practice of friendship in one's personal life. Through Hermes, Plato shows us the way to go outside of ourselves so that we can both find ourselves and practise friendship with others. Tocqueville diagnoses the failure of friendship in democracy and points to Hermetic paths that open up our potential for friendship.

5

Evoking Friendship as the Form of Politics in Plato's Laws

FRIENDSHIP AS THE FORM OF POLITICS

Platonic politics is predicated on friendship. To act according to reason, to act with moral intent, is to act for the purpose of friendship, however short we fall of actualizing that purpose. Friendship is part of both the constitution of reason, and the rule of reason. Friendship is the telos of the moral act, and, as we saw in our chapter on the *Lysis,* mysteriously the telos of the intellectual act as well. The soul, the Athenian Stranger states in the *Laws,* is both "the thing that is most one's own" (726a) and "a most divine thing" (728b). Love of one's own and love of the good, the two poles of Platonic thinking about politics, are combined in various efforts to identify the good with one's own. The Athenian Stranger explains that "a man who is to attain greatness must be devoted not to himself or what belongs to him, but to what is just – whether it happens to be done by himself or by someone else … So every human being should flee excessive self-love, and should instead always pursue someone who is better than himself, without putting any feeling of shame in the way" (732a–b). On one level, the Athenian Stranger's counsel to befriend someone better than oneself is straightforward. Kleinias and Megillus partially befriend the Athenian Stranger, and, similarly to the argument of the *Lysis,* the Athenian Stranger befriends Nous. Friendship is inseparable from the ceaseless quest for moral and intellectual improvement, and this improvement is inseparable from the practice of friendship. Friendship seems to be the horizon of our intellectual and moral aspirations, and as such, we seem incapable of fully reaching it, even though it makes its presence felt in all of our actions.[1]

1 See Spaemann, *Happiness and Benevolence,* 109.

At a deeper level, the Athenian Stranger's statement betrays the insight that because one's soul is not simply a thing that might be possessed by an undefined object or another soul or self, one's soul *is* one. Or, as Socrates describes in the *Symposium*, the restlessness of eros characterizes our souls; we are always in motion. This invites the reader to reconsider how the Athenian Stranger regards the relationship of love of one's own, and love of someone who is better, to love of the good. That "divine thing" is strung between oneself and the good, moving restlessly between resource and poverty, as Socrates has Diotima relate in the *Symposium*. Thus the very constitution of the soul is in motion, moving and being moved toward the other. A soul not deformed by "excessive friendship for oneself" (*Laws* 731e) is in friendship with another. The soul finds its completion in friendship.

The *Laws* elaborates a polity whose first principle is friendship, that moral practice in which one is most likely to identify the just man with the happy man (see 661d–664b). It is the best practical polity based on fulfilling the good of friendship. Like the *Republic*, the city of the Laws, Magnesia, is founded on the "old proverb" that "things of friends really are in common" (*Laws* 739c).[2] Like Socrates's, the Athenian Stranger's opinion of this proverb is ambiguous. On the one hand, neither the Athenian Stranger nor Socrates seems to claim this view as his own, however much their conversations with others lead toward it. On the other hand, all of Socrates's own views are ambiguous. For example, Socrates's oath, "by the dog," is a case of deflection or indirection, as it is an oath to an Egyptian god, Anubis (Hermes to the Greeks). He does not seem to have friends, but says instead that "when it comes to the acquisition of friends I'm quite passionately in love" (*Lysis* 211e). Finally, he claims that "it has been given [*hermeta*] to me from a god – to be able quickly to recognize both a lover and a beloved" (*Lysis* 204c). In all of these paramount instances of what counts as Socrates's "own," it is ambiguous what this own is – just as the nature of the Socratic self, to which one might attribute subjectivity as the condition of ownership, is ambiguous. Socrates and the Athenian Stranger are like the uncanny silenus statues that Alcibiades compares Socrates to in the *Symposium*. So we should not be surprised that Socrates, the wayfarer, does not claim the proverb as his own: his own is radically ambiguous. One can see how the man with the paradoxical name, the Athenian Stranger, is similarly ambiguous.

2 See *Republic* 424a and 449c; and *Phaedrus* 279c. See also Euripides, *Orestes*, 725.

Political action aims at bringing regimes "as close as possible" to the proverb that "things of friends are in common" (*Laws* 739e). The Athenian Stranger explains what the proverb entails:

> If women are common, and children are common, and every sort of property is common; if every device has been employed to exclude all of what is called the "private" from all aspects of life; if, insofar as possible, a way has been devised to make common somehow the things that are by nature private, such as the eyes and the ears and the hands, so that they seem to see and hear and act in common; if, again, everyone praises and blames in unison, as much as possible delighting in the same things and feeling pain at the same things, if with all their might they delight in laws that aim at making the city come as close as possible to unity – then no one will ever set down a more correct or better definition than this of what constitutes the extreme as regards to virtue. (*Laws* 739c–d)

In his critique of Plato, Aristotle claims that a city with such an extreme degree of unity is no longer political. The *Laws* represents Plato's agreement with Aristotle, insofar as Magnesia is the closest practical approximation of this rule of friendship that still bears a resemblance to anything like a polity.[3] The political friendship of Magnesia is a form of unity leavened by different bodies and associations, and by liberty.[4] The *Republic* depicts a city ruled despotically by reason. It is despotic because it suppresses the non-rational, especially eros and bodies. The *Laws* presents a city ruled politically by reason (Nous). It is political because it finds a place for the non-rational. Through music, it creates friendship and "consonance" (*symphonia*) between reason and the passions, and eros is ruled in such a way that its main public manifestation is friendship

3 Aristotle's criticism of Plato in *Politics* 1260b36–61a22 seems to draw from Plato himself (see Michael Kochin, "The Unity of Virtue and the Limitations of Magnesia," and Zuckert, *Plato's Philosophers*, 104n106).

4 Seth Benardete argues that the difference between the *Laws* and *Republic* is negligible because in applying the proverb, each has as its model not two friends but a single individual. The problem with applying the friendship standard to the "second best" regime is that "The best city is a matter of becoming, friendship just is" (*Plato's "Laws": The Discovery of Being*, 166). Benardete's comprehensive reading of the *Laws* examines the distinction between the "eidetic structure of the good and the genetic structure of law" (18), which in turn is the distinction between immortal and mortal, and between what is eternal and what is within time. The collapse of this distinction turns on the double-meaning of *nomoi* as law and song (202). This collapse, as well as the effort to reduce the "old proverb" to a single individual, seems to me an instance of an overly close association of dialectics with technique. For a discussion of this difference, see Planinc, "Tracking the Good in Plato's *Republic*."

(*philia*) (653b). Like the *Republic*, Magnesia is still "utopian" because the city is presented "as a dream" (*Laws* 969b), whose founding does not depend on violence or killing or exiling "incurables" who are deemed too evil to join.[5] Even so, the *Laws* evokes a political order that recognizes that all political orders are grounded in, and aspire to, the highest kind of friendship, virtue-friendship.

"Things of friends really are in common" is the extreme rule, or outer limit, that informs the noetic constitution of Magnesia. It might be an "old proverb," but for Plato it expresses a fundamental truth about the act of *noesis*, which is communal, as seen in our examples of *sunaisthesis* in chapter 1, and our discussion of Aristotle in chapter 2. In our own time, some explanation is needed as to why it should serve as a standard not only for politics, but also for friendship. Indeed, this extreme unity seems a recipe for totalitarianism and homogeneity, and even if Plato did not regard the unity of Magnesia or of *kallipolis* in the *Republic* as a practical possibility, one still wonders why such a thing should serve as a standard for politics at all. It is also unclear why it should serve as an expression of friendship, considered as an ethical standard.

As an expression of consubstantiality in the quest for wisdom, the proverb points to a paradox that runs through the Platonic dialogues and through the constitution of the polis in the *Laws*. If knowledge is sought together, it cannot be implanted by one soul into another, any more than sight can be implanted into the eyes of another (*Republic* 518b). Insight must be experienced, or received, independently by each individual searcher (see *Laws* 968e). One cannot be one another's benefactor in thought. This is a fundamental Socratic commitment. Our erotic and friendly attachments to one another and to the good are punctuated by the deep freedom we experience both as individuals, restlessly questing between resource and plenty, and with each other.

5 We are told that Kleinias has been assigned to found a Cretan colony. He has the power to pick and choose suitable future citizens: "There isn't any need to devise a colonizing expedition or some purgative selection at present; instead, just as in the case of a single reservoir formed by the flowing together of many springs and mountain torrents, we are compelled to turn our minds to insuring that water flowing in will be as pure as possible, partly by drawing off some and partly by diverting some in side-channel" (*Laws* 736a–b). The Athenian Stranger notes the dreamlike or speculative character of their inquiry next when he states: "But it's likely that toil and danger are present in every political project. Since things are being done now in speech but not in deed, let's assume that our selection has been carried out and that the purification has happened according to our manner of thinking" (*Laws* 736b).

The Athenian Stranger's elaboration of the proverb extends the act of *noesis* into our affections and our body, signifying that the rule of reason seems to extend throughout our entire being. Like the *Republic*, the Athenian Stranger's statement conflates internal goods of the soul with external goods of the body. This is less like the noetic constitution of Magnesia, but the latter still reflects this conflation as far as it is possible by instituting the political rule of Nous in consonance (*symphonia*) with the non-rational strata of reality, including the affections and bodies. The best way to understand the non-despotic, political rule of Nous over bodies is by observing the attention that the three men of the *Laws* give to choruses, where citizens sing and dance. By singing and dancing, citizens display political action in the body's willing obedience to being ruled by Nous. As this and the next two chapters will show, learning to dance is the Magnesian way of noetic political rule. Choral dance is the characteristic form of political action of the Magnesian regime.[6]

The Athenian Stranger states that the choral gifts of the Muses and Apollo "should be the first things one tells everyone" when founding a new city (*Laws* 796e). The choruses are the beginning of civic life, civic education, and civic friendship in Plato's *Laws*, but they also point to the end. The end is a vision of Magnesia as an ikon of Nous, the rule of reason, whose aim is friendship.[7] The contents of the dialogue (the argument and the action), as well as its very writing by Plato and the performance of it by his readers, consist in the demiurgic act of bringing forth the rule of Nous. The dialogue dramatically represents the genesis of Nous as the transformation of a point into a completed sphere – an image of the completion of the cosmos itself – when, as the Athenian Stranger later states, "the original cause ... allows of perception by perceivers" (894a). The *rhythmos* and *harmonia* of the choruses – the form of civic action in Magnesia – are an image of the "everflowing [*aenaos*] existence by a motion that receives its coming-into-being" from soul (966e). The character of this friendly noetic theology will be elaborated upon in chapter 7.

6 This study focuses on chorality at the expense of the Athenian Stranger's discussion of the physicality of sports and war-games because my focus is on the intellectual or visionary component of friendship. On sports and war-games, see Michael S. Kochin, *Gender and Rhetoric in Plato's Political Thought.* On sports and spectatorship in general, see Michael Novak, *The Joy of Sports: End Zones, Bases, Baskets, Balls, and the Consecration of the American Spirit,* and James Schall, "On the Seriousness of Sports, Watchers All."

7 Planinc, *Plato's Political Philosophy*, 165.

Magnesia, an ikon of the cosmos ruled by Nous, is a theater in which friends behold one another while simultaneously beholding the first cause through varying degrees of mediation. As we saw in chapter 2, it is the perfection of what Aristotle, at the height of his teaching on virtue-friendship, calls *sunaisthesis,* or joint perception of the good. The polity brought into being by speech in the *Laws,* which is the image of the spherical cosmos, is an image of friendship, the form of politics. By focusing on the connection between the *nomoi* of this polity, its festivals, the three elderly interlocutors, and the cosmic first cause, this discussion of the *Laws* (while not comprehensive) traces a sphere sector that illuminates the nature of political friendship. The vision of political friendship that the Athenian Stranger brings forth, playfully as if in a dream, holds true of the practice of politics for us. The dialogue's drama, concerning the genesis of the regime of friendship, reminds us that, at least in politics if not in other realms of life, friendship is generated out of what is not friendship, even enmity. One cannot emphasize enough the difficulty of peacemaking, of reconciling the infinite distance between beings who are opposites if not enemies. In chapter 4 we saw how Plato invokes Hermes to illuminate the miracle of friendship. Hermes is not explicitly present in the *Laws,* but the problem that Hermes represents – of how to reconcile dissimilars at nearly the highest intellectual, and thus emotional, level in the genesis of political order – is the main concern of the dialogue.

PRELUDES

This sphere sector of friendship – the one that draws a line from civic festive dance to the first cause of the cosmos – can be seen in a statement the Athenian Stranger makes in Book IV, immediately after noting that the day's conversation has taken them to noon, when the sun reaches the highest part of the sky, on the day of the solstice. He states:

> It seems to me that we have only just begun to enunciate laws, and that everything said before consisted of our preludes to laws. Why have I said these things? What I wish to say is this: all speeches, and whatever pertains to voice, are preceded by preludes – almost like warming up exercises – which artfully attempt to promote what is to come. It is the case, I suppose, that of the songs sung to the kithara, the so-called "laws" or *nomoi,* like all music, are preceded by preludes composed with amazing seriousness. Yet with regard to things that are really "laws," the laws we assert to be political, no one has ever either uttered a prelude or become a composer and brought one to light – just as if it were a thing that

did not exist in nature. But the way we've been spending our time has shown us, it seems to me, that such a thing really does exist. (*Laws*, 722d–e)

The "revelation at noon," as Voegelin describes this passage,[8] consists of the Athenian Stranger's proclamation of the political rule of Nous over the universe. Indeed, the Athenian Stranger not only proclaims it, but he effects it, such that the *Laws* itself is a dialogue that effects the political rule of Nous. As he indicates, no one before has ever brought the phenomenon of preludes to light, "just as if it were a thing that did not exist in nature." The *Laws* "completes" nature by being the first instance of genuinely begetting preludes, in a manner more complete, self-conscious, and differentiated than in the *Hymn to Hermes* (discussed in chapter 4), where Hermes completes the theogony by singing his own song. The significance of this bringing forth, or founding, is that it effects, without violence, the rule of Nous over the forceful and violent elements of nature. It is the kind of rule that is most in accord with nature: "the natural rule exercised by the law over willing subjects, without violence" (*Laws* 690c).[9] For the first time in history, Nous is shown and made to rule. Just as the rule of Kronos gave way to Zeus, so too now does the rule of Zeus give way to Nous.[10]

Indeed, Plato's refiguring of the mythological birth of Zeus in the drama of the *Laws* highlights this revelatory and demiurgic process. The dialogue takes place during the long walk of the three men from Knossos, the dancing ground that Daedalus built for Ariadne, to the cave of the birthplace of Zeus. Hesiod describes the scene of Zeus's birth, when Rhea, his mother, "hid him [from Cronus] deep in a cave, deep within the hollows of sacred Earth, deep beneath the Aegean mountain, dense with woodland."[11] Rhea subsequently presents Cronus with a rock instead of baby Zeus, who swallows it in the belief he is killing his son, whom he knows will one day destroy him. However, Cronus vomits out the stone, which Zeus later fixed "in the wide-open ground, for the Pythian oracle at sacred Delphi, under the mountain glens of Parnassus. Ever since, the rock remains a sign of his rule, a wondrous attraction for

8 Voegelin, *Plato and Aristotle*, 253–7.

9 Or at least the violence is hidden from sight, as one would expect in such a "dream." See Waller Newell's discussion of the "hidden founding" of the *Laws* (*Tyranny: A New Interpretation*, 108–18).

10 Voegelin, *Plato and Aristotle*, 215–68.

11 Hesiod, *Theogony*, lines 482–3.

mortals to see."[12] Other sources, such as Apollodorus, describe Rhea as having the Corybantic dancers protect Zeus in the cave by dancing around him: "clashing their spears on their shields in order that Cronus might not hear the child's voice."[13] Thus, the journey of the *Laws* re-enacts and refigures the birth of Zeus – complete, as we shall see, with choruses, which also shelter and protect Nous, since it is always undergoing birth. Plato seems to be playfully associating the choruses with the Corybantic dancers. In similar fashion, he playfully derives chorus from *charis* (joy). Furthermore, in Greek the chi can become a kappa (as Chronus and Kronos), and the vowels can slide into one another.[14] One might even fancifully regard the three old men as representing the young Corybantic dancers – initiates and daimons – who dance around the newly born Nous and stand guard against the forces of violence, as the original Kouretes stood guard against Kronos.

The *Laws* as a demiurgic act can perhaps be seen most vividly when the Athenian Stranger suggests that the conversation be recorded and used by the Magnesians to help them govern themselves (811c–d; see also 859a). In establishing the political rule of Nous, the dialogue *Laws* is demiurgic in addition to being diagnostic. It is the very act of political creation it describes.

The preludes are evocations, enchantments, or even prayers to induce hearers to practise friendship and thus be amenable to the rule of Nous in their souls. Plato is refiguring the meaning of *prooimion* as it comes down from Greek lyrical poetry, and the Homeric Hymns in particular. Gregory Nagy explains the Hermetic background and the political function:

> The archetypal virtuoso performance of Apollo, where he first struck up the lyre and then "sang beautifully, in accompaniment" (*Hymn to Hermes* 502), is morphologically a *prooimion*, which can be translated roughly as "prelude" but which I prefer to render with the more neutral Latin borrowing, "prooemium." The *prooimion* is a framework for differentiated virtuoso singing by the individual "lyre

12 Hesiod, *Theogony*, 497–500.

13 Apollodorus *Library*, 1.1.6–7; Hyginus *Fabulae*, 139. They guarded Dionysius as well (Nonnos, *Dionysiaca*, 9.160ff., 13.135ff.). See also Homer, *Iliad*, 18.591–2; Callimachus, *Hymns*, i.52ff.; Strabo, *Geography*, 10.3.11; Diodorus, *The Library of History*, 5.70, 2–4; Lucretius, *On the Nature of Things*, ii.633–9; Virgil, *Georgics*, 3.150ff; Jane E. Harrison, *Epilegomena to the Study of Greek Religion and Themis: A Study of the Social Origins of Greek Religion*, 1–29. Harrison regards the ritual hymn of the birth of Zeus at Palaikastro on Crete as the centre of her inquiry into the origins of Greek religion (2). I thank Rebecca LeMoine for pointing out the presence of the Corybantes in the *Laws* to me.

14 I thank Michael Davis for suggesting these puns.

[*kitharâ*] singer," and it literally means "the front part of the song [*oimê*]" (just as *pronâos* means 'the front part of the temple [*nâos*]'). The *prooimion* or prooemium took the form of a prayer sung to a given god who presided over the occasion of a given seasonally recurring festival where the song was performed in competition with other songs. A clear reflex of this form can be found in the actual structure of the *Homeric Hymns.* In fact Thucydides (3.104.3–4) uses the word *prooimion* in referring to the version of the Homeric *Hymn to Apollo* that he knew. That the dramatized context of these *Hymns* is one of seasonally recurring festivals where contests in song are held is clear from the use of 'seasonal time' (*hôrâ*) in *Hymn* 26.12–13 and of *agôn* 'contest' in *Hymn* 6.19 ... To sum up the essence of the *prooimion,* I quote the wording of Quintilian (*Institutio oratoria* 4.1.2): "that *oimê* is song and that the *kitharôidoi* refer to those few words that they sing before their contest proper, for the sake of winning favor, as *prooimion.*"[15]

Nagy's historical and philological examination of the *prooimion* (or prooemium) demonstrates its choral, performative, and civic function in Greek culture, and illustrates Plato's basic assumptions in adapting its meaning in the *Laws,* including the Hermetic source text of the *Homeric Hymns* which is also apparent in the *Lysis.* Indeed, as shown below, the choruses themselves are refigured versions of the choral practices described in those hymns.

For the Athenian Stranger, the preludes function as the reasons the lawgiver provides to his citizens for the laws he enacts. It is tyrannical merely to command. Laws must also persuade by giving their reasons, and the preludes to laws serve this purpose by acknowledging the dual purpose of a good polity, which is freedom and friendship among citizens (*Laws* 701d). Thus, shortly before the revelation at noon, the Athenian Stranger indicates that the first law, which commands citizens to marry between the ages of 30 and 35, exists so that citizens may partake in the type of immortality appropriate for mortals – namely, having children (*Laws* 721c–d). On its own, however, the reason provided by this prelude is unconvincing. At best it is only partially true, as immortality is usually not at the forefront of people's minds when they engage in sexual relations.

Kleinias seems to overlook the incomplete nature of this prelude when, immediately after the revelation, he speaks of preludes as a kind of statement of purpose distinct from "just any chance sort of speech" (*Laws* 723e). Yet, as evidenced by the Athenian Stranger's reference in the revelation at noon to preludes as "everything said before," preludes

15 Nagy, *Pindar's Homer: The Lyric Possession of an Epic Past,* chapter 12, §33.

are neither statements of purpose (which would, after all, be commands) nor "just any chance sort of speech." The entire dialogue is a prelude, a way of preparing the ground in people's souls for the political rule of Nous. At the same time, preludes are not quite dialectic either. Dialectic is a combination of the two types of speech Kleinias seems to have in mind – purposeful, but also seemingly governed by chance.[16] Preludes, by contrast, are preparatory: they prepare souls to engage in dialectic, to have Nous govern them. Indeed, the Athenian Stranger distinguishes "argument" (*logos*) from prelude (*prooemium*) by stipulating that the latter puts those who receive the law "in a frame of mind more favorably disposed and therefore more apt to learn anything" (*Laws* 723b). These warming-up exercises or enchantments prepare our psyches to receive the *logos*, which means that they also prepare the non-rational parts of our soul. This is why choruses play such an important role in education in the *Laws*. As Socrates states in the *Republic*, music reaches the inmost part of our souls (*Republic* 401d). Right (*ortho*) music is preparatory because it mysteriously attaches souls to Nous by means of "enchantments" (*epoidai*) (*Laws* 655d). Yet enchantments are not magical or irrational. Rather, as Glenn Morrow shows, "if there is magic in them, it is the magic of meaningful words addressed to an intelligent soul, when accompanied by rhythm and melody and the other adornments of musical art; and they are designed to produce an effect, not upon the gods, but upon the souls of the citizens. They are peculiarly effective means of persuasion."[17]

Another way of thinking about preludes' preparatory nature is that each law, speech, or "whatever pertains to the voice" comes with its own set of assumptions and premises. In the case of the founding laws of Magnesia, the preeminent prelude postulates that the gods are good, and thus that they care for humans and cannot be bought off (*Laws* 897b–c). Despite Kleinias's assertion that a brief prelude can establish this (*Laws* 723e), demonstrating this prelude requires a long road if it can be demonstrated, rather than evoked or enchanted, at all (I shall argue in chapter 7 that it cannot). Preludes, then, point but do not necessarily lead to highest and first principles. They point to dialectic, but they themselves are not dialectic. The task of preparing souls to receive the political rule of Nous is endless.

Preludes are preparatory speeches and enchantments, but they are also acts or deeds. "Everything said before" in the dialogue also refers to

16 Zuckert notes that the word "dialectic" (*dialektike*) does not occur in the *Laws* (*Plato's Philosophers*, 108).

17 Morrow, *Plato's Cretan City*, 310.

the action of three old men: an Athenian, a Cretan, and a Spartan leisurely walking through the Cretan countryside. Their discussion ranges over various topics, including wine-drinking, choruses, courage, prudence, law, and so forth; but throughout their walk, the conversation itself transforms them and their relationship with each other. I think Planinc is correct to argue that the relationship between the three men is an icon of the symphonic relationship of Nous, *psyche*, and *soma* (body), and that the Athenian Stranger moulds the other men to be as receptive to the rule of Nous as possible.[18] Kleinias and Megillus represent the extent to which non-philosophers are governed by Nous. This may be shown most vividly in the dialogue's last lines, when Megillus, who represents body (*soma*), tells Kleinias that "either the city's founding must be abandoned, or this stranger here must not be allowed to go, and by entreaties and every contrivance he must be made to share in the city's founding" (*Laws* 969c). In a scene that echoes the opening of the *Republic*, when Polemarchus has his slave force Socrates to stay and speak with their group, *soma* here pleads to be ruled by Nous. The body is receptive to the rule of Nous when it wants to learn how to dance: it wants to learn to dance together with other bodies and souls. The body pleads for friendship – embodied friendship.

CONVERSANTS STRIVING TO BEFRIEND ONE ANOTHER

The dialogue is made up of dual dramas, insofar as it is about the colony that Kleinias is to establish, but also about the relationship of the three founding Greeks. Their conversation, while leisurely, is bound by the practical necessity of Kleinias's learning how best to found a city, and in a timely fashion. The conversation is also disrupted by Kleinias's and Megillus's non-philosophical natures, which obliges the Athenian Stranger to skip over or abbreviate discussion of fundamental questions, including the idea that the gods are good and that the beautiful and the good are identical (*Laws* 655a, 664a). He must resort to sophisms to get Kleinias and Megillus, as well as future citizens, to believe "just about anything": the noble lie (*pseudos mythos*) or "magnificent myth" that is also true (*Laws* 663d).

Beneath the friendliness of the three men flows intra-Greek rivalry. Each man displays admiration for the city of the others, but each thinks his own is superior; Kleinias and Megillus become indignant when the Athenian Stranger points out weaknesses in their cities' constitutional

18 Planinc, *Plato's Political Philosophy*, 227.

orders.[19] In addition, hanging over their walk in the country is an awareness that Crete is mountainous and dangerous. Kleinias reminds them how proficient his fellow Cretans are at mountain warfare while articulating the perspective that nature is strife, and therefore that politics is about total war and "peace is only a name" (*Laws* 626a).[20] One can imagine that during his long silences, Megillus is watching the other two and on the lookout for ambushes. The three men must walk far before their proclamations of friendship for one another can be meaningful (many fail to be reciprocated[21]).

Preludes are preparatory conversations and enchantments to make the recipients of laws "more apt to learn something," but they refer also to deeds. Perhaps the preeminent deed in "everything said before" is Kleinias's apparent *metanoia* in Book I (*Laws* 628a). Throughout the first part of Book I, Kleinias has been asserting a pre-Socratic view of the universe whereby all beings are in a state of flux and strife. The purpose of politics is war. For this reason the warlike Lacedamonians are constitutionally obliged to eat their meals in common, in barracks. The purpose of their city, and all cities, is war. War characterizes more than just a city's outward stance toward others. It also characterizes a city's internal composition, the internal composition of its units (such as families), and, it seems, the internal composition of a human being. Human beings seem always to be at war with each other and with their own souls.

Part of the action of Book I involves the Athenian Stranger demonstrating the implausibility of such a view, and how, in fact, Kleinias goes astray in his theoretical understanding of both the universe and politics.

19 See throughout Book I of the *Laws*, especially 625e to 626b.

20 Zuckert suggests that the Athenian Stranger's argument in Book X that the gods exist is directed against Kleinias himself (*Plato's Philosophers*, 126). I consider this argument in chapter 7.

21 See *Laws* 641d, 642d, 648c. The gentlemen's attitudes toward each other's cities is related to the dramatic dating of the dialogue. Zuckert argues that it must be dated before the Peloponnesian War because no one mentions it (*Plato's Philosophers*, 53). It would be surprising for them to cooperate as much as they do during or immediately after the war. However, it should be noted that at least one event in the war is alluded to, Pericles's Funeral Oration, when the Athenian Stranger speaks of the laws as a "despotic mistress" – an object of eros according to Pericles, but under the constitution of Nous, laws become an object of *philia* (*Laws* 698b). Indeed, while it would be surprising for the gentlemen to cooperate during or immediately after the Peloponnesian War, it would not be impossible. Voegelin's suggestion that the *Laws* represents Plato's endeavour to create a pan-Hellenic empire or consciousness is plausible in light of what probably every intelligent Greek understood after the war, which is that the Greek city-state was no longer tenable as a political form, if indeed it ever was (*Plato and Aristotle*, 223–8). If this was Plato's goal, then it would be quite reasonable, as Basil Fawlty also understood, not to mention the war.

For Kleinias, political order is based on courage alone, which is only one part of virtue. Yet his actions betray his speech because he is conversable, peaceable, leisurely, and a good companion to the two other men (his references to the proficiency of mountain warfare among the Cretans notwithstanding). His opinion that the universe is war conflicts with his deeds, as it must. His tyrannical dream that happiness consists of satisfying all his desires also conflicts with his deeds, as it must (*Laws* 661c–d). Moreover, unlike other interlocutors in the Platonic corpus who espouse similar views, including Thrasymachus and Callicles, Kleinias is easily persuaded by the Athenian Stranger's demolition of his arguments. It is as if Kleinias wants to have his theory disproven. The *nomoi* and the *logos* must match existence. Turning Kleinias around and making him more conversational is part of the Athenian Stranger's political founding of Nous.

It is startling but not altogether surprising when the Athenian Stranger poses three alternatives for the best method of establishing political rule, and Kleinias chooses the one involving friendship. The Athenian Stranger asks which method is best: (1) destroying the wicked and letting the better rule themselves, (2) enslaving the wicked and letting the better rule themselves, or (3) "reconciling [*diallagon*] them by laying down laws for them for the rest of time and thus securing their friendship for one another" (*Laws* 627e; see 628b). In the first mention of friendship (*philia*) in the dialogue, Kleinias, almost with relief, jettisons his view of the universe as war and strife and embraces the political view that friendship is the telos of politics (though he fails to understand its full implications). This view also points toward more cosmological possibilities later in the dialogue.

With this admission, Kleinias and the Athenian Stranger can get on to the task of inquiring into the nature and scope of politics, and what makes the best regime. But this is made possible by their developing practice of friendship with one another and with Megillus. They are not yet friends, and perhaps, due to the inequality between the Athenian Stranger and the other men, true friendship is not possible for them. Even so, as with the third political option Kleinias chooses, they go about performing the political deed among themselves of "reconciling [*diallagon*] them by laying down laws for them for the rest of time and thus securing their friendship for one another."

The gap between them is one that the Athenian Stranger mentions at the conclusion of the dialogue. In the situation in which the lawgiver stands before learners, it is

> vain to discuss these matters ... for it wouldn't be clear to the learners themselves whether the subject were being learned at the right time, until knowledge of the

subject had, presumably, come into being within the soul of each. Thus, while it would be incorrect to speak of all that pertains to these matters as indescribable secrets, they are incapable of being described beforehand, because describing them beforehand would clarify nothing of what is being discussed. (*Laws*, 968d–e)

One might say that the preludes the Athenian Stranger offers to Kleinias and Megillus are a more gentle version of the forceful *periagoge* described in the *Republic*, where the prisoner is forcibly turned around and dragged out into the light by the teacher (*Republic* 518c–d). The preludes of the *Laws* are "some safe cable" that the gods, via the Athenian Stranger, hold out to the other men, to help them cross the "rather swift and perhaps almost unfordable" argument that establishes the political rule of Nous (892e–893b). However, as we shall see, the "safe cable" of the gods involves an element of injustice on the part of the Athenian Stranger.

The conversation and leisurely walk of the three men is sprinkled with gestures and claims of friendship that are often reciprocated but just as often not. Most tellingly, the Athenian Stranger argues that they, as fellow founders, cannot be friends unless they can agree, or are in "consonance," on one fundamental matter: that the just man is also the happy man (*Laws* 661d–664b). Kleinias has great difficulty understanding this prelude, and so to believe it he relents to the Athenian Stranger's authority. This prelude is the foundation of their city. The justice of their laws depends on it. Indeed, it is the article of faith that any founder, any ruler of a regime, must hold. For Americans, the American citizen is the happy citizen. For Canadians it is the Canadian. For the Chinese it is the Chinese – and so on. All political regimes are predicated on the principle that their laws are the most just and most conducive to happiness. Only the regime predicated on the entirety of virtue, purportedly Magnesia, can truly be happy, it seems.

To summarize so far, the Athenian Stranger, with Kleinias and Megillus in tow, founds the political rule of Nous. The preludes are the expression of this political rule: they prepare people to receive it by enchanting them and by educating them to be amenable to persuasion, as much as possible. The political rule of Nous is revealed, at noon on the longest day of the year, when the men realize that Nous can rule independently and over coercion. This is the possibility of political rule, over and against tyranny, in our world. The revelation at noon is the culmination of the argument and the action of the dialogue, in which the three men discuss wine-drinking, choruses, law, and come to agree that the purpose of the good regime is friendship. They themselves may not be friends, but they aspire to friendship, the outer limit and ordering force of moral action.

Their practice of friendship is the prelude that enables them to reveal the political rule of Nous. In Voegelin's terms, *philia* is a pretheoretical experience that enables love of the good and beautiful.[22] Its practice is a reminder of how the love of the good and the beautiful is a practice too, and one whose good surpasses our capacity to theorize about it. Friendship is the deed that is the prelude to establishing the political rule of Nous. Friendship is the prelude to the laws, and to the dialogue entitled *Laws* (*Nomoi*). The rule of Nous establishes friendship as the form of politics.

NOMOI

A final comment is needed regarding the revelation at noon. The Athenian Stranger observes that the word *nomoi* refers to the ancestral songs sung with the accompaniment of the kithara (see *Laws* 700b). *Nomoi* carries numerous meanings in the dialogue, including what we would call legislation and customary law, but also music, song, and poetry. *Nomoi* reminds us of the cosmological significance of music to Plato, in both the order of the universe and political order. The Athenian Stranger's reference to songs accompanied by the kithara is an indication that at least part of his effort in founding the rule of Nous is refiguring the ancestral Greek customs and myths for a new age. The innovation of the revelation at noon is not a *novus ordo seclorum,* nor is it comparable to a new revolutionary calendar along the lines of the French Revolution. Rather, it is a refiguring of tradition, a way of fulfilling the possibility of that tradition by anchoring it to Nous. To borrow from Augustine, the political rule of Nous is ever ancient, ever new.[23]

The paradigm of the prelude with the kithara that the Athenian Stranger probably has in mind is Odysseus's proclamation to the Phaikians that banqueting and listening to the bard is the "crown of life."[24] Odysseus's song about his deeds starts with a self-reflective prelude stipulating that the best thing for men to do is be leisurely while listening to the bard sing, likely with the kithara, about great deeds. Having just been entertained by Demodocus, the bard of the Phaikians, Odysseus sets out to sing the greatest of all stories, his own. He refigures the tradition. The self-reflective song of Odysseus compares with the one

22 Voegelin, *Science, Politics, and Gnosticism*, 259. Leo Strauss's study *The Argument and Action of Plato's Laws* presents the most detailed account of the "argument and action" of their discussion.

23 Augustine, *Confessions,* X.27.

24 Homer, *Odyssey,* IX.1–12. See discussion of this text in chapters 1 and 3.

sung by the Athenian Stranger, who is himself adapting the song of Odysseus sung by Homer.[25] Even so, it is noteworthy that the paradigm of life being held up is one in which humans reflect on great deeds, rather than perform them. Or more accurately: it is both the performance and the reflection upon those deeds, together with friends. Thought succeeds action. Thinking together, allowing "perception by perceivers" (*Laws* 894a; examined in chapter 7), is the epitome of life. The political form of such reflection is conducted in songs sung by those aspiring to *symphonia,* with one another and within their own souls. The form of politics is the practice of friendship. As we saw in previous chapters, it is for this reason that Aristotle quotes this line from the *Odyssey* as expressing the "pastime of free persons" (*Politics* 1338a28–30). As Odysseus sings his own song, the citizens of Magnesia will sing theirs, which will be a better tragedy than anything a poet can produce (*Laws* 817b). Indeed, the *Laws* seems to take up Socrates's invitation for a lover of poetry to defend it without meter, while retaining the Socratic perspective that only those educated by philosophy can truly be the judges of poetry (*Republic* 607d–e). As with Odysseus, the mimicry of the Magnesian chorus is ambiguous because it seems both to mimic a paradigm of good action and to constitute good action. The dialogue *Laws* describes and effects the rule of Nous.

25 Planinc argues that the *Laws* refigures Odysseus's homecoming (*Plato's Political Philosophy*, 250).

6

Political Friendship as Learning to Dance Together

At the still point of the turning world. Neither flesh nor fleshless;
Neither from nor towards; at the still point, there the dance is,
But neither arrest nor movement. And do not call it fixity,
Where past and future are gathered. Neither movement from nor towards,
Neither ascent nor decline. Except for the point, the still point,
There would be no dance, and there is only the dance.
I can only say, *there* we have been: but I cannot say where.
And I cannot say, how long, for that is to place it in time.[1]

CHORUSES: DANCING TOGETHER

Just as Kleinias regards common feasts as the paradigmatic way in which the Lacedaimonians come together as a city (though he initially regards them as serving the city's primary aim of war),[2] the Magnesians will spend their days in festivity. The principle distantly glimpsed within the inferior Lacedaimonian practice will come to fruition in superior Magnesia. Choral festivity is their form of civic life: "That every man and child, free and slave, female and male – indeed, the whole city – must never cease singing, as an incantation to itself, these things we've described, which must in one way or another be continually changing, presenting variety in every way, so that the singers will take unsatiated

1 T.S. Eliot, "Burnt Norton," in *Collected Poems, 1909–1962,* 173.

2 Even so, he can agree with the Athenian Stranger that feasts and drinking parties are acts of friendship: "friends communing with friends in peace and with goodwill" (*Laws* 641b).

pleasure in their hymns" (*Laws* 665c).[3] The Athenian Stranger restates his point later: "One should live out one's days playing at certain games – sacrificing, singing, and dancing – with the result that one can make the gods propitious to oneself and can defend oneself against enemies and be victorious over them in battle" (*Laws* 803e).

The Athenian Stranger's point is important. Not only will this particular regime, Magnesia, perform these paradigmatic actions, but, because Magnesia is the best practical regime on account of being based upon the entirety of virtue (i.e., wisdom, justice, moderation, and courage), he also claims that civic virtue per se takes this form: "the good man is very noble, very good, and most efficacious for a happy life, as well as preeminently fitting, if he sacrifices to and always communes with the gods – through prayers, votive offerings, and every sort of service to the gods" (*Laws* 716e). Civic action is paradigmatically liturgical.

Because he thinks that festivity is the paradigmatic civic action of a regime based upon the entirety of virtue, or at least of civic virtue, the Athenian Stranger employs numerous devices to ensure that the choruses are governed by Nous instead of passion or Dionysius (in fact, Dionysius is brought in only to be tamed by Nous). Among these devices is the musical education that forms their loves, and which encourages choruses to take delight in each other and their shared vision of the good in a manner characteristic of friendship-love. Their education in music, in which they mimic good character, teaches them the practical judgment to discern good character, as well as to take proper pride in their own regime, which is dedicated to the goal of cultivating virtue. The Athenian Stranger's insight regarding choral education might appear strange from the perspective of our less musical age, but in fact it coheres with some contemporary research that associates participating in choirs with moral aptitude.[4] The dances of the Magnesians will be

3 For details, see Morrow, *Plato's Cretan City*, 302–18. Morrow's exposition of the choruses and their central role in civic education is thorough, except he fails to illuminate how citizens experience choral life collectively. That is, he treats choruses as assemblages of individual choreuts singing and dancing in isolation, with little guidance as to how they experience themselves singing and dancing together, and thus he misses the significance of the chorus as the centerpiece of political friendship. Other helpful discussions include Steven H. Lonsdale, "Dance and Play in Plato's *Laws*: Anticipating an Anthropological Paradigm"; Lucia Prauscello, "Patterns of Chorality in Plato's *Laws*" and, more recently, *Performing Citizenship in Plato's Laws*, chapters 3–4; Anastasia-Erasmia Peponi, ed., *Performance and Culture in Plato's Laws* (especially the essays by Claude Calame, Leslie Kurke, and Barbara Kowalzig).

4 John Bingham, "Perfect Harmony: How Singing in a Choir Can Make Us More 'Moral,'" *Daily Telegraph*, 27 February 2015, http://www.telegraph.co.uk/news/religion/

ecstatic but their ecstasy will be drawn out by Nous. Nous will not teach them to sing the song of philosophy, but it will teach them a large amount of practical wisdom, which will enable them to discern the virtues in others and share that discernment with their fellow citizens.

Readers of the dialogue do not see these friendships directly, but rather see the channels through which the personal friendships of Magnesian citizens will flow. The three gentlemen will describe the political friendship of the Magnesians, but not the inner workings, as it were, of their private practices of friendship. They also treat the prospective citizens as an undifferentiated whole, not as individual persons, as we saw in Socrates's treatment of Lysis and his friends in chapter 4. One major reason for this is that the three of them are legislators. They recognize the distinction between knowledge and law: "For no law or order is stronger than knowledge, nor is it right for intelligence to be subordinate, or a slave, to anyone, but it should be ruler over everything, if indeed it is true and really free according to nature ... That is why one must choose what comes second, order and law – which see and look to most things, but are incapable of seeing everything" (*Laws* 875c–d).[5] As Socrates points out in the *Phaedrus*, lawgiving is comparable to writing insofar as both are, relative to dialectic, blind to the particular souls of the one with whom one converses (277d). This is a major reason why, in the *Gorgias*, he tells Callicles that he alone possesses the "true political art" (521d). Law treats people as a group at the expense of their individuality; dialectic is the most genuine encounter of person to person.

According to the Athenian Stranger, two reasons explain why people have not noticed that festivity and chorality make up the quintessential form of civic action; and these reasons also explain why cities have not yet fully devoted themselves to the life of festivity. First, most cities are dominated by an erotic love of wealth that precludes leisure (*Laws* 831c). The erotic love of wealth enslaves cities to the ceaseless pursuit of putative necessities: a quasi-Hobbesian quest for power after power that ceaseth only in death, or war. In chapter 3 we examined Aristotle's argument that political societies typically regard play and festivity as mere respite from occupation – their supposedly real form of action. Moreover, for the Athenian Stranger, this erotic love of wealth also marginalizes spirited people in cities (and the spirited parts of citizens' souls), whose actions

11437624/Perfect-harmony-how-singing-in-a-choir-can-make-us-more-moral.html. Bingham is reporting on a study published by the Jubilee Centre for Character and Virtues at the University of Birmingham, England (http://www.jubileecentre.ac.uk/).

5 See Kochin, *Gender and Rhetoric in Plato's Political Thought*, 109, and Seth Benardete, *Plato's "Laws,"* 143–52.

are more likely to be the kind that cities would praise in song and dance. Excessive love of wealth undermines leisure, and the spiritual freedom required for festive play.

The second reason the Athenian Stranger gives for the lack of festivals among citizens follows from the first. Most entities we currently call cities or regimes are in fact composed of warring factions, most notably the rich versus the poor (*Laws* 832e). They are based upon partial virtue, which marginalizes those who possess the other virtues. Thus there is no basis for them to come together in the moments of unity and self-reflection characteristic of festivals. Only a city based upon the entirety of virtue, and not just a part of it, can fully be considered political. Only a city based upon the entirety of virtue is capable of being present to itself in festivity.[6] This argument is similar to the one made by Aristotle in *Politics* VII–VIII that leisure is the self-sufficient activity to which political societies must aspire, but which they also fail to achieve in nearly every case.

The Athenian Stranger expresses anger when recounting these reasons, and the fact that Kleinas chastises him for immoderation here is noteworthy. Kleinias complains that the Athenian Stranger's criticisms of cities based on the pursuit of wealth "make those who are courageous into pirates, housebreakers, temple robbers, warriors, and tyrannical types"; on such a view, the latter are condemned "to live out their lives with their own souls always hungry" (*Laws* 831e). Kleinias adds that the Athenian Stranger gives "the impression that you're so filled with hatred that you chastise this sort of disposition more than is required by the present argument" (*Laws* 832b). The Athenian Stranger is moderate throughout the entire dialogue except at this point. This is a sign of the importance he attaches not just to festivity, but to how festivity reflects the city that is genuinely committed to virtue, and the great injustice that less virtuous cities commit against, in this case, the courageous. The passage is reminiscent of one of the only other instances in the Platonic dialogues when Socrates vents "spirited anger against those who were responsible" for unjustly spattering philosophy in mud, for making her appear as sophistry (*Republic* 536a). The connection between these two manifestations of the Platonic philosopher's anger or indignation seems to be that in each case, vitriol is directed at an injustice committed against what is best in human beings. For Socrates, this is philosophy; for the more politically minded Athenian Stranger, it is the completion of virtue in the life of the polis. For both, the target of their ire is

6 For details see Morrow, *Plato's Cretan City*, 352–89. Josef Pieper's theoretical exposition of festivity is based largely on the *Laws* (*In Tune With the World* and *Leisure: The Basis of Culture*).

injustice against the capstone of human perfection, or that which makes us truly human.

The Magnesians will spend the majority of their time in festivity. There will be 365 festivals per year – one for each day (*Laws* 828b). This includes twelve festivals for the twelve Olympian gods, with each of the twelve tribes of Magnesia taking responsibility for one (*Laws* 828c). In addition, there will be separate festivals appropriate for men and for women: "They'll make sacred monthly sacrifices to each of these, along with choruses, musical contests, and gymnastic contests" (*Laws* 828c). The focus here is on choruses, but one must keep in mind that they partake in festivals along with musical contests and gymnastic choruses, by which the Athenian Stranger means primarily pyrrhic dances that mimic combat (and Corybantic dancers), as well as spirited war games in which death is a real possibility.[7] Festivals are leisurely and free, but also engage the virtues of the citizens. They practise courage in war games; they practise moderation by dancing and singing in the spirit of friendship instead of eros; they practise justice in choral competition and by living out the mathematical composition and proportion of their city; and they practise wisdom by imitating good characters and beholding the cosmos in wonderment.

A chorus is a "combination of dance and song taken together as a whole" (*Laws* 654b). The Athenian Stranger claims that choruses, along with festivals in general, are gifts given by the Muses, Apollo, and Dionysus as a way to get human beings to remember the proper measure of pleasures and pains that forgetfulness has caused to become slack, unstrung, or shapeless (*khalatai*) (*Laws* 653c–d).[8] Thus the gods "move us, and lead us in choruses, joining us together [*suneirontas*] with songs and dances" to return us to the proper constitution of our souls and communities. In this way the gods help re-form our souls. Choruses get their name from the enchanted sense of joy (*chara*) that we experience when dancing with the gods and with one another. They are the quintessential expression of our social, political, and rational natures as embodied beings.

The city is to be composed of three, or possibly four, choruses. They each sing together and "before the whole city," organized in concentric

7 *Laws* 815a and 829b–c. Morrow argues that pyrrhic dances were central to ancient Greek civic festivals (*Plato's Cretan City*, 360–1). See also Harrison, *Epilegomena*, 1–29.

8 The Athenian Stranger seems to take the Homeric Hymn to Apollo as the paradigm of a festive chorus (Kurke, "Imagining Chorality: Wonder, Plato's Puppets, and Moving Statues," 147–9; Calame, "Choral Practices in Plato's *Laws*: Itineraries of Initiation?," 97; and Prauscello, "Patterns of Chorality in Plato's *Laws*," 140–1).

circles with the children's chorus in the middle (*Laws* 664c).[9] They are the city being present to itself. The children's chorus is dedicated to the Muses (*Laws* 664c). The chorus for those up to the age of thirty is dedicated to Paean as "witness to the truth of what is said" (*Laws* 664d). The third group consists of those between thirty and sixty. The fourth consists of those who are older and can no longer "bear the toil of singing" (*Laws* 664d). In the subsequent discussion between the Athenian Stranger and Kleinias, the lines between the third and fourth choruses will blur, because the educators and elders will be drawn from them, to compose, in the end, the Nocturnal Council.

The chorus is a *symphonia* of soul and body, and a *symphonia* of souls and bodies together. Choruses imitate good character, the substance of which I shall elaborate below. Their songs should consist of "auspicious" or "reverential" speech (*euphemia*) (*Laws* 801a), and they should consist largely of hymns to the gods, demons, heroes, and finally esteemed citizens, including the founders themselves (*Laws* 801e). It is crucial that the subject of a hymn be dead: "It isn't safe to honor through encomia and hymns those still living (before a person has run through the entire course of his life and arrived at a noble end)" (*Laws* 802c). The Athenian Stranger does not explain why, but it is reasonable to assume that someone still living may fall into evil and thereby cause the city to regret hymning to him. Moreover, the dead have completed their lives, so friends may observe the totality of their actions and gain a clearer picture of their characters. The living may not serve as paradigms of characters for citizen chorus members, the choreuts. However, in learning to imitate their actions in rhythm and harmony, the choreut citizens will develop an understanding of how moral character appears in motion. They will develop the practical wisdom to discern form in movement: a musical education that mimics the dialectical education that gives mathematics priority in the *Republic,* in which the guardians must learn to discern the good in itself before they are capable of discerning its instantiations in the realm of becoming.[10] This can be inferred from the Athenian Stranger's statement that the choruses will compete to determine which one is the best at mimicking good characters. This, with the

9 See Calame, "Choral Practices in Plato's Laws," 92.

10 Socrates: "I'm just not capable of regarding any other study as making a soul look upward than one that's concerned with what is and is invisible; if someone attempts to learn anything from perceptible things, whether with wide-open eyes gazing up or with squinty eyes peering down, I'd never claim he was learning, because knowledge has nothing to do with things of that sort, or that his soul was looking up rather than down" (Plato, *Republic* 529b–c).

help of the judges of the choruses, requires choreuts to know the original first, and then discern how it is present in the choral song and dance. The manner of their rhythmic discernment, the practical wisdom that is specific to them as citizens, will be elaborated below.

The dead serve as forms for the flowing souls and bodies of citizens. Evoked by Apollo, they should sing of how the just man is also the happy man (*Laws* 664c), the postulate upon which the goodness of the laws is based.[11] The just and happy man is likely the Athenian Stranger, the primary founder of their polis. However, his case is complicated because he is anonymous. The reasons for this, and their implications for political friendship, will be considered below. But to consider the issue of his anonymity in relation to his injunction against singing hymns to the living, his being a stranger reminds us of the way in which we are always present and absent to one another, in the sense that our characters are in continual flux until death. If, as Aristotle states and the Athenian Stranger would agree, our characters are "made" by our moral choices, then our character cannot be complete until our lives are complete (a paradox noted in our previous chapters on Aristotle). For the Athenian Stranger, "it isn't safe" to honour the living because we lack sufficient knowledge about the objects of the hymns until their characters are fully made. Yet when their characters are finally present, that is, complete, they are absolutely absent, that is, dead.

David Walsh makes this point in another context when discussing how it is that the dead have dignity on account of the irreducibility of personhood:

> For [persons] allow us to relate directly to them in all their invisibility. By saying nothing they have said everything. They show that above all persons are, most of all when they are not expressed in anything present. Even without consciousness, they give themselves through their breathing until they yield up their last breath. Theirs is the dignity in which they can be contained. This is why we reverence their remains as what still speak to us even after the person is gone. Not even death can defeat the person who, somehow, is deathless. This is why the distinctive mark of all human societies is remembrance of the dead. We are inclined to think that thinking about the afterlife is the result of religion, but it is really the converse. Religion arises because we already know about the afterlife

11 Calame, "Choral Practices in Plato's *Laws*," 95. The three postulates of the so-called minimum dogma in Book X serve this need: (1) that the gods exist, (2) that they care for human beings and their affairs, and (3) that the gods cannot be bribed. See chapter 7 for discussion.

through our experience as persons who are never fully here and therefore are never fully departed.[12]

The daimonism of the departed and the living means that Magnesia is indeed a communion of the living and the dead. This is why the second postulate of the so-called minimum dogma, that the gods care for human affairs, cannot easily be dismissed, as we shall see in chapter 7 (see *Laws* 904d–e).

The Athenian Stranger largely leaves it up to the Dionysian elders over 50 years of age to supervise the composition and performance of songs sung by the younger citizens. The latter are divided into children's choruses and Apollonian choruses: "By interpreting the intentions of the lawgiver, they should put together dance and song and choral performance as a whole in a way that comes as close as possible to the intentions in his mind" (*Laws* 802c). With the assistance of poetic and musical men, the Dionysian elders are to take up and rework the "many ancient and beautiful creations in music, and also for the bodies, dances of the same quality" (*Laws* 802a–b). They are to refigure ancestral songs so that they conform better to the rule of Nous, which means that their sung components, and their rhythms and harmonies, must be moderate and guided by reason. As Morrow argues, the choruses are to sing and dance to songs already enjoyed in Greece, but, as it were, in a new noetic key.[13]

Despite the Athenian Stranger's admiration for the Egyptian law that creates music according to timeless and unchanging principles (*Laws* 657a–b), the Magnesian choruses sing and dance to songs "which must in one way or another be continually changing, presenting variety in every way, so that the singers will take unsatiated pleasure in their hymns" (*Laws* 665c). The Athenian Stranger seems to have in mind neither a static and unchanging musical form, nor the "theatocracy" whose innovative music appeals to whichever random emotions and impulses uncultured people have. Instead, the "correct" (*ortho*, as in orthodox) music of Magnesia is predicated on a view of the craft of music that requires practitioners always to return to first principles – that is, to the perspective of "a god or someone divine," which can stand the test of time in the way that Egyptian music is said to. This understanding of the craft of music is closer to the approach of composers like Mozart or Bach, whose music is radically innovative while remaining "old fashioned." Singleminded devotion to innovation undermines knowledge of the musical fundamentals. Genuine innovation requires a mastery of tradition, which

12 Walsh, "Dignity as an Eschatological Concept," 254.
13 Morrow, *Plato's Cretan City*, 310.

includes ascending to the greatness of past masters.[14] Extreme, and thus shallow, innovation is like sawing off the branch one is sitting on: it is the viewpoint of philistinism, not excellence. Even so, the excellence of Magnesian music does not consist in its virtuosity. Rather, it consists in its imitation of virtue and the relative ease with which citizens can perform it in chorus. As Warren Anderson, suggests, it cultivates a certain high-minded amateurism among citizens.[15]

Rhythms and harmonies conducive to learning, especially for the young, are crucial. The kithara and lyre are best suited to accompany singing because the range of stringed instruments is closest to that of the human voice. The flute and other instruments that prevent individuals from simultaneously playing and singing are inappropriate. Also inappropriate are harmony, dissonance, and atonality, because their elements "contradict one another," and so fail to cultivate the exercise of reason, at least among the young. Finally, it is inappropriate to separate rhythm and postures from melodies, to write words in meter without accompaniment, and to play the kithara or aulos alone, which makes it "very difficult to know what it intended and which worthwhile imitations are being imitated by this rhythm and harmony" (*Laws* 669e). Such practices are instances of a wonderful epithet: "unmusical virtuousity" (*Laws* 670a).

"*APAIDEUTOS ACHOREUTOS*"

"So the uneducated man will in our view be the one untrained in choral performances, and the educated ought to be set down as the one sufficiently trained in choral performances?" (*Laws* 654b). So asks the Athenian Stranger, and Kleinias's positive response sparks a discussion that equates choral education with education as a whole: "Presumably, the choral art as a whole is for us the same as education as a whole" (*Laws* 672e).[16]

With joy (*charis*), choruses enchant singers and listeners together. Their joint enchantment mimics the wonder of perceiving the unmoving source of the cosmos (see *Laws* 893b–e),[17] and the goodness that enables gods, demons, heroes, and esteemed citizens, including their

14 The Athenian Stranger's discussion of how music is to be refigured – something he himself is doing in his performance of the dialogue – can be compared with Eva Brann's discussion of the paradox of returning to the first principles of a tradition in order to participate in that tradition (see *Paradoxes of Education in a Republic*, 64–119).

15 Anderson, *Ethos and Education in Greek Music*, 64–110.

16 For details of this choral educational project and its influence on notions of education and philosophy in classical antiquity and early Christianity, see James L. Miller, *Measures of Wisdom: The Cosmic Dance in Classical and Christian Antiquity*.

17 Planinc, *Plato's Political Philosophy*, 211.

founders and themselves, to partake of that order. The enchantment of the choruses is not irrational ecstasy, as modern sociologists such as Emile Durkheim imagine communal participation to involve, but a musical enchantment that attaches Magnesians to Nous in the way that lead filings attach to a magnet (*Laws* 666c).[18] Indeed, the simplicity of the music, coupled with the injunction that prevents citizens from becoming expert performers (and so playing complex melodies and harmonies with the potential to appear divinely inspired at the expense of the *logos*), helps ensure that its enjoyment is rational or at least capable of being uplifted by reason. One might compare this to the simple Christian hymns of Martin Luther and Isaac Watts, which constitute the musical memory of many generations of Protestant Christians. Their simplicity means that individuals of varying degrees of musical expertise are still able to sing them, and be uplifted by them. As Anderson argues, "The spectator ought properly to be hearing about what is superior to his own ethical code. For Plato, education which does not uplift men is not education; to uplift oneself he considers an impossibility."[19]

One might argue that the educational program of the *Laws* strives to purge people of eros by attaching it to reason, but this makes no sense.[20] Instead, the educational program uplifts eros into *philia*, making friendship-love the basis of society (837d). Citizens' enchantment with each another and with their *nomoi* is an image of the wonder that Plato and Aristotle say is the beginning of philosophy. It is an image of the turning-around (*periagoge*) of the soul that Socrates describes as the beginning of education in the *Republic*; as we saw in chapter 5, the preludes are gentler versions of that turning-around. Barbara Kowalzig argues that the encounter of Magnesian citizens with each other has its philosophical counterpart in the loving encounter between the philosopher and his beloved that Socrates describes in the *Phaedrus*: "And so each person picks out from the beautiful ones his love after his fashion; and he constructs and adorns for himself a sort of statue of that one, as a god, for him to honor and celebrate. So then, those of Zeus seek someone heavenly [*dios*] in soul to be the one loved by them; therefore they look into whether he is in his nature philosophic and capable of leadership, and whenever they find him and fall in love, they do everything so that

18 Barbara Kowalzig, "Broken Rhythms in Plato's *Laws*: Materialising Social Time in the Chorus"; Kowalzig writes that Durkheim focuses only on "psychical exaltation not far removed from delirium" that does "violence to the organism" (178, citing Durkheim, *Elementary Forms of the Religious Life*, 258–9).

19 Anderson, *Ethos and Education in Greek Music*, 92.

20 See Calame, "Choral Practices in Plato's *Laws*," 105.

he will be such."[21] What is going on in the *Phaedrus* between individual, manic lovers whose souls have been formed by the divine, is very different from what is going on in the *Laws,* where the choral education of the Magnesian citizenry as a whole is a mediated version of that divine formation. Comparing the two would require a separate, extensive study.[22] Even so, Kowalzig is correct to see the friendly encounter of mutual recognition and love as a paradigm of what the Athenian Stranger has in mind. It is a form of *sunaisthesis* comparable to that examined within the context of Aristotle's writings in chapter 2.

The delight that Magnesians are supposed to enjoy with one another seems similar to the delight that Michael Oakeshott associates with friendship, as well as contemplation:

> Friends and lovers are not concerned with what can be made out of each other, but only with the enjoyment of one another. A friend is not somebody one trusts to behave in a certain manner, who has certain useful qualities, who holds acceptable opinions; he is somebody who evokes interest, delight, unreasoning loyalty, and who (almost) engages contemplative imagination ... What is communicated and enjoyed is not an array of emotions – affection, tenderness, concern, fear, elation, etc. – but the uniqueness of a self.[23]

Unlike erotic love, delight is not associated with need. It is an emotion of freedom and exuberance drawn from the plenitude of being, which enables one to behold another at a distance that affirms the other's freedom without severing emotional ties. Delight in another person, like the act of relishing, is the act of a being who is capable of rationally ordering her loves toward other persons, and other things.[24] The choruses are governed by Nous.

21 Kowalzig, "Broken Rhythms in Plato's *Laws,*" 174. The passage quoted above is *Phaedrus* 252d–e (Nichols translation). The beloved as the revelation of the beautiful can also be seen in the *Lysis,* as explained in chapter 4 and by Rhodes, "Platonic *Philia* and Political Order."

22 On the *Phaedrus,* see Rhodes, *Eros, Wisdom, and Silence,* 460–517. On the consistency between the presentation of friendship in the *Laws* and of eros and friendship in the *Phaedrus,* see Dimitri El Murr, "*Philia* in Plato," 13–17.

23 Oakeshott, "The Voice of Poetry in the Conversation of Mankind," in *Rationalism in Politics and Other Essays,* 537.

24 "Wine, properly drunk, transfigures the world at which you look, illuminating that which is precisely most mysterious in the contingent beings surrounding you, which is the fact that they are – and also that they might not have been" (Roger Scruton, *I Drink Therefore I Am,* 115). See also Scruton's discussion of how only the rational being is capable of the act of relishing wine because only he can reflect rationally upon his sensory experience (123–7). The Athenian Stranger claims that wine inspires awe (*Laws* 672d).

Choruses are to mimic the actions of good characters (*Laws* 655d) – indeed, characters superior to the individual choral members (*Laws* 659c). According to the Athenian Stranger, we become the types of character we mimic and delight in (*Laws* 656b). Thus it is necessary to habituate citizens to mimic and delight in good action (*eu prattein*), as a way of educating them in virtue (*Laws* 657c). They hymn primarily to the just man who is also the happy man (*Laws* 664c), the lynchpin of Magnesia's legislation. However, their own city and its laws (*nomoi*) is the manifestation of justice and happiness combined, so their songs are also about their city and themselves (*Laws* 817b). That they mimic themselves along with good characters is indicated by the Athenian Stranger's assertion that the gods dance together with them (*Laws* 654a). J.-M. Bertrand explains that "the chorus is at once, thus, addressee and addressor of what it sings: it enchants itself according to the rules laid down by the legislator, but it also knows how to enchant the city-state as a whole."[25] Similarly, Leslie Kurke argues that "choral performance is a machine for conjuring of absolute presence, whereby gods, chorus members, and audience are all linked or joined together by a single (mimetic) chain."[26]

The ambiguous nature of this mimesis is also noted when the Athenian Stranger points out, in a discussion of poets, that one cannot mimic anything that one does not already know. Indeed, we know from our own popular culture that the best parodies are usually a loving homage to the original.[27] The truest form of mimesis, it seems, is not mimesis at all, but action based upon wisdom. Or perhaps the philosopher comes closest to being the true mimic because he comes closest to knowing the unmoved mover. Mimetic action on the part of non-philosophical choreuts appears to be hymning and dancing to the cosmic demiurge that creates order out of disorder, and friendship through reconciliation (*diallogon*). The choreuts mimic the actions of their founders, especially the Athenian Stranger. However, the Athenian Stranger is anonymous to them. Their only knowledge of him is in the text of the conversation he and his interlocutors left behind, which resembles the "strong cable" that the gods provide to human beings to ascend to wisdom. Knowledge of the Athenian Stranger can only arise in the choreuts' own souls. Mimesis, paradoxically, seems only possible with wisdom.

Because of the Athenian Stranger's anonymity (if not self-annihilation), it is unclear just what form the songs take that the choruses will sing and

25 J.-M. Bertrand, *De l'écriture à l'oralité: Lectures des Lois de Platon*, 400, quoted and translated by Calame, "Choral Practices in Plato's *Laws*," 107n16.

26 Kurke, "Imagining Chorality," 127.

27 I thank Travis D. Smith for pointing this out to me.

dance. How does one praise an unknown human being? How does one hymn to an unknown founder, unknown prophet, or unknown god? It seems impossible to create an image of his likeness. How does one hymn to someone without name or image, without forging an idol that is nothing but a self-image, unless that self-image is itself constituted by Nous? There seems to be deliberate instability or perplexity in the mimetic practices of the choruses, because the drawing of souls that the Athenian Stranger defines as education involves the slow and gentle revelation of Nous in the souls of the inhabitants. Mimesis is paradoxical because it must ultimately be based on their own knowledge, which is perhaps why the Athenian Stranger suggests that the record of their dialogue be left as a record for citizens, and serve as a model for their conversable polity. Conversation, like that conducted in the "Nightly Meeting," noetically orders the souls of the citizens.[28]

WONDROUS PUPPETS

In chapter 2, we saw how Aristotle thought of the moral life that friends share as analogous to sculptors impressing the forms of their characters upon one another (and also being ready to receive the form of their friends upon themselves). This is central to the role mimesis plays in moral and political education, as we saw in chapter 3. Similarly, in Plato's *Laws*, the Athenian Stranger's strategy of education through choral mimesis can be fruitfully approached by considering one of the icons he suggests in the dialogue – that of human beings as puppets of the gods.

> Let's consider each of us living beings to be a divine puppet [*thauma*], put together either for their play or for some serious purpose – which, we don't know. What we do know is that these passions work within us like tendons or cords, drawing us and pulling against one another in opposite directions toward opposing deeds, struggling in the region where virtue and vice lie separated from one another. Now the argument asserts that each person should always follow one of the cords, never letting go of it and pulling with it against the others; this cord is the golden and sacred pull of calculation [*logismon*], and is the common law of the city; the other cords are hard and iron, while this one is soft, inasmuch as it is golden. (*Laws* 644d–645a)

28 See V. Bradley Lewis, "The Nocturnal Council and Platonic Political Philosophy." Lewis argues that "nightly meeting" is a more accurate translation of *nukterinos sullogos* than the sinister-sounding "nocturnal council," which is the more common translation.

This is one of Plato's famous icons for the human soul. Unlike in the *Republic,* where citizens are divided into gold, silver, and bronze classes, here it seems that all human beings are endowed with a golden cord and it is up to them to find a way to follow it, as it is the softest.[29]

It is curious that Plato chooses to use the term *thauma* to signify the puppet. It literally means "object of wonder" and is etymologically related to *thaumazein,* to wonder, which associates it with the beginning of philosophy.[30] Kurke notices that other terms are available to Plato, which he does use in other parts of the dialogue.[31] Here he could have used "*paignion*" (plaything, used at *Laws* 803c) or "*ta neurospasta*" ("things drawn by cords" or "marionettes"), which is the term Xenophon uses in his *Symposium.*[32] Kurke argues that Plato uses the term he does (and amplifies his meaning throughout his description of the *thauma*) to emphasize the uncanny and wondrous nature of human beings, and the "doubleness" with which we face one another. "The designation *thauma* points us to something essential about puppets, focalized (as it were) through the credulous gaze of very small children: though we know them to be mechanical and inanimate, we simultaneously believe that puppets are alive, for they are infused with motion and voice."[33] Something similar goes on when small children enjoy a visit from Santa Claus. They know it is just a fellow in a red suit and that it is not really Santa Claus. Yet it is Santa Claus. As with the divine puppets, they play along because it is all play.

Kurke cites Richard Neer's insight about the wonder that Greek sculptors sought with their images: "In Greek as in English, one wonders at wonders; and literary texts from Homer on suggest that the quintessential wonder is a spectacle of brilliant radiance, flashing speed, and radical 'otherness.' Uniting these qualities is a basic effect of twofoldness or doubleness in viewing: the statue should seem simultaneously alien and familiar, far and close, inert and alive, absent and present."[34] Kurke suggests that the reader regard the puppet icon in a manner comparable to the way ancient Greeks viewed statues. This is a mode that Plato would have invited, since his terms for ideas or forms (*eidos*) draw on the

29 Voegelin, *Plato and Aristotle,* 230–6.

30 It also refers to Thauma, father of Isis, messenger of the gods, similar to the Greek god Hermes (Hesiod, *Theogony* 780).

31 Kurke, "Imagining Chorality," 126.

32 Xenophon, *Symposium* 4.55, in *Memorabilia. Oeconomicus. Symposium. Apologia.*

33 Kurke, "Imagining Chorality," 126.

34 Kurke, "Imagining Chorality," 126, citing Richard Neer, *The Emergence of the Classical Style in Greek Sculpture,* 4.

vocabulary for seeing statues. Kurke is correct, but more must be said about our manner of looking at the *eidos.*

Eva Brann explains that *eidos* literally means "looks" – "in that eerily active sense in which a thing that has looks or is a sight *presents* itself to our sight and our looking."[35] Similarly, in his discussion of how *theoria* is the peak experience for philosophy and for Greek religion, Kerényi elaborates on this active sense of a sight presenting itself with the term "radiance," which gets carried over into the *Laws.*[36] In mythology, especially in Homer, the divine radiates throughout the cosmos; forms radiate in their sensual instantiations. Indeed, bodily representation and art are identical, which explains why art (*poesis*) is a "bringing forth." In his description of radiance, Kerényi writes that "the looking which is here meant is not 'looking through,' it referred not to the transparency of the medium but to the primary, immediate object of vision – the forms of the gods."[37] This is because the world "is quite simply known by any being upon whom it has an effect."[38] Achilles "knows like a lion savage things"; Cyclops "knew things against the law of nature" when he devoured men; and "friends are 'knowing of friendly things towards one another.'"[39] Radiance is the intellectual dimension of music's revelation to and from the inmost parts of our soul.

As we saw in chapter 2, *episteme* is a passive experience because it expresses our experience of divine Nous knowing through our own act of knowing:

> *Noein,* just as much as *eidenai,* perhaps even more so, can mean the disposition, the mentality, the direction in which one is driven by a higher power. This is proved by the mythological names ending in -noos or -noe, like Hipponoos or Hipponoe, 'being driven by a horse's nature' ... By *noein* the object of perception is apprehended from that quarter which escapes the organs of sense, but which can yet be apprehended by the vehicle of *noein,* by the nous. Nous directs itself toward the world in *noein* just as the eyes do in seeing.[40]

Episteme is experienced as a windfall (*hermiaon*), a revelation, whose meaning we examined in our discussion of Plato's *Lysis*: "In Greek the

35 Brann, *Music of the Republic,* 323 (emphasis in original).

36 The following is a partial summary of my essay, "The Intermediaries of the Eranos Festival: Orpheus and Hermes."

37 Kerényi, *Religion of Greeks and Romans,* 151.

38 Ibid., 146.

39 Kerényi, *Religion of Greeks and Romans,* 147, citing *Odyssey* 3.277.

40 Kerényi, *Religion of Greeks and Romans,* 147–8.

occurrence of knowledge that sees can be formulated as follows: it is God when such a thing occurs."[41] *Theos* is frequently a predicate in the Greek language, which helps us to understand how the gods are fellow-dancers with the choruses.[42] The most famous example in Greek philosophy is probably to be found in Aristotle's *Nicomachean Ethics* X, where he states that the life of contemplation is the most divine; it imitates the Greek style of religion in which Zeus contemplates the cosmos. However, my favorite example of *theos* as a predicate is in Euripides's *Helen*, where we find the line, "O gods! For the recognizing of friends is a god."[43] *Theos* as predicate is key to understanding the epiphanies of the gods and Nous in the *Laws*, including the participation of the gods in the choruses, and the assistance the gods provide to the three gentlemen in their conversation. It is also the key to understanding the peculiar assumptions built into the three postulates of the civil religion that will be discussed below.

Put simply, choruses are composed of human beings, puppets who are radiantly conducted by, and together with, the gods. Yet this apparent simplicity betrays a deep uncanniness. Kurke notes that Plato juxtaposes the inanimate object, *thauma*, with *ton zoon* ("living creature"), and again with *theion*: "This collapse or uneasy fusion of three normally mutually exclusive categories – divine, mortal human, and artifice or object of skilled crafting – is indeed a 'wonder' that is also, I suggest, very much at the core of the Greek imagination of chorality."[44] The Athenian Stranger seems to think that adults retain (or at least *should* retain) the same wonder toward fellow human beings that children have toward wonders.

In fact, an authentic beholding of other human beings necessitates such wonder. As a child knows that a puppet is inanimate, yet lets herself believe it is animate for the sake of participating in the greater story, so too does an adult know that another human being is mortal, yet divines that human beings have a connection to immortality.[45] Such divining is the only way to ascribe meaning to the daimonic actions of both the puppet and the human being, and to establish a connection between them. Like the Hermetic symbols in the *Lysis*, the icon of the puppet player, characterized by a "doubleness in viewing," is an example of Plato symbolizing the metaleptic and daimonic participation of humans in a divine order. Referring to the golden cord as the cord of calculation (*logismon*) reinforces the fact that the enchantments of the chorus have

41 Ibid., 147.
42 Ibid., 147, 151.
43 Euripides, *Helen*, 560.
44 Kurke, "Imagining Chorality," 127.
45 Walsh, "Dignity as an Eschatological Concept," 254.

a noetic core. As divine puppets, we make sense of ourselves by recognizing that our golden cords extend upward toward the gods, and also secure our union with one another. As Kurke suggests: "The image of dancing puppets suggests at once a direct vertical connection between each puppet and the divine and a horizontal linkage of a group of bodies in perfectly synchronized, coordinated motion."[46] Moreover, we can only make such conjectures when we wonder at the mystery of ourselves while beholding the mysteries of others – a dynamic that finds its fullest expression in virtue-friendship.[47]

We noticed earlier that the Athenian Stranger refigures the ancestral *nomoi* to formulate the choruses of Magnesia. Kurke reads the Athenian Stranger's prescriptions through the *Hymn to Apollo,* the main surviving account of the inauguration of festive choruses in the Greek world.[48] He claims that the divine puppet icon allows the Athenian Stranger to replicate the *Hymn to Apollo*'s vision of the divine presence in the context of the choreuts: "The choreuts of a perfectly performing chorus are assimilated simultaneously to the divine and to precious works of art or of uncanny crafting … *Choreia* is a machine for the production of pure presence, which, through mimesis links together and merges the gods, the dancers, and the human spectators. This is what makes it a *thauma.* The engine or motor of this mimetic chain in eros."[49] Finally, the beauty of the choral song brings together the god, chorus, and spectators: "The power of this magnetic attraction is so strong that the audience almost identify themselves with the performers, ultimately feeling that they themselves are speaking."[50]

Kurke bases much of his analysis on Plato's understanding of Greek choral practices, elaborated most of all in the *Hymn to Apollo.* This is a good way to understand Plato's refiguration of his literary tradition; but it is important to note that Plato is not simply replicating that tradition. In favour of Kurke's interpretation of the choruses, it is at least consistent with the brief statements the Athenian Stranger makes concerning choral composition. These include his claim that the gods "move us, and lead us in choruses, joining us together [*suneirontas*] with songs and

46 Kurke, "Imagining Chorality," 134.

47 See Socrates's statement concerning how a human being is more wondrous than "a more curious monster than Typhon or a friendlier and simpler being, by nature sharing something divine" (*Phaedrus* 230a). And see Kierkegaard's comments on this, in the voice of the pseudonymous Climacus (*Philosophical Fragments/Johannes Climacus,* 37).

48 Kurke, "Imagining Chorality," 146–50.

49 Ibid., 147.

50 Ibid., 148.

dances" (*Laws* 654a), as well as his prescription that the choruses perform for the entire city (*Laws* 664c), and the city perform with them.

However, Kurke is incorrect to attribute the attractive power of the choruses – gods, choreuts, spectators – to eros, because the Athenian Stranger is adamant throughout the dialogue that the city is to be based on *philia*, the attraction of souls instead of bodies (*Laws* 837a). Mixing eros with *philia* produces "total confusion and obscurity" (*Laws* 837a). The joy (*charis*) and enchantments experienced by the citizens is based on their friendship-love for one another. It is the heightened intellectual love of people who enjoy each other and their lives together, and the sublime awe they have for the laws that join them (*Laws* 699c). In addition to understanding the choruses in light of Greek culture, it is necessary to understand them in light of what Plato is reorienting those traditions toward, namely the rule of Nous. We need to consider the choruses as participating in the light of Nous in order to gain full appreciation of their character as the starting points of civic education and action, as well as of civic friendship.

PLATONIC "WITHNESS" AND MODERNS WHO DANCE ALONE

Let us gather together our picture of the choruses before moving on to see the order of friendship-love in which they participate. The choreuts sing and dance together in a circle before the city. Choreuts simultaneously behold one another and the vision of the good that they share, and they behold and are beheld by the spectators, their fellow citizens, thus nearly eliminating the distinction between choreut and spectator. The songs (*nomoi*) of the choreuts are the laws (*nomoi*) of the city, hymns to the causes of their coming-into-being and to the people and their virtues who brought them about. Their civic friendship is rooted in the awe inspired by the laws (*Laws* 698c).

The Athenian Stranger's view of the choruses, and the central role they play in civic education and friendship, resonates with twentieth-century accounts of the priority of musical performance as a social form. Alfred Schütz, for example, regards musical performance as the "paramount situation" of communication, whose perfection is grounded in friendship: "This sharing of the other's flux of experiences in inner time, this living through a vivid present in common, constitutes … the mutual tuning-in relationship, the experience of the 'We,' which is the foundation of all possible communication."[51] Schütz goes on: "Both share not only the inner *durée* in which the content of the music played actualizes

51 Schütz, "Making Music Together," 173.

itself; each, simultaneously, shares in vivid present the Other's stream of consciousness in immediacy. This is possible because making music together occurs in a true face-to-face relationship – inasmuch as the participants are sharing not only a section of time but also a sector of space."[52] Put in simpler terms, musical performance is shared intellectual and emotional perception. It is also embodied, because performers perform better when they can see one another (face-to-face) and respond to one another's gestures: "the Other's body and its movements can be and are interpreted as a field of expression of events within his inner life."[53] Moreover, the meaning of such gestures only makes sense to the performers when they know each other, or, as Schütz indicates, they grow old together. Their musical performances mimic the life of virtue-friendship that Aristotle describes as a life of "living together and sharing conversation and thinking" (*NE* 1170b10–12). Schütz speaks of musical performance along the same lines as Aristotle's formulation of *sunaisthesis*, or joint perception of the good, as the peak of virtue-friendship. This is how the Athenian Stranger describes the foundation of the *nomoi* for Magnesia, whose primary civic expression is found in the choruses.

Even so, Schütz's account does not quite capture the communal element of friendship that the Athenian Stranger strives for in the choruses. It is difficult to compare the choruses to any contemporary musical experience, because moderns simply lack what Roger Scruton calls the "withness" of more archaic versions of song and dance. One comparison that might prove fruitful is with Mediterranean circle-dances, including the Syrtos Kalamatianos of modern Greece, which Anderson suggests "affects dancers in a way which shows vividly the end that Plato had in mind. Thrasybulos Georgiades describes it thus: while watching the dancing or taking part in it 'one feels the ancient tradition in the attitude of the dancers. They exhibit a dignity otherwise foreign to them; their faces become mask-like ... The dancers convey a primeval tradition ... their reverence for their forefathers and their unity with them become manifest.'"[54]

Moderns do not sing and dance together, consciously and under the rule of reason with simple rhythms and harmonies, and hymn to the just and happy man.[55] The Christian hymns of Isaac Watts or Martin Luther,

52 Ibid., 176.

53 Ibid., 177–8.

54 Anderson, *Ethos and Education in Greek Music*, 247n49, citing Georgiades, *Greek Music, Verse and Dance*, 139–40.

55 Modern scholarship barely understands what ancient Greek music sounded like. According to Armand D'Angour, its melodies and harmonies are closer to the sounds of Middle Eastern music than anything found in the West ("How Did Ancient Greek Music Sound?," *BBC News*, 23 October 2013, http://www.bbc.co.uk/news/business-24611454).

which are simple and familiar enough to many churchgoers that they feel comfortable singing them with others, approximates the musical dimension of the chorus, but there is no corresponding dance component. Some tribal dances that express attunement with the cosmos, including the Maori haka dance, have been taken up in a modern setting.[56] Alexandr Onishenko's impressionistic painting, "Jewish Dance," which is based upon Mario Giacomelli's series of photographs from 1962, "Il Pretini [Little Priests]," also conjures up this attunement by portraying the religious believers dancing in a circle while holding hands.[57] The "withness" of the Magnesian choruses is probably better compared to Scottish reels. With freedom and friendship being the goals of Magnesia, the Athenian Stranger would likely appreciate Friedrich Schiller's observation of the reel:

> The first law of gentility is: have consideration for the freedom of others. The second: show your freedom. The correct fulfillment of both is an infinitely difficult problem, but gentility always requires it relentlessly, and it alone makes the cosmopolitan person. I know of no more fitting image for the ideal of beautiful relations than the well danced and multiply convoluted English dance. The spectator in the gallery sees countless movements which never cross each other colourfully and change their direction willfully but never collide. Everything has been arranged so that the first has already made room for the second before he arrives, everything comes together so skillfully and yet so artlessly that both seem merely to be following their own mind while never impeding the other. This is the most fitting picture of a maintained personal freedom, which respects the freedom of others.[58]

This paradoxical blend of cooperative friendship and individual freedom also lies at the heart of the friendship between the Magnesian choreuts, which is itself modelled on their friendship with the Athenian Stranger, the subject of their songs. As founder and teacher, he knows us most intimately and yet stands at an infinite distance from us. As we saw in the last chapter on the *Lysis*, this is the paradox of Socratic friendship.

Modern life offers few opportunities for such experiences of "withness" in song and dance. We veer between the extremes of the crowd-forming (rather than society-forming) ecstasies of popular music, and

56 Geoffrey Ingersoll, "The New Zealand Army Mourns its Dead With an Ancestral War Dance," *Business Insider*, 30 August 2012 (http://www.businessinsider.com/watch-the-new-zealand-army-mourns-their-dead-with-ancestral-war-dance-2012-8).

57 I thank William French for this example.

58 Quoted in Roger Scruton, *Understanding Music*, 69.

the rationalist contempt of Jane Austen's Mr. Darcy, who refuses to join Elizabeth Bennett and her circle in dancing to "Scotch and Irish airs": "Every savage can dance," he sneers.[59]

In Hermetic fashion, Magnesia's choruses steer between the Apollonian and the Dionysian by subsuming both under Nous. They do so by regarding the communal side of human life in terms of play. The Athenian Stranger tries to attach the souls of citizens to Nous – not directly, as a philosopher seeks wisdom, but indirectly, through enchantments or incantations (*epoidai*) and play. "To prevent the child's soul from becoming habituated to feeling delight and pain in a way opposed to the law and to those who are persuaded by the law, to make the child's soul follow and feel the same joys and pains as an old man, the things we call songs (*odes*), but which are really incantations (*epoidai*) for souls, have now come into being ... But since the souls of the young cannot sustain seriousness, these incantations are called 'games' and 'songs'" (*Laws* 659d–e). The most important lesson in which citizens need to be steeped through incantation (*epaidein*) is that "the most pleasant life and the best life are the same" (*Laws* 664b–c). The Athenian Stranger's play on words, mixing enchantments or incantations (*epoidai*) with education (*paideia*), is purposeful and illuminates the role that the choruses play in civic education.[60] Theirs is a rational enthusiasm, one in which the choreuts are lifted above themselves into a higher state of intellection, self-awareness, and awareness of others. It is one in which choreuts "delight" in the object of their songs and dances, a delight that includes not just exuberant joy, but also involves a degree of reflective distance from its objects. The choreuts are not lost in the experience, but their intellection is enhanced through delight and noetic guidance.[61] They are a civic version of the moment of *sunaisthesis*, wherein friends face one another in "effortful holding of oneself in readiness."

Choral education is also anchored in citizens' noetic awe (*aidos*) of the laws (*Laws* 698b–c, 699c). Speaking of the Athenians (though the point is general), the Athenian Stranger argues that in the past, "all these things instilled in them a friendship for one another: fear, both that

59 Austen, *Pride and Prejudice*, 18. For an overview of modern rationalism's banishment of "collective joy," see Barbara Ehrenreich, *Dancing in the Streets: A History of Collective Joy*. Her analysis is flawed because the only forms of collective joy she sees (and celebrates) are the irrational ones, explained in Durkheimian terms. James Schall's discussion of the "theoria" of modern sports provides a useful corrective ("On the Seriousness of Sports, Watchers All"), as do Pieper's works on leisure and festivity.

60 Calame, "Choral Practices in Plato's *Laws*," 93.

61 See Roger Scruton's comparable discussion of wine, discussed above.

which came at the time and that which sprang from the laws they already had – the fear which they possessed as a result of their enslavement to those previous laws, which we have often in the arguments before called 'awe,' and which we claimed those who are going to be good must be enslaved to" (*Laws* 699c). Awe here is not simply the fear of Leviathan. It is an aesthetic experience rooted in the perception of the laws as beautiful and as a gift received by citizens. The fear that inspired citizens to band together to defend themselves, their "temples, the graves, the fatherland, and their relatives, as well as their friends" – rather than run away and be "scattered from the rest at that time" – is borne of shame about not living up to the gift of those laws (*Laws* 699c). Such awe is rooted in a proper pride about partaking in the good and the beautiful, and wishing to act in a way that is worthy of such partaking. It is like the love and shame Winston Churchill drew upon in his many World War Two speeches to inspire his countrymen to carry on with their great "island story," including his famous speech to Cabinet in May 1940 where he convinced them Great Britain could not negotiate a separate peace with Hitler: "If this long island story of ours is to end at last, let it end only when each one of us lies choking in his own blood upon the ground."[62] The great "island story," which began with the great deeds and sacrifices of their ancestors, could never end with shameful surrender, but only with their deaths. Churchill's "island story" and Magnesia's *nomoi* are comparable because they are both the song that one sings, and the song itself. They are an instance of the only type of "fabrication" that Hannah Arendt regards politics as being capable of: "[political action] 'produces' stories with or without intention as naturally as fabrication produces tangible things."[63] In response to prospective poets who would tell their story, the Athenian Stranger advises Magnesians to say: "Best of strangers … we ourselves are poets, who have to the best of our ability created a tragedy that is the most beautiful and the best; at any rate, our whole political regime is constructed as the imitation of the most beautiful and best way of life, which we at least assert to be really the truest tragedy … We are your rivals as artists and performers of the most beautiful drama, which true law alone can by nature bring to perfection – as we hope" (*Laws* 817b–c). The enchantments are anchored by the noetic awe that Magnesians have for their laws, the "most beautiful and best way

62 Winston Churchill, *The Churchill War Papers*, 2: 182–4.
63 Arendt, *The Human Condition*, 184.

of life" that can be perfected by nature. It would be a tragic shame to fall short of that standard.[64]

RHYTHMOS METHODOS

The Athenian Stranger's treatment of rhythm (*rhythmos*), the complement of harmony (*harmonia*) (*Laws* 653e), illuminates the noetic governance of the choruses: it is the choral method of instilling political and practical wisdom into citizens of a regime based upon the entirety of virtue. As we have seen, the joy (*charis*) experienced by the choreuts is not simply irrational exuberance, or ecstatic, self-annihilating absorption into the collective. The practice of *rhythmos* in choral dance cultivates practical wisdom because *rhythmos* is an act of discerning order within the flow of motion. Emile Beneviste argues that the notion of rhythm, as "continuous activity broken by meter into alternating intervals," is Plato's invention.[65] Socrates's description of *rhythmos* in the *Philebus*, which focuses on the mind-body mystery, is key:

> You have grasped certain corresponding features of the performer's bodily movements, features that must, so we are told, be numerically determined and be called 'rhythms' and 'measures' [*rhythmous kai metra*], bearing in mind all the time that this is always the right way to deal with the one-and-many problem – only then, you have grasped all this, have you gained real understanding, and whatever be the 'one' that you have selected for investigating, that is the way to get insight about it. (17d)[66]

64 Michael Kochin argues that the political friendship of the Magnesians tends toward excessive self-love because they lack inducements to regard their laws as anything less than the best and the most wise. Notably, such friendship is excessively spirited on account of it being based upon self-image (*Gender and Rhetoric in Plato's Political Thought*, 124–5). Kochin's analysis focuses on the role of *thumos* in the psychological make-up of the Magnesians, whereas my analysis focuses on the degree to which *noesis* makes itself felt musically in their souls. He does argue that "The Athenian Stranger legislates manly songs, moderate songs, but no just songs ... If justice is human excellence, as Socrates states in the *Republic* (335c4), Magnesia and its choruses know nothing about it" (117, citing Anderson's *Ethos and Education in Greek Music*, 80). Yet the choruses hymn about the just man who is also happy, which, as we have seen, is paradoxical because that man is also the unknown Athenian Stranger. If there are no songs about justice, then it might be more accurate to suggest that the just man is the condition of the "right music" of Magnesia.

65 Kowalzig, "Broken Rhythms in Plato's *Laws*," 185.

66 Hackforth translates "*rhythmous*" as "figure," which I have replaced with "rhythms." However, "figure" is suitable because, as shown below, *rhythmos* is "figure." Both terms signify the discernment of form in motion.

Contemplating festive dance together is a key method of discerning the one or unity within the flow of motion, which is the message concerning practical reason that the Athenian Stranger offers in the *Laws*.

Kowalzig suggests that Plato's attempt to control rhythm under the temporal order "stands in the larger service of the dialogue's concern with both social integration and civic permanence."[67] She elaborates:

> Rhythm underlies what I shall call the 'bodily social,' a physical property of community while it dances, a transcendent force realized in the convergence of individuals' rhythmic impulse in the chorus. The key point is that the physical properties of the individual body merge with those of collective rhythmicity; in a somewhat materialist turn, this collective rhythmicity becomes the nexus where 'nature' and 'culture' meet in society. It is this integration of nature and culture, of individual and collective rhthymic feeling, in the 'bodily social' that ultimately affords the permanence of the city-state in the *Laws*.[68]

We have seen the role of rhythm, and choruses in general, in constituting, expressing and cultivating political friendship among citizens. However, I contend that Plato brings the chorus not so much under the temporal order, as under the experience of wonder about the unmoved mover, the "most divine of all things which are provided with everflowing [*aenaos*] existence by a motion that receives its coming-into-being" (*Laws* 966e). The noetic core of this statement will be examined in chapter 7. For now, however, the *rhythmos* of the choruses mimics the *rhythmos* of the everflowing (*aenaos*) nature of the unmoving mover's creativity, which humans experience when their souls turn around (*periagoge*) from darkness to light, from ignorance to the pursuit of wisdom (*Republic* 518c–d). This enables us to see the true extent of Plato's linguistic innovation with *rhythmos*.

Beneviste demonstrates that *rhythmos* had little to do with the understanding of rhythm in ancient Greece prior to Plato. Deriving from *rhein* ("to flow"), its meaning for pre-Socratic philosophers, historians, and a few poets had more to do with the movements of rivers (though apparently not the sea[69]). In general, the term was used to designate form in movement, "the particular manner of flowing."[70] For instance, the atomist philosopher Democritus speaks of the forms of political constitutions

67 Kowalzig, "Broken Rhythms in Plato's *Laws*," 185.

68 Ibid., 173.

69 Beneviste, "The Notion of 'Rhythm' in its Linguistic Expression," 281; Kowalzig, "Broken Rhythms in Plato's *Laws*," 182.

70 Beneviste, "The Notion of 'Rhythm' in its Linguistic Expression," 182.

as *rhythmos,* on the assumption that since human affairs are always variable, constitutions are expressions of entities in flux, as "river" is an expression of water particles in flux. It is not insignificant that Plato himself describes constitutions in similar terms, that is, as entities in flux rather than in a static state. For example, in the *Republic* Socrates describes democracy as being between oligarchy and tyranny, and each of these are in between other regimes, with *kallipolis* and tyranny serving as the two poles between which all constitutions exist. Similarly, the Athenian Stranger describes all constitutions as lying between democracy and monarchy: "There are, as it were, two mothers of regimes. It would be correct for someone to say that the others spring from these, and correct to call one monarchy and the other democracy ... All other regimes ... are woven from these. Both of them should and must necessarily be present if there is to be freedom and friendship, together with prudence" (*Laws* 693d–e).

Tilo Schabert explains the importance of understanding the movements of political forms:

> All forms of political order are phenomena of movements. The classical typology of political constitutions that Plato elaborated and Aristotle modified to an extent therefore represents both: a description of the different constitutions identified – monarchy, aristocracy, oligarchy, and so forth – *and* the passages from one constitutional form to another, as from an aristocracy to an oligarchy, for example. In the realm of human action there is no stability, Aristotle stated, as if it were a cosmo-political law, and the constitutional forms that arise from such action are no exception to this law. Their status in political reality is an institutional presence between foundation and decay. They appear to be bodies of firm structures and yet, measured against the real forces in human life, they have no greater weight than that of fictional edifices.[71]

The "cosmo-political law" that one must be able to discern forms "between foundation and decay" – that is, forms undergoing genesis and destruction – has important consequences for political practical wisdom, as well as for citizenship. The Athenian Stranger seems to be delivering this wisdom on the wings of music, which is perhaps the best way for it be delivered, since music is the primary means of replicating the cosmos. Discerning the *rhythmos* of moral character, and perhaps of constitutions as well, seems to be a crucial ingredient in political prudence that the

71 Schabert, "The True Form of Governments: The Constitutional Movements of Power," 3, citing Aristotle, *Nicomachean Ethics* 1104a5, and Plato, *Statesman*, 269d.

Athenian Stranger wishes to instill through choral education, at least in a preliminary way.[72]

Other instances of pre-Socratic usages of *rhythmos* include Aeschylus's description of Xerxes changing the shape (*rhythmos*) of the Hellespont.[73] Kowalzig suggests that Herodotus' usage in particular captures its meaning of being a "particular manner of flowing" when he speaks of the early Greek alphabet. "At first the Phoenicians (who had settled in Greece) used the same letters as all the other Phoenicians; but as time went on, as they changed their language, they also changed the shape (*rhythmos*) of the letters. The Greeks ... learned the alphabet from the Phoencians, and, having made a few changes in the form of the letters (*metarrhythmisantes*), used these letters."[74] As Beneviste summarizes the general pre-Socratic meaning of *rhythmos,* it refers to "the form in the instant that it is assumed by what is moving, mobile and fluid, the form of that which does not have to organize consistency; it fits the pattern of a fluid element, of a letter arbitrarily shaped, of a robe which one arranges at one's will, of a particular state of character or mood. It is the form as improvised, momentary, changeable."[75] This seems to be Socrates's point in the *Philebus* regarding the motion of a dancer, and it captures the intellectual formation that the Athenian Stranger has in mind for the citizen choreuts, modelled on the rhythms of dialectic.

Beneviste and Kowalzig argue that Plato's innovation is to distinguish *rhythmos* as a kind of bodily movement governed by mathematical proportion. Kowalzig suggests that this is part of Plato's attempt to take control of time, to prevent the dissolution of Magnesia by hindering musical innovation. However, her claim about Plato's desire to control time conflicts with her suggestive, and largely extra-textual, comments concerning the "subversive" and spontaneous elements within the *rhythmos* of the choruses.[76] We have seen how the Athenian Stranger blends order and

72 Xenophon treats *rhythmos* as a manner or attitude of an action (*Memorabilia* 3.10.10).

73 *Persians,* 747, cited by Kowalzig, "Broken Rhythms in Plato's *Laws,*" 182.

74 Herodotus, *History,* 5.58, cited by Kowalzig, "Broken Rhythms in Plato's *Laws,*" 182–3. Aristotle speaks of the shape of letters as "*rhythmos*" (*Metaphysics* I.985b16–17, in *The Collected Works of Aristotle*).

75 Beneviste, "The Notion of 'Rhythm' in its Linguistic Expression," 285–6.

76 "Plato seeks to freeze the passage of time" (Kowalzig, "Broken Rhythms in Plato's *Laws,*" 194). See also: "Rhythm, when scrutinized more closely, is not mindless repetition. It is itself a form of variety: it is the succession of the quasi-identical. It is variety within a regularity-there is an element of progression in it because of the passage of time" (188). Kowalzig bases her claim regarding the "subversive" aspect of *rhythmos* in the *Laws* in large part on a Philostratean tableau, *Hymnetriai,* which she then takes to be a general Greek cultural view of *rhthymos* that she then imputes to the *Laws.* Part of the confusion might be

innovation in music. His praise for the Egyptian law of music has less to do with it making music static than with cultivating great music that transcends the fashions of the theatocracy. He also encourages the musical educators to innovate (*Laws* 655c). As Andrew Barker suggests, the Athenian Stranger is not as concerned with delineating types of appropriate music as he is with discovering the qualifications a reliable judge of music will need to identify the best music.[77] Good rule in Magnesia is based on practical wisdom, which, like pre-Socratic *rhythmos*, discerns the pattern in the flux; humans cannot put a stop to flux. Indeed, the Athenian Stranger's introduction of the topic of the choruses points to the legislator's act of discerning the *rhythmos* of citizens when he observes that education "tends to slacken [*khalatai*] in human beings," a development that necessitated the introduction of festivals by the Muses, Apollo, and Dionysus (*Laws* 653c). *Khalatai* literally means "lose shape," as in having lost *rhythmos*.[78] Humans tend to lose *rhythmos*, both in the pre-Socratic and Platonic meanings of the term. The choruses are designed to re-in-form those souls about *rhythmos*.

EXUBERANT LEAPING TO NOETIC GESTURES: EFFECTING THE RULE OF NOUS IN CHORUS

Nous is the ordering force of bodily and psychological *rhythmos*. This can be seen in the Athenian Stranger's comparisons between cosmic rhythms and those experienced by human beings. At the beginning of a more extended discussion of the choruses in Book VII, he claims, as "a sort of fundamental principle that applies to both body and soul," that it is beneficial for small children to be rocked in a rhythm "as if they were always on a ship at sea" (*Laws* 790d). He compares this motion with the rhythm and melody of the choruses: "For presumably when mothers want to lull their restless children to sleep they don't provide stillness but just the opposite, motion; they rock them constantly in their arms, and not with silence but with some melody. It's exactly as if they were charming the children with aulos-playing, even as is done for the maddened Bacchic

resolved if we bear in mind Planinc's argument that the *Laws* takes place within "mythic time": "The genesis of Magnesia in deed from the Athenian's speech seems to require only a few days because it occurs in myth" (*Plato's Political Philosophy*, 249). Thus whether Plato freezes time or permits variety needs to be judged in light of the dramatic presentation of time within the dialogue.

77 Barker, "The *Laws* and Aristoxenus On the Criteria of Musical Judgment," 400–1.

78 Kowalzig suggests that with *khalatai* the Athenian Stranger is "playing with the traditional meaning of *rhythmos*" ("Broken Rhythms in Plato's *Laws*," 192).

revelers, to whom they administer this same cure which consists of the motion that is dance and music" (*Laws* 790d–e).[79] This is not the first time the Athenian Stranger suggests this "fundamental principle" (*oion stoicheion*).[80] Earlier in his introduction to the choruses, he suggests that the argument sings (*logos hymneitai*) that according to nature (*kata physein*), choruses have their origin in the fact that "every young thing, so to speak, is incapable of remaining calm in body or in voice, but always seeks to move and cry: young things leap and jump as if they were dancing with pleasure and playing together, and emit all sorts of cries" (*Laws* 653d–e).

However, later he attributes the origin of dance to the tendency of human beings to make bodily gestures to amplify the meaning of their spoken words: "In general, no one who is using his voice – whether in songs or in speeches – can remain very calm in his body. That is why, as the imitation through gestures of what is being said came into being, it gave rise to the whole art of dancing" (*Laws* 816a). Though he initially suggests that dancing derives from the proclivity of the young to "leap and jump" as if at sea, he changes this to suggest that logos drives bodily motion in dance. This change is noteworthy. It indicates the extent to which the Athenian Stranger and his interlocutors acknowledge the scope of Nous's governance, and the extent to which Nous governs them and their argument. These two statements on the origin of dance indicate how Nous has been brought forth in the souls of the three founders and thus in the cosmos. The Athenian Stranger introduces the choruses in terms that suggest that they find their origin in cosmic motion, which his interlocutors would understand largely in terms of pre-Socratic atomism. His later claim concerning "gestures of what is said" retains this connection between the choruses and the cosmos, but now their noetic core is acknowledged because music has helped establish the rule of Nous. The rhythmic flow of the choruses reflects cosmic coming-into-being, as well as the experience of the dialecticians of having the *logoi* "poured over us" (*Laws* 793b).

79 Kowalzig suggests that Plato refigures the "flow" of *rhythmos* as the rhythm of sailing: "Plato's reconceptualization of rhythm does seem to play with the metaphors of 'flowing' versus 'sailing' in describing rhythmic processes of social life" ("Broken Rhythms in Plato's *Laws*," 196).

80 *Stoicheion* refers to indivisible elements of speech, matter, or proof. For proofs, see Aristotle, *Metaphysics* 1014b1 (*The Collected Works of Aristotle*). It is also the part of the sundial that casts the shadow.

7

"The Argument Is Singing to Us Now": Founders' Friendship and Cosmic Friendship in Plato's Laws

Gesang ist Dasein.[1]

LEARNING THAT THE JUST MAN IS THE HAPPY MAN

The Athenian Stranger wants us to regard the choruses as imitations of the conversation he has with Kleinias and Megillus. Frequently the men speak of the argument (*logos*) singing to them (e.g., *Laws* 653d). Theirs is a noetic version of the experience in which the gods "move us, and lead us in choruses, joining us together [*suneirontas*] with songs and dances" (*Laws* 654a). The *logos* sings to them, and they sing together, just as choreuts simultaneously sing and dance with one another, their spectators, and the gods. The elderly men of the *Laws* belong to the chorus that does not sing and dance, but rather which watches and supervises the other choruses. Their conversation founds the polity and provides the choruses with their script.[2] As founders, they place their imprint onto the souls of the citizens. Their conversation, qua script for the conversable Magnesian colony, can be compared to the correspondence between Thomas Jefferson and John Adams, which began as an effort to reconcile their broken friendship. Benjamin Rush, who brought them together, called the two men the North and South Poles of the American Revolution. In opening his correspondence, Adams wrote to Jefferson: "You and I

1 Rainer Maria Rilke, *The Sonnets to Orpheus*, III.

2 "It's probably not surprising for me to have had such a feeling, to have been very pleased at the sight of my own speeches; brought together, as it were" (*Laws* 811c–d).

ought not to die before we have explained ourselves to each other."[3] Likewise, the founders of Magnesia give an account of themselves (*logon didonai*) and the polity they create.

The elderly men are on a leisurely walk to the cave of Zeus on the day of the summer solstice. They proclaim that they can walk slowly, due to their age and for the sake of the leisure they may enjoy while discussing laws. Even so, we noticed earlier that their leisure is leavened by a sense of necessity, because it is Kleinias's responsibility to form a Cretan colony and he must learn the best way to legislate. Their contemplation is constrained by the practical necessity of his having to act politically, just as their leisure is constrained by the fact that, as old men, their lives are nearing their end. The choruses cannot hymn to them until after they die. Their speeches, then, might be considered their death masks.[4] We also noticed in chapter 5 that their peace and leisure are in tension with the hostility of the Cretan countryside, which is compounded by Kleinias's initial view that nature is strife, and all social order is war.

Just as the choreuts are educated by their elderly teachers, Kleinias and Megillus are led by the Athenian Stranger. The argument appears to lead them in circles, just as the choreuts move in circles, and just as soul rotates the cosmic sphere: "It seems to me the argument has come around again for the third or fourth time to the same thing, namely, that education is the drawing and pulling of children toward the argument that is said to be correct by law and is also believed, on account of experience, to be really correct by those who are most decent and oldest" (*Laws* 659d; see also *Laws* 664e). Yet the argument's "circle" is more like a spiral, starting with, and always coming back to, Kleinias's view that common meals are paradigmatic of the way in which a regime comes together. Returning to this idea moves the interlocutors toward deeper insights into the *nomoi*.

3 Letter of John Adams to Thomas Jefferson, July 15, 1813, in Cappon, ed., *The Adams-Jefferson Letters*, 358. I thank Geoffrey Kellow for suggesting this comparison to me in the chapter on the *Laws* in his forthcoming book, *The Wisdom of the Commons: The Education of Citizens from The Republic to The Wealth of Nations.*

4 "Each text, it might be said, is the death mask of its creation. Once it has been finished and its author has bid it farewell, as it were, the *text* will continue to be contemplated and studied as the existing work of a creative deed that has all but vanished behind it – and this even to the eyes that read it. In the perception of those who now read it, the creative life from which the text originally emerged has been replaced by the finite concreteness, the formal rigidity of a text that endures both in time (being infinitely the authoritative document apart from its author) and in the reading process (being necessarily the normative guide for the act of its being read). Following its creation, the life of the created work begins: an extended and varied life, indeed" (Tilo Schabert, "Eric Voegelin's Workshop: A Study in Confirmation of Barry Cooper's Genetic Paradigm," 232–3, emphasis in original).

As we have seen, there is a vast epistemological chasm between the Athenian Stranger and the other men (*Laws,* 968d–e). The gods must offer "some safe cable" to Kleinias and Megillus to help them cross the "rather swift and perhaps almost unfordable" argument establishing the political rule of Nous (*Laws* 892e–893b). Such is the difference between the prophet of Nous and men still living under the rule of Zeus.[5] The Athenian Stranger must perform the Hermetic task of serving as the bridge between gods and men, and of bringing Nous to them – though, paradoxically, they already have Nous within them. We saw in the chapter on the *Lysis* an elaboration of this problem.

The Athenian Stranger insists that there is one matter above all that they must sing about in consonance, which is the idea that the just life is the happy life, and the just man is the happy man (*Laws* 661d–664b).[6] This also happens to be the most difficult question for them to settle, and the one the other two men have the most difficulty understanding. As the Athenian Stranger says, "my friends, if some god were to give us consonance – for now, at any rate, we sing pretty much at variance with one another. For to me, dear Kleinias, these things appear more necessary than the proposition that Crete is manifestly an island" (*Laws* 662b). The claim that the just man is the happy man is also the hardest for Kleinias to accept because, in Zuckert's assessment, he believes "at bottom, that pleasure is the good and it is best to be a tyrant."[7]

Thus, the most important proposition for founding a regime is also the most difficult for the other men, and the regime's citizens, to understand. It is the proposition that best illuminates the gaping divide between the Athenian Stranger and his interlocutors.

The Athenian Stranger explains that it will be easy to convince citizens of this "noble lie" (*agathos pseudos, Laws* 663d). "It is possible to persuade the souls of the young of just about anything, if one tries ... and he should discover every device of any sort that will tend to make the whole community speak about these things with one and the same voice, as much as possible, at every moment throughout the whole of life, in songs and myths and arguments" (*Laws* 664a). Using the same term Socrates employs in the *Republic* to describe that dialogue's "noble lie" (414c), the

5 At least Moses could rely on Aaron to speak for him (Exodus 4:27). See Winston Churchill's remarks on their political friendship ("Moses as Political Leader," 305).

6 See *Crito* 49d (in Plato, *Four Texts on Socrates*), where Socrates claims he can find no "common counsel" with those who think they can repay injustice with additional injustice.

7 Zuckert, *Plato's Philosophers*, 71. She continues: "It is probably not an accident that Plato gave the old Cretan the same name as Alcibiades's father (and son). In this case the son inherited and acted out his father's desire" (71n39).

Athenian Stranger asserts that people are so gullible that they can be persuaded of "about anything," including that the just life is also the most pleasant.

It is easy to see why this proposition is so useful for the founding of a regime. If it were accepted, the regime's laws would be seen as the most just and therefore the most conducive to happiness. Every regime claims that its justice ensures happiness: for example, the laws of liberal democracy ensure "life, liberty, and the pursuit of happiness," and "peace, order, and good government." At one level, then, this proposition is useful.

But is it true? Calling it an *agathos pseudos* suggests that, at the very least, it might not be. It is easy to appreciate the sense in which it is not true. The just man is not necessarily the happiest. Even though he is just, he can, and likely would, still suffer the deprivation of external goods such as his reputation, wealth, and even friends and family. As Glaucon asserts in Book II of the *Republic*, the just man can suffer the most extreme of injustices: that of having a reputation for being the most unjust man, and thereby suffering all the harms that go along with it (361a). One thinks here of the accusations against Socrates, or Jesus Christ. Indeed, the Platonic dialogues all come back to the question of whether the just man, Socrates, is also happy. They seem to suggest that he is, because the philosopher who seeks wisdom has the best claim to being the just man, and he is happiest when philosophizing. That he is happiest when philosophizing is the reason Socrates gives the Athenian jury for his refusal to give up philosophizing; that the philosopher has the best claim to being just was the basis of the Delphic Oracle's claim, and what prompted him to philosophize.[8]

Even so, the claim that the just man is also the happy man holds true at a level not recognized by the other two men. They fail to see it because it results from witnessing the rule of Nous, which they have yet to fully experience. Their leisurely walk and conversation about the rule of Nous is their initiation into its mysteries, and their expansive willingness to converse for the entire day is a sign of their willingness to learn how to dance to the song of Nous.[9]

8 *Apology* 28b–30a.

9 The Athenian Stranger holds out the possibility that the proposition might be demonstrable: "Even if what the argument has now established were not the case, could a lawgiver of any worth ever tell a lie more profitable than this (if, that is, he ever has the daring to lie to the young for the sake of a good cause), or more effective in making everybody do all the just things willingly, and not out of compulsion?" (*Laws* 663d–e). The question is predicated on the conversants' view that in fact the argument has established its truth, though the Athenian Stranger recognizes that a longer argument is required to establish it.

However, the Athenian Stranger must not only provide and act as a "safe cable" for them to cross the river; he must also drag them along contrary to their understandings. The two men are required to put their whole trust into the Athenian Stranger, because they appear to agree with his proposition without understanding it to be true. This means that they will not be among those who think "things are otherwise," and whom the Athenian Stranger invites, "let him not hesitate to carry on the controversy through argument" (*Laws* 664a).[10] We see this in their assent to his proposition that the just man is also the happy man, as voiced by Kleinias: "It seems to me that with regard to what you've now said, at least, neither of us would ever be able to dispute you" (*Laws* 664b). The two Dorians seem to be in a position comparable to that of the founders vis-à-vis the citizens hearing the *agathos pseudos.* The epistemological gap between the Athenian Stranger and the other two men requires the kinds of Hermetic strategies of communication and communion that we saw in the *Lysis* to reconcile them and sustain their friendship.

When considering the Athenian Stranger's use of the *agathos pseudos,* it is worth recalling the description of eros that Socrates imputes to Diotima in the *Symposium*: "He plots to trap the beautiful and the good, and is courageous, stout, and keen, a skilled hunter, always weaving devices, desirous of practical wisdom and inventive, philosophizing through all his life, a skilled magician, druggist, sophist" (203d–e). Diotima's comparison of eros the philosopher to a sophist is puzzling, but it holds true upon reflection. First, it is extremely difficult for non-philosophers (and students) to distinguish the philosopher from a sophist because both share the characteristic of leading students into dialectical dead ends, as Adeimantus complains (*Republic* 487b–d). Part of the opposition to Socrates is that non-philosophers simply lack the experience to distinguish philosophers from sophists – that is, distinguish those who do not make the weaker argument the stronger (the philosophers), from those who do (the sophists). The *nomoi* of Magnesia will inculcate in citizens a mediated capacity to distinguish the two. Second, nearly all good teachers know that they must resort to sophisms sometimes, in order to purge students of falsehoods and secure a deeper insight. Indeed, the first two books of the *Laws* centre on such a sophism. In them the Athenian Stranger must get Kleinias the Cretan and Megillus the Lacedaimonian, both very puritanical, to speak and think seriously about

10 See also the Athenian Stranger's avoidance of "a very lengthy discussion" on whether the good is the same as the beautiful (*Laws* 655b).

drinking wine in order to purge them of their excessive moderation.[11] The Athenian Stranger must purge these unduly moderate appetites so that the two men may become more immoderate in thought. Used in the service of a philosopher's authentic desire for truth, instead of a sophist's desire for rhetorical victory, a skilful sophism shows students the extremes to which their premises lead. Socrates uses sophisms all the time in his dialogues, and frequently sends his interlocutors to ridiculous conclusions so that they may see the fallacies in their opinions.

One of the differences between Socrates's use of sophisms and that of the Athenian Stranger is that the latter is less willing to humiliate his interlocutors. He resorts to flattery instead.[12] Indeed, Abraham Lincoln adopts a similar strategy in his 1842 Temperance Address. There he explains to the Springfield Temperance Society that they would better advance their cause if they avoided scolding people for their drinking habits. Befriending them and persuading them is more effective than berating and commanding them:

> When the conduct of men is designed to be influenced, *persuasion,* kind, unassuming persuasion, should ever be adopted. It is an old and a true maxim, that a "drop of honey catches more flies than a gallon of gall." So with men. If you would win a man to your cause, *first* convince him that you are his sincere friend. Therein is a drop of honey that catches his heart, which, say what he will, is the great highroad to his reason, and which, when once gained, you will find but little trouble in convincing his judgment of the justice of your cause, if indeed that cause really be a just one.[13]

Likewise, it seems praise or flattery is more effective than humiliation in bringing about the political rule of Nous. Befriending one's interlocutors is even better.

From the perspective of those who have not had Nous revealed to them, the claim that the just man is the happy man appears as an *agathos pseudos* indeed. This is how it strikes Kleinias and Megillus, for whom the notion that nature is *not* continuous strife, but rather is governed by Nous, is something new and bewildering. The Athenian Stranger spends Book I refuting Kleinias's argument to that effect. As we saw above, Kleinias may

11 After their extended discussion, the purgation of their excessive moderation is signified by the Athenian Stranger's "Carthaginian law" on drinking that will be stricter than even the Cretan and Lacedaimonian (*Laws* 674a–c).

12 Zuckert, *Plato's Philosophers,* 67.

13 Lincoln, "Temperance Address," *Abraham Lincoln Online,* http://www.abraham lincolnonline.org/lincoln/speeches/temperance.htm.

not really believe his stated view, because his pre-philosophical understanding of political and moral reality does not reflect it. He talks tough but he practises friendship, and is glad to finally make sense of friendship (*Laws* 628a–c). If politics involves "friendship as well as peace brought about through reconciliation [*diallogion*]" (*Laws* 628b), the conversation of the three men is an emblematic practice of politics.

As indicated above, the Athenian Stranger convinces the others that the just man is the happy man, but he does not demonstrate why. Indeed, after agreeing to the proposition, the two men are eager to return to the more comfortable topic of choruses, which sits more comfortably within the horizon of the citizen's perspective, as well as their own (*Laws* 664b–c). Kleinias in particular has more to say about the composition and arrangement of the choruses than he does about their central proposition, the object of their hymns and dances. Yet, conceding to that central proposition will carry the three men into a longer argument that leads to the Athenian Stranger's demonstration that Nous does indeed rule, and that its rule necessitates that the stronger argument cannot become the weaker. The central proposition of the *nomoi* will show them that the rule of Nous is also necessarily the rule of, and for, friendship.

FRIENDSHIP OF NOUS: "PERCEPTION BY PERCEIVERS"

The three men return to the foundations of the *nomoi* in Book X after considering the variety of injustices and punishments. The question of the rule of Nous arises when they ask why injustice, especially insolence against the gods, occurs. The Athenian Stranger proposes the following three claims, or dogmas: "No one who believes in gods according to the laws has ever voluntarily done an impious deed or let slip an illegal utterance unless he is suffering one of three things: either this, which I just said, he doesn't believe; or second, he believes they exist but that they do not think about human beings; or, third, he believes they are easily persuaded if they are brought sacrifices and prayers" (*Laws* 885b). These three propositions are commonly known as the "minimum dogma" or civil religion that underwrites the *nomoi* of Magnesia.[14] As we shall see, they also express, in compact form, the constitution of reason in the cosmos and human souls, and as such the expression of friendship. Their dogmatic formulation (that is, their mention of the gods) also reflects the Athenian Stranger's noetic and daimonic experience of reality.

14 Voegelin, *Plato and Aristotle*, 263–5; V. Bradley Lewis, "Gods for the City and Beyond: Civil Religion in Plato's *Laws*."

Though he and Kleinias state their satisfaction at having demonstrated the truth of these propositions in their noetic form, that truth, by the very terms of the propositions, cannot be demonstrated so much as pointed to or acknowledged by having Nous rule and act upon one's soul.[15] One is only in a position to assent to their truth by already being in the process of assenting to the rule of Nous. The claims of the minimum dogma express the identity, if not the priority, of the ethical over the metaphysical, of the practical over the theoretical. This is because, as the basis for the *nomoi* and their preludes, they are the expression of the practical truth of reason at work, and primarily of friendship at work: "It makes no small difference, if somehow or other there is some persuasiveness in our arguments that the gods exist and are good, honoring justice differently from human beings. For this would be just about our noblest and best prelude on behalf of all the laws" (*Laws* 887c). The three propositions point to the "spring of all wonders" that enchants the choruses, whose "joy" (*charis*) mimics the wonder of perceiving the unmoving source of the cosmos (see *Laws* 893b–e).[16] They are the fundamental prelude holding that the just life is also the happy life, and as such, they cannot be compared to dialectical argumentation, but rather to the evocations of the soul that the Athenian Stranger has been conducting all along.

Because they reflect the highest things, the claims of the minimum dogma can only be contemplated as the core of our experiential order, in a manner that it is inadequate to speak or write about. They are comparable to the "most important things" that Plato, writing in his own name in *Letter VII*, refuses to write or speak about.[17] They are beyond words. Indeed, in the discussion of psyche (or Nous) as motion, the Athenian Stranger mentions name and definition as two things that one needs in order to understand the essence of a thing. In *Letter VII*, Plato mentions image and science in addition to these. But that is not all. The interlocutors of the *Laws* are speaking about ultimate reality, and because one cannot ascend to an Archimedean point above it, the best one can hope to attain is some "flash of understanding" (as Plato says in *Letter VII*,) or insight into its nature. Indeed, Socrates in the dialogues does not speak of the essence of eros, the most fundamental reality. It is beyond essence, or put more literally, it is the "eternal really being." The Athenian Stranger does not speak this way to Kleinias and Megillus

15 See Strauss, *The Argument and the Action of Plato's Laws*, 147–50.

16 Planinc, *Plato's Political Philosophy*, 211.

17 *Letter VII*, 341c–344d. For explanation, see Rhodes, *Eros, Wisdom, and Silence*, 113–81.

but the insight is the same. The entire dialogue is an effort, a prelude, to provoke a flash of understanding in them without actually drawing them up to the "eternal really being." Instead, the Athenian Stranger draws "eternal really being" down to them, through the mediated preludes, as a cable across the swift dialectical river. While they never become the dialecticians that the Athenian Stranger appears to be, they are willing followers of the argument, which presupposes some kind of flash of understanding or insight. We have already noticed Kleinias's experience of *metanoia*, when he recognized how friendship could be the telos of political life after recognizing it in the patterns of his own life. The ultimate realities, about which the three dogmas or propositions sing, are not demonstrated but evoked. They are preludes of the highest kind. They express the daimonic experience of reality.

The Athenian Stranger and Kleinias consider the noetic version of each of these dogmas. The noetic expression of the claim that the gods exist is that psyche is the unmoved mover of the cosmos. This gets expressed in various ways: "the best soul supervises the entire cosmos and drives it along such a path as that" (*Laws* 897c). Or: soul is the eldest and "most divine of all things which are provided with everflowing [*aenaos*] existence by a motion that receives its coming-into-being" (*Laws* 966e).

The materialist pre-Socratic philosophers got backwards the first cause of the *genesis* and passing away of all things. "It is soul, comrade, that almost all of them have dared to misunderstand ... How it is among the first things, how it comes into being before all bodies, and how it is, more than anything, the ruling cause of their change and of all their reordering. And if these things are so, isn't it necessarily the case that the things akin to soul would come into being before the things belonging to body, since it is elder than body?" (*Laws* 892a–b).[18] Rather than "fire or air ... it's soul that has come into being among first things, it would be most correct, almost, to say that it is especially by nature" (*Laws* 892c). At stake in this metaphysical dispute is the possibility of human freedom and thus of moral action. If the cosmos is not subject to random material processes, neither are human beings. The import of soul's priority over the

18 According to Zuckert, the Athenian Stranger's "arguments concerning the priority of the soul and the importance of the orderly motions of the heavens are based on, and formulated primarily in reaction to, the doctrines of the pre-Socratic cosmologists," especially those of Archelaus, a pupil of Anaxagoras and teacher of Socrates (*Plato's Philosophers*, 56). She adds that everything about this pre-Socratic philosophy is compatible with Kleinias's initial belief that human beings are always at war: "The suspicion arises, therefore, that the Athenian's argument to show that the gods exist is ad hominem" (126).

body is the priority of freedom over necessity, of the exercise of practical reason and moral choice, and of moral responsibility.[19]

To demonstrate this strange new argument, the Athenian Stranger compares their task to that of crossing a dangerous river. They must invoke, "in all seriousness," the aid of the god, to grasp hold of "as if to some safe cable" (*Laws* 893b). The gods must descend to help them, for Nous is about to reveal its rule. The conversant founders are choreuts with the gods, with Nous, with Hermes to guide them across the gap.

The Athenian Stranger proceeds to give an account of coming into and passing out of being, and of motion and rest, by describing the motion of the cosmic sphere around whose middle "the circumference turns in circles that are said to stand still ... In this rotation such motion carries the largest and the smallest circles around together, distributing itself proportionally to the small and the large, being less and more according to proportion. That is how it has become a source of all wonders, conveying the large and small circle at the same time, at slow and fast speeds that are in agreement" (*Laws* 893c–d). The Athenian Stranger's description reflects Pythagorean principles of proportion, which in turn represent the justice of the cosmos.[20] He describes *genesis* as a matter of beings travelling around the spheres, and then coalescing (*sugrinetai*) with one another. "Now the coming into being [*genesis*] of all things takes place when what experience occurs? Clearly, when the original cause, obtaining growth, proceeds to the second transformation, and from this, to the next, and, when it arrives at the third, it allows of perception [*aisthesis*] by perceivers [*aisthanomenois*]. By this transformation and change everything comes into being" (*Laws* 894a).[21] The coming into being of the cosmic sphere that expresses the proportions of justice is completed when it admits of "perception by perceivers."

Genesis is incomplete until it is known, until it is rationally reflected upon and becomes reflective upon itself. This is not dissimilar to the Hebrew Bible's description of God beholding His creation and calling it good and very good.[22] In Greek mythology it is comparable to the image

19 The three noetic propositions function similarly to Kant's three postulates of practical reason (freedom, God, and the immortality of the soul), except that Kant would reject the Athenian Stranger's attempt to incorporate them into metaphysics.

20 Planinc, *Plato's Political Philosophy*, 221–32; Ernest McClain, *The Pythagorean Plato: Prelude to the Song Itself*, 97–116.

21 The Athenian Stranger explains *genesis* as the motion of the cosmic or divine sphere: "The god [who] just as the ancient saying has it, holding the beginning and the end and the middle of all there is, completes his straight course by revolving, according to nature" (*Laws* 715e–16a).

22 Genesis 1:25, 31.

of Zeus beholding the cosmos, and more generally with the Olympians taking great interest in the affairs of human beings.[23] The human manner of partaking in cosmic coming into being is by telling stories, forming choruses, and philosophizing together. The cosmos has not fully come into being until reason has appeared and can tell its own story. As we saw in Plato's *Lysis*, this capacity to tell the cosmic story is expressed in the *Hymn to Hermes*'s description of Hermes, the last Olympian, singing the first theogony and thus signifying the completion of the cosmic order. By affording "perception by perceivers," the original cause enables beings to perceive it and each other. *Sunaisthesis* is built into the noetic order of the cosmos, and it is brought about by the process of *genesis* in which beings coalesce with one another. The rational structure of the cosmos is just, and its purpose is friendship – regardless, it seems, of the numerous ways life shows us the opposite.

Soul is "motion capable of moving itself" (*Laws* 896a). This quality means that soul is not simply alive, but is also life itself, or its principle (*Laws* 895c–d). This equation of soul with life points to the special mode in which the statement of soul's priority over body is to be understood. We cannot prove we are alive so much as experience it, or be in a condition of it. Life is the basis of our capacity to prove that we live. This seems to be point of a comment Socrates makes to Gorgias and Polus: "And indeed I would not be amazed if what Euripides says is true in these lines, where he says, 'Who knows, if living is being dead, and being dead is living?' And perhaps really we are dead; for I'm sure I have also heard from some one of the wise that we are now dead and our body is a tomb."[24] Life is less a datum of experience than the condition of experience, which cannot be contained by our understanding. Similarly, soul is the condition of our capacity to distinguish soul from bodies. Our capacity to know presupposes soul. Existence incorporates the friendly rule of soul within it, which is a point we saw in our consideration of Aristotle on *sunaisthesis* in chapter 2.

The Athenian Stranger is the paramount example of the first cause's perceiver enabling it to be perceived. He not only reveals the first cause of soul, he enacts it and completes it by his demonstration.[25] Nous becomes known through him. Its rule becomes effective through him. He is a prophet, but, necessarily, he must be unknown or unnamed, even though the choruses will hymn to him along with the other founders. He

23 Heyking, "The Intermediaries of the Eranos Festival: Orpheus and Hermes." See also Kerényi, *The Religion of the Greeks and Romans*.

24 Plato, *Gorgias* 492e–493a, citing a lost play of Euripides (either *Phrixus* or *Polyidos*).

25 He enacts the Hermetic drama that Socrates enacts in the *Lysis*. See chapter 4.

is unknown or unnamed because, as efficient cause of the noetic constitution, his causation must come into the souls of Magnesia's citizens as if of their own accord. This is the paradox of teaching that he asserts at the conclusion of the dialogue:

> It is vain to discuss these matters in writings, for it wouldn't be clear to the learners themselves whether the subject were being learned at the right time, until knowledge of the subject had, presumably, come into being within the soul of each. Thus, while it would be incorrect to speak of all that pertains to these matters as indescribable secrets, they are incapable of being described beforehand, because describing them beforehand would clarify nothing of what is being discussed. (*Laws* 968e)

The greatest gift a friend can give, the revelation of Nous, must go unacknowledged, because otherwise it would distort Nous. If, as Jesus says, the greatest gift a friend can give is to die for his friend (John 15:13), the Athenian Stranger's greatest gift is his self-annihilation. We can never know him. The greatest act of friendship-love is to acknowledge one's infinite distance from one's friend.

FRIENDSHIP WITH THE "OLD MAN"

The noetic version of the second proposition, that the gods care for men, is already implied in the first proposition, that soul as first cause means that soul governs the universe and everything in it, big and small (*Laws* 898d–905d). Reason is identical with reason's rule. The atheist's objection to this is that the gods are too noble and great to care for such small matters as human affairs, and that it is inconsistent for the gods to care about human affairs while allowing for so many evils (*Laws* 900b). The Athenian Stranger dismisses the objection by suggesting that it is an excuse for committing injustices. It is based on a rejection of one's moral responsibility, one's capacity for practical wisdom and moral choice, just as the objection to the first dogma is a rejection of one's moral freedom. The Athenian Stranger's other response, that the atheist fails to appreciate that the good of the whole is greater than the good of its parts (*Laws* 903c), is less convincing, especially since he attempts to demonstrate the second proposition by arguing that the gods' care for great matters also makes them capable of caring for small (human) matters.

Even so, the rule of soul is providential in the basic sense that it governs the general and the particular, the large and the small. Ruling for the good of the whole is the demiurgic act of bringing things into being through coalescence, and enabling them to pass away by dissolution.

The cosmos cannot be a cosmos without a ruler, first cause, or king (*Laws* 903e–904a). It is in the nature of the cosmos for good to triumph over evil (*Laws* 904b–e).

Judging and being judged seem to be the main noetic concerns of the second proposition. In responding to the atheist's objection, the Athenian Stranger alludes to the wishes of particular persons to seek their places in the cosmos designed by "our King," to be judged: "For the sake of the whole he has, in fact, contrived it so that when a certain sort of thing comes into being it must always take a certain place, and then dwell in certain regions. And he has assigned to the wishes of each of us the responsibility for what sort of person comes into being: the way one desires and what one is in one's soul just about determines each time, the type of character every one of us, for the most part, becomes" (*Laws* 904c). While the Athenian Stranger emphasizes that the working of the whole requires individual parts, individual persons, to "take a certain place," he also indicates that we as individuals desire to take responsibility for the types of characters we are to become. The providential care for the whole incorporates the parts' desires to find their places, become what they are, and fulfill their potentials. This principle is consistent with statements that Socrates makes in the *Republic* regarding the individual's experience of his or her own completion within a greater whole. In Book X, we read that individual souls choose their own lots in the afterlife. They, not the god, are responsible for their choices (617e). Similarly, the principle of "one man, one job" that animates the just city requires that each individual loves his or her only job: "When we claim someone loves something, if it's being said correctly, it has to be clear that he doesn't love part of it and part not, but is devoted to it all" (*Republic* 474c). "Vocation" is probably a better term than the more instrumental "job" – the former signifies one's moral, intellectual, and spiritual aspirations for one's work.

Just as the Athenian Stranger counsels that we should "always pursue someone who is better than himself, without putting any feeling of shame in the way (*Laws* 732a–b), so too are "things that partake [*metaxos*] of soul transformed, possessing within themselves the cause of the transformation, and, undergoing transformation, are moved to the order and law of destiny" (*Laws* 904c). Soul as "life" exists between the divine and the bodily, and thus always in motion and undergoing transformation, though it contains within itself the "cause of the transformation," which is freedom. This movement is made possible by the soul's "own wishing and familiarity with others," who are either better or worse. "Then, when by mingling [*homilia*] with a divine virtue it comes to be such in an exceptional degree, it undergoes an especially great transformation in locale and is borne along a hallowed path to some other, better place; and when the opposite things occur, it transfers its own life to the opposite sorts of places" (*Laws* 904d–e). The act of coalescing with others is described in terms of friendship; the very way that the Athenian Stranger conceives of soul is essentially in terms of leaning towards others, whether better or worse. People do these things "while they're alive and dreaming, and when they've become separated from their bodies" (*Laws* 904d). As with the judgment of the dead at the end of the *Republic*, this judgment occurs not simply in the afterlife, but at every moment and every second. It is now. We stand eternally in responsibility under the light of judgment. The second dogma shows how the demiurgic act of "coalescing" in creation is experienced by us mortals as a transformation into the better whom we love and befriend.

The second proposition of the so-called minimum dogma is probably the most contentious to moderns. Moreover, it seems to violate the Aristotelian assertion that gods and human beings cannot be friends.[26] Philosophers and scholars have good reason to reject this proposition. The Athenian Stranger does not demonstrate it (or any of the other of the three propositions), so much as point to it or evoke it, as he evokes preludes. His motivation for putting it forward seems to be that it supports the moral basis of the laws and thus secures citizens' commitment to them. Citizens can take comfort that their moral striving has cosmic support, despite potentially equally valid arguments to the effect that "we humans would appear to be set adrift in a fundamentally indifferent, if not hostile environment."[27] One's commitment to living the just life receives sustenance when one sees it as under divine care, especially amidst life's trials and tribulations. That said, there are also good reasons to dispute the veracity of the second proposition, not the least of which is that it can serve as a club for messianic lunatics claiming divine support for their political ambitions, however terrible. "God is on my side" and "History is on my side" are the claims of many tyrants.

Even so, neither statesmen nor political philosophy itself can altogether reject the second proposition because of its daimonic quality. We have seen how Plato conceives of the soul as "in-between," and so cannot provide a fully demonstrable account of its genesis or its end. It is between the resourceful gift of the gods, and the poverty created by their thefts from us. This is the Hermetic dimension of human eros considered in

26 *Nicomachean Ethics* VIII, chapter 7. However, see chapters 2 and 4, on Aristotle and sunaisthetic friendship and on Plato's *Lysis* respectively, for reasons why this argument requires qualification.

27 Zuckert, *Plato's Philosophers*, 145. See also 126–7.

chapter 4. It is also reflected in the Athenian Stranger's account of divine judgment and the manner in which souls transform when they "mingl[e] [*homilia*] with a divine virtue" (*Laws* 904d–e).

But the experience of divine care is not restricted to Platonic philosophers under the spell of Hermes, or to messianic tyrants. Sensitive statesmen also speak of it. Winston Churchill was such a statesmen. His disbelief in the eternity of the soul is well-known and documented, as is his disbelief in the redeeming power of Jesus.[28] However, different beliefs seem to be betrayed by his actions, which were ever hopeful. Indeed, Churchill once stated: "Whether you believe or disbelieve, it is a wicked thing to take away Man's hope."[29] "Never give in, never, never, never, never!" is his most famous expression of this.

Indeed, Churchill seems to have held a strong belief in Providence, and one might even go so far as to characterize his religion in terms of the second proposition's civil religion. Geoffrey Fisher, archbishop of Canterbury during Churchill's peacetime years as prime minister, describes it in terms the Athenian Stranger would readily identify with: "Churchill had a very real religion but it was a religion of the Englishman. He had a very real belief in Providence; but it was God as the God with a special care for British values. There was nothing obscure about this, it was utterly sincere, but not really at all linked on the particular beliefs which constitute the Christian faith and the life which rests on it."[30] Churchill's faith in Providence extended to the special care he thought was given to him.

Paul Addison argues that Churchill's ego, as well as the "emotional need for support and protection" that stemmed from his difficult relationship with his father, played no small role in shaping his creed. Addison cites Churchill's firm belief, starting in 1897, that he was destined to become prime minister, and a letter he wrote to his mother after narrowly escaping death in battle on the northwest frontier of India: "I am so conceited I do not believe the Gods would create so potent a being as myself for so prosaic an ending."[31] "Ambition," as Addison observes, "was the instrument of Providence: what was good for Winston Churchill

28 After his stroke in June 1953, he spoke to Harold MacMillan and his doctor, Lord Moran, of "black velvet-eternal sleep" (Paul Addison, "Destiny, History and Providence: The Religion of Winston Churchill," 238). See Kenneth Young, *Churchill and Beaverbrook: A Study in Friendship in Politics*, 314. See also Socrates's suggestion that death might bring eternal sleep (*Apology* 40b–c).

29 Meacham, *Franklin and Winston*, 29. David Walsh provides a powerful meditation on hope in action ("Hope Does Not Disappoint").

30 Edward Carpenter, *Cantuar: The Archbishops in Their Office*, 489.

31 Addison, "Destiny, History and Providence," 241.

was good for Britain."[32] Churchill interpreted his escape from a Boer prisoner-of-war camp as the most vivid example of divine protection:

> Finding himself alone in the wilderness and fearful of recapture, he prayed to God for guidance. Having made his way to some lights in the distance he knocked on a door to discover his salvation: a friendly English mine manager who concealed him from the bottom of a mineshaft. Churchill was also delighted to discover that the engineer at the mine, a Mr. Dewsnap, was from Oldham, the constituency in which he was the prospective Tory candidate. As he entered the cage to descend into the mine, Dewsnap whispered to him: "They'll all vote for you next time." Churchill believed – as he confided to Leo Amery many years later – that God had answered his prayer.[33]

As with Joseph sitting in the pit his brothers tossed him into, we do not know what Churchill was thinking at the bottom of that mineshaft. Perhaps he was reconsidering his youthful atheism. Even so, throughout his career he regarded his political life as under providential care. His exclusion from office during the 1930s, the so-called wilderness years, was no less providential: "Now one can see how lucky I was. Over me beat the invisible wings."[34]

John Colville, his secretary, reports that Churchill regarded World War II as guided by "some overriding power which had a conscious influence on our destinies."[35] Addison points out that this belief was confirmed by Churchill in his speech on the eve of the Battle of Alamein: "I sometimes have a feeling, in fact I have it very strongly, a feeling of interference. I want to stress that. I have a feeling sometimes that some guiding hand has interfered. I have the feeling that we have a guardian because we have a great cause, and that we shall have that guardian as long as we serve that cause faithfully."[36] Finally, in June 1950, on the eve of the Korean War, as leader of opposition he told his shadow cabinet: "The old man is very good to me. I could not have managed this [Korean] situation had I been in Attlee's place. I should have been called a warmonger." Asked by Sir David Maxwell Fyfe who the "old man" was, Churchill replied, using his nickname for Maxwell Fyfe: "God, Sir Donald."[37] As

32 Addison, "Destiny, History and Providence," 243.

33 Ibid., 241–2.

34 Churchill, *The Gathering Storm*, 141.

35 Colville, *Fringes of Power*, 128.

36 Addison, "Destiny, History and Providence," 248, citing a speech to a conference of delegates of coalmine owners and miners on October 31, 1942.

37 Addison, "Destiny, History and Providence," 248.

Odysseus had his Athena, as Socrates had his daimon, and as Moses had God, so too did the daimonic Churchill have his "old man."

If we are to take the daimonism of human existence seriously as a fundamental outlook of Plato's political philosophy, we cannot discount the sentiments of providential care expressed by otherwise clear-headed statesmen like Churchill. He seems to have understood the term, daimon, to describe military genius, the capacity to discern the form of a battle or grand strategy in an ineffable manner that transcends the discernment of its individual parts. This is consistent with a Platonic view;[38] indeed, Clausewitz draws the analogy with Plato.[39] Churchill seems to attribute such daimonism to himself. In his characteristically self-referential essay on Moses as a political leader, published during the wilderness years, he advances a subtle understanding of miracles as simultaneously explicable and inexplicable according to natural causation. Locusts, frogs, and the parting of the Red Sea are not significant as miracles. What is truly miraculous is the daimonic passion of Moses and the Israelites' act of covenanting with God: "[The Burning Bush] burned, yet it was not consumed. It was a prodigy. The more it burned the less it was consumed; it seemed to renew itself from its own self-consumption. Perhaps it was not a bush at all, but his own heart that was aflame with a fire never to be quenched while the earth supports human beings."[40] Then God, "now inside the frame of Moses," said, "I will endow you with superhuman power. There is nothing that man cannot do, if he wills it with enough resolution. Man is the epitome of the universe. All moves and exists as a result of his invincible will, which is my Will." Later Churchill writes: "This wandering tribe, in many respects indistinguishable from the numberless nomadic communities, grasped and proclaimed an idea of which all the genius of Greece and all the power of Rome were incapable. There was to be only one God, a universal God, a God of nations, a just God, a God who would punish in another world a wicked man dying rich and prosperous; a God from whose service the good of the humble and of the weak and poor was inseparable."[41] Curiously, Churchill also emphasizes the friendship between Aaron and

38 Churchill, *Life of Marlborough*, vol. 1, 569.

39 "If we then ask what sort of mind is likeliest to display the qualities of military genius, experience and observation will both tell us that it is the inquiring rather than the creative mind, the comprehensive rather than the specialized approach, the calm rather than the excitable head to which in war we would choose to entrust the fate of our brothers and children, and the safety and honor of our country" (Carl von Clausewitz, *On War*, I.3).

40 "Moses: The Leader of a People," 304.

41 Ibid., 309–10.

Moses, though the Hebrew Bible indicates that they are kin. This is part of his general view of politics as the activity of great individuals with their friends.[42]

Statesmen of this stature engage in the greatest of political acts and take the greatest of risks. Despite or because of their ambition, they have a special sensitivity to the precariousness of their endeavours and the fragility of human projects, and the very real possibility that the cosmos is indifferent or hostile. As Churchill wrote in *The River War*, "every incident is surrounded by a host of possibilities, any one of which, had it become real, would have changed the whole course of events … In the flickering light of conflict the outlines of solid fact throw on every side the vague shadows of possibility. We live in a world of 'ifs.'"[43] So when, out of the dark of the deepest mineshaft, such people's prayers are answered, they would regard their salvation, and the salvation of their nations, as the result of providential care. Why did we succeed when we really ought to have failed? The statesman who has endured the wilderness years is grateful for the care he has been given. Thus Harry Jaffa says of Churchill and the intelligibility of his life of action: "Contemplating life as a whole must give us faith that, in the long run, chance is not merely indifferent to human excellence"[44]

The third proposition of the minimum dogma, logically entailed by the first (and second), is that the gods cannot be appeased by the unjust with gifts (*Laws* 905d–907d). The noetic version of this proposition is an injunction against sophistry, of making the weaker argument the stronger: "The reason, dear Kleinias, why they were animated by a fondness for victory was a concern lest the bad should believe that if they ever were stronger in arguments, they could act in the ways they wish, according to the sorts of notions they have about gods" (*Laws* 907c). Both versions are injunctions against excusing unjust behavior by buying off the gods (*Laws* 906d). One cannot cheat reason. Obedience to reason acknowledges its rule, and enables us to enjoy friendship. The three propositions are the dogmatic articulation of the rule of friendship in Magnesia. They point to their noetic counterparts, which shows how the moral practices of the polis, including its choruses, are inherently practices of friendship.

42 See my *"Comprehensive Judgment" and "Absolute Selflessness": Winston Churchill on Politics as Friendship.*

43 Churchill, *The River War*, I.235.

44 Jaffa, "Can There Be Another Winston Churchill?" *Claremont Review of Books*, February 2004, https://www.claremont.org/basicPageArticles/can-there-be-another-winston-churchill/.

CONCLUSION

The Magnesian choruses are the nexus in which the Athenian Stranger's revelation of Nous refigures Odysseus's claim that the best of life is found in human beings feasting and listening to the bard sing of their deeds.[45] The chorus is the emblem of political friendship that consists in reflecting, in music, on the greatest deeds of the regime. The choreuts' play, freedom, and conscious participation in the noetic order has them mimic the dialectical ascent of the conversant founders. Their reasoned singing and dancing, conducted in friendship, mimics the freedom of the unmoved mover, whose creation of a cosmos that "allows of perception by perceivers" (*Laws* 894a) is a creation of friendship.

The choruses' hymn to the unmoved mover is also a hymn to the founders of Magnesia, an act that not only replicates cosmic creation but enacts it as well. Nous is unknown and ineffective before the Athenian Stranger reveals it in this dialogue, which itself creates a citizenry conversant with it.

The Athenian Stranger's friendliness, then, is the paradigm of friendship that the choruses mimic. He brings peace to disparate elements, to friends and enemies, via reconciliation (*diallogion*). He brings about *symphonia* among friends and enemies, through the inculcation of virtue. He brings about *symphonia* between body and soul as well, by having soul govern the body. The presence of all the virtues – justice, prudence, moderation, and courage – enables the soul's rule over the body to be friendly. A sign of this is in the body's metaphorical willingness to be ruled, by seeking to learn to dance. This is seen in the choruses, and it is seen in the final proclamation of Megillus (who signifies body, *soma*) that they must force the Athenian Stranger to stay and continue teaching them.

But the Athenian Stranger's friendship is paradoxical because he annihilates himself. He is anonymous. Making the reasonable inference that he is Socrates is no less paradoxical because Socrates himself is a paradox. Moreover, from the perspective of the non-philosopher citizen, both the Athenian Stranger and Socrates appear as sophists who lead them astray. The Athenian Stranger's safe cable, which he and the gods throw to the two men and the rest of us, is one that we must grasp in trust. It gets tossed to us despite the Athenian Stranger's knowing full well that it clarifies nothing unless we possess knowledge of Nous beforehand (*Laws* 968e). The Athenian Stranger knows us more intimately than we know ourselves, yet also stands at an infinite distance from us.

45 Homer, *Odyssey*, IX.1–12.

This is the paradox of Socratic friendship that we saw in the *Lysis*. Even so, this very paradox might also be the paradigm of all human friendships, including those of the choreuts holding hands together, singing and dancing in a circle, both friendly and free.

The *Laws* puts forth the case that friendship is the form of politics. Magnesia is founded upon the old saying that friends share all things in common. Strange as this claim is, and strange as the Magnesian regime is, the practices of statesmen, ancient and modern, seem to acknowledge this. They do not replicate Magnesia exactly or in detail, but they seem to acknowledge its constitution as the ordering force of their political understanding and practice. We saw in the introduction that statesmen often conceive of friendship as the primary category of their political activity. A few more observations that pertain to the Magnesian choruses illuminate this further.

We have seen how the choruses' rhythms and harmonies are hymns, and how some traditional Christian hymns might be comparable to them. Christian hymns are reverential, and they are about the paradigmatic action of the just man: in this case, Jesus. The hymns of Isaac Watts or Martin Luther, with their moderate melodies, harmonies, and rhythms, facilitate moderation and awe, and the relative ease of singing them facilitates widespread participation among the congregation. Some hymns are even somewhat warlike, as is, for instance, Luther's "A Mighty Fortress is Our God." Indeed, the composition of hymns was instrumental in the development and spread of Lutheranism during the Protestant Reformation; it enabled popular participation in the theological movement and provided solidarity to members.[46] The Jewish and Christian tradition of singing the Psalms might also compare. However, Christian hymns do not usually involve dance. We have also examined how modern dance is more crowd-inducing than friendship-inducing – at least in its popular forms, or in the forms that blur any distinction between performer and spectator. Schiller's description of the Scottish reel seems to nominate it as a good candidate for a modern equivalent of the Magnesian chorus.

However, these modern and Judeo-Christian examples are not political, as the Magnesian choruses are. Since the choruses involve play and celebrate justice, one must rule out, as their modern counterparts, political festivals such as the Nuremberg rallies and the festivals spawned by

46 Christopher Brown, *Singing the Gospel: Lutheran Hymns and the Success of the Reformation*.

the French Revolution.[47] One of the best examples of a Magnesian chorus in modernity is Estonia's "Singing Revolution" between 1988 and 1991, when half the country came out in defiance of Soviet troops and tanks to sing nationalist songs for Estonian independence. These events are a good example of the Magnesian synthesis of freedom and friendship.[48]

From this citizen-driven chorus, we can turn our attention to the "choruses" of modern statesmen. Neither Lincoln nor Churchill was talented at music, but they were inherently musical or daimonic, as Socrates argues statesmen must be.[49]

Lincoln's speeches, especially his Gettysburg Address, are examples of musical choruses. Their rhythms, cadences, and arguments are drawn from the King James Bible and from Shakespeare. Lincoln loved music, especially opera. He also loved the song "Dixie," which he made into a quasi-national song in an act of reconciliation with the South after the Civil War. In his personal bearing he always seemed to keep a rhythm. Julia Taft, a family friend, remarks that while reading, Lincoln would sway his legs, "as if in time to sing inaudible music."[50] Additionally, he conceived of the American Republic, not in terms of a Lockean social contract, but in terms of political friendship: "We are not enemies, but friends. We must not be enemies. Though passion may have strained it must not break our bonds of affection."[51] His subsequent reference, in the first inaugural address, to "mystic chords of memory," compares with Churchill's notion of England as an "island story," and the Athenian Stranger's observation that the awe inspired by the laws also provides the basis for civic friendship. I shall address another example of such a civic festival in the conclusion.

47 See Hamilton Burden, *The Nuremberg Party Rallies, 1923–39*; and Mona Ozouf, *Festivals and the French Revolution.*

48 Guntis Smidchens, *The Power of Song: Nonviolent National Culture in the Baltic Singing Revolution*; Clare Thomson, *The Singing Revolution: A Political Journey through the Baltic States*; and see the documentary, *Singing Revolution,* written by James Tusty, Maureen Castle Tusty, and Mike Majoros. Complicating this example is that the "Singing Revolution" occurred during a revolutionary time, whereas the Magnesian choruses take place during "normal" times, 365 days a year.

49 See *Phaedrus* 248d.

50 Goodwin, *Team of Rivals,* 335.

51 Lincoln, "First Inaugural." On Lincoln's conception of political friendship and music, see Eva Brann's "A Reading of Lincoln's 'Gettysburg Address'"; see also Matthew S. Holland, *Bonds of Affection: Civic Charity and the Making of America; Winthrop, Jefferson, and Lincoln,* 161–240.

Churchill's speeches also follow the rhythms and cadences of the King James Bible. Indeed, in writing out his speeches, he would adopt the "psalm" format: blank verse with all lines but the first indented.[52] Churchill had a keen sense of musical ritual. An important example of this was when he chose the hymns that were played and sung at the first meeting between him and Roosevelt as world leaders and friends (along with their senior naval staffs), aboard the *Prince of Wales* off the coast of Newfoundland.[53] He selected "O God Our Help in Ages Past" by Isaac Watts, "Onward Christian Soldiers," and "Eternal Father Strong to Save." In the spirit of Magnesian choruses, John Martin noted in his diary that this service "seemed a sort of marriage service between the two navies."[54] Finally, like Lincoln's mystic chords of memory, Churchill's island story is an example of the *nomoi* instilling awe that serves as the basis for freedom and friendship for the city. And in addition, like the *nomoi*, it is an instance of the polis singing its own song, that is superior to anything a poet could create. Indeed, Churchill is the bard of the island story at the same time that he is the demiurgic statesman who guides the action. He creates the island story while he writes its histories.[55]

The acts of friendship of great statesmen and citizens follow the logic that the *Laws* seems to outline. The dialogue lays out the form in which their actions participate. It invites us to consider the possible shapes that politics and friendship may take. The *Laws* treats music as the bridge between form and instantiation, by creating *symphonia* between body and soul, between soul and Nous, between citizens and lawgivers, and between citizens themselves. All of this is predicated on the music of the "measure," the gracious and divine "middle course" between the extremes, upon which we dance (*Laws* 792d).

The *Laws* concludes with Megillus the Spartan, who does not speak much, insisting that he and Kleinias prevent the Athenian Stranger from departing. The scene resembles the beginning of the *Republic*, when Polemarchus has his slave boy force Socrates to stay with the group. Megillus dramatically signifies body (*soma*), as Kleinias signifies soul (*psyche*) and the Athenian Stranger signifies Nous.[56] The conclusion of

52 I thank Allen Packwood, director of Churchill Archives at Churchill College, Cambridge University, for this information.

53 Martin Gilbert, *Finest Hour, 1939–1941*, 1158–9.

54 Ibid., 1159.

55 It is for this reason that complaints that Churchill's historiography is insufficiently scholarly are beside the point. Indeed, his histories are mythic, but his myth is better understood in the Platonic terms outlined here. For details, see my *"Comprehensive Judgment" and "Absolute Selflessness": Winston Churchill on Politics as Friendship.*

56 Planinc, *Plato's Political Philosophy*, 227.

the *Laws,* then, has the body demanding that both it and psyche be ruled by Nous. The sign of the body's readiness to be governed politically – not despotically, as it is in the *Republic* – is its willingness to be taught to dance in chorus. Reason's rule is the rule of friendship.

Voegelin reports that on the evening of Plato's death at the age of 81, he had a Thracian girl play the flute to him: "The girl could not find the beat of the *nomos.* With a movement of his finger, Plato indicated to her the Measure."[57] The Athenian Stranger continues to conduct us in the rhythms of our chorus.

57 Voegelin, *Plato and Aristotle,* 268.

8

Conclusion: Dwelling Together

"I will do this [engage in philosophic questioning] to whomever, younger or older, I happen to meet, both foreigner and townsman, but more so to the townsmen, inasmuch as you are closer to me in kin."[1]

LOOKING FOR LOVE IN ALL THE RIGHT PLACES

In this book, I have attempted to recover the understanding of virtue-friendship in Aristotle and Plato, and its relationship with political order. The chapters have shown how each philosopher regards *sunaisthesis* as the pinnacle or crown of friendship, in spite of some paradoxes involved in the phenomenon. I have also shown how both Plato and Aristotle thought that a political society requires its citizens to share in this experience to some extent. While political friendship is not the same as *sunaisthesis,* we do see a political version of the latter in the way that these philosophers regard festivity as the culmination of, or even regulative ideal for, political friendship. Political friendship itself is not the most "intense and best" – a description Aristotle reserves for sunaisthetic friendship. However, a political society in which citizens lack personal experience of sunaisthetic friendship will be distorted and convulsed by utopian and ideological attempts to seek that kind of friendship in the political sphere. Communism, socialism, general will, and other forms of collectivism are instances of such distorted passions, variations of which Plato and Aristotle understood and criticized in their writings. Utopian ideologues look for love in all the wrong places, to cite the country song by Johnny Lee. The ancient views of festivity that we have examined do not fall prey to this misplaced political longing, but rather put it into its proper context.

1 Plato, *Apology* 30a.

In previous chapters, I have attempted to draw out the contemporary implications of various aspects of Aristotle's and Plato's thinking. I have noted the difference between Aristotle's understanding of sunaisthetic friendship and our own, and for the most part I regard ours as deficient. Thus Aristotle provides us with moral teachings about friendship that we can draw from to make us better at practising friendship, and especially at knowing what it is when we encounter it. I find that this, more than anything else I teach, is what undergraduates find to be the most personally compelling in the teachings of Plato and Aristotle. Most undergraduates are at an age when their friendships are the most important relationships they have, and they are trying to understand what count as the best forms of friendship. Both Aristotle and Plato teach us how to navigate the treacherous waters of our times, which are so laden with false conceptions of both *eros* and *philia*. Their teachings on friendship teach us something vital. The most crucial, and perhaps the most challenging to our own age, is their view that friendship (and *eros*) is weakened and deformed when not guided by the proper flourishing of a mature intellect. Opposing our romantic view that friendship is love without wings may be the most subversive teaching Plato and Aristotle have for us.

I hope that my exposition of Plato and Aristotle on political friendship as festivity has demonstrated that this view cannot be rejected *tout court* as utopian or wishful thinking, and that it is not completely foreign to our experience as citizens of a modern liberal democratic state. In some ways it is this teaching that is the most foreign to us, because we so rarely come together as citizens (as opposed to coming together as sporting spectators, or in other festivals celebrating different cultures within our society). I have attempted to demonstrate how traces of Plato's and Aristotle's fundamental insight that festivity is the completion of civic virtue still can be found in the forms and formalities of our own society, as well as in civic festivals that are not simply a form of rest from our "more important" business of, well, going about our business. That these forms, formalities, and festivities reside outside our usual scope of attention – that they filter into it as distant lights get filtered through dense atmosphere or through window panes – shows, perhaps, how our own liberal democratic regime is predicated upon partial virtue, a reason the Athenian Stranger notes when he complains that so few regimes take festivity seriously.

METAXIC RIDING

To conclude, I shall apply some of these insights to a contemporary example of a civic festival: the world-famous Calgary Stampede, which takes place every July in Calgary, Alberta, Canada. It affords a unique insight into the possibility of festivity (in the sense described by Plato and Aristotle) in a liberal democracy, because it is a civic festival that expresses a fundamental like-mindedness but also prizes individualism and tolerance. It seems to succeed at the Hermetic task of reconciling opposites, from like-mindedness and tolerance to the principles of liberty and equality. In doing so, it reflects the Athenian Stranger's view that political friendship entails leavening two different types of equality: (1) equality according to "nature" or excellence, and (2) "equality of the lot" (*Laws* 757b–e). Mixing these two types of equality, though with the first being more prominent, is a recipe for political success and friendship.

Two recent events that took place in my hometown, Calgary – among my "kin," to use Socrates's term – illustrate how it might be possible to conceive of the reconciliation of tolerance and common life. The first was the catastrophic flood of June 2013 that displaced between 75,000 and 100,000 people from their homes, and severely damaged the facilities of the Calgary Stampede. The second is the city's accommodation of its numerous Muslim taxi drivers, who in 2013 faced the dilemma that Ramadan overlapped with the Stampede – meaning that a period of fasting and resting coincided with a dramatic increase in demand for their services.[2]

Begun in 1912, the Calgary Stampede is an annual festival that celebrates the West by holding a professional rodeo, agricultural exhibition, carnival midway, and numerous other cultural and economic activities. Despite initial worries, Stampede officials proclaimed that the flood of 2013 would not cause it to be cancelled. "Come hell or high water" became the rallying cry not only for the Stampede but for the city as a whole, as its citizens take great pride in it. Indeed, many observed that the Stampede, which is a non-profit organization run at arm's-length from the civic politicians, depends on its army of roughly 2,500 volunteers, many of whom worked to clean and rebuild the facilities.[3] As mayor Naheed Nenshi, an Ismaili Muslim, declared after the flood, "all of those volunteers that make it happen every single year will make it

2 "City Looks to Accommodate Stampede Taxi Drivers for Ramadan," *CBC News*, 20 June 2013, http://www.cbc.ca/news/canada/calgary/story/2013/06/20/calgary-ramadan-taxi-drivers-hth.html.

3 "Volunteers Heart of the Calgary Stampede," *Calgary Journal*, undated, http://www.calgaryjournal.ca/index.php/ourcity/1762-stampede-volunteers.

work."[4] Indeed, the volunteer effort to clean up the city was astounding. As Ray Pennings observed, "it is significant that only 1,500 of the 75,000 evacuated people utilized the municipally-provided shelters – all the others were taken care of through their own social contacts or by strangers who offered their homes. Monday morning the city needed 600 volunteers to do a door-to-door drop-off; 2,500 people showed up at McMahon Stadium ready to help."[5] The Stampede is emblematic of the can-do, volunteering spirit of Albertans, and that the cleanup and rebuilding effort took place independently and well in advance of government efforts reveals something important about the regime.[6]

The City of Calgary set up a temporary prayer tent for its Muslim taxi drivers, who compose roughly half of all its taxi drivers. Even so, observing Ramadan proved a challenge for many of them. As one driver explained, "We can't skip Ramadan, we can't skip Stampede. How am I going to do this?"[7]

These two events illustrate something crucial about the Calgary Stampede and the question of tolerance and faith in the common life. First, regarding Ramadan, the Stampede, though a festival celebrating the West, is also one that celebrates the founding principles of western civilization, namely ordered liberty, and this includes tolerance. Second, regarding the response to the flood, the Stampede is an expression of civic friendship, as illustrated by its central role in the community as well as the importance of volunteers.

Moreover, the Calgary Stampede is something rarely found in modern civilization: a civic festival, or a festival of the civil religion of a specific area, namely, Calgary and southern Alberta. Its festivities embody principles and stories specific to a particular regime, but ones practised across western liberal polities devoted to liberty and, less obviously, to

4 "Flames Arena on Stampede Grounds Flooded 10 Rows Deep," *National Post*, 21 June 2013, http://news.nationalpost.com/sports/nhl/flames-arena-on-stampede-grounds-flooded-10-rows-deep.

5 Ray Pennings, "Reflections from the Calgary Flood Plain," *The Cardus Daily Blog*, 24 June 2013, https://www.cardus.ca/blog/2013/06/reflections-from-the-calgary-flood-plain.

6 Jen Gerson, "No Waiting For the Government: Calgary Community Makes it Work, Pitches in to Help," *National Post*, 24 June 2013, http://www.nationalpost.com/m/wp/news/blog.html?b=news.nationalpost.com/2013/06/24/gerson-floods-monday&pubdate=2013-06-24.

7 "Ramadan Fasting During Stampede Hard For Some Taxi Drivers," CBC *News*, 9 July 2013, http://www.cbc.ca/news/canada/calgary/story/2013/07/09/calgary-ramadan-stampede-el.html.

civic friendship. It is a civic festival in the sense that it embodies the principles of the regime's civil religion, of liberty. This is rare because most festivals today are cultural and therefore reside in the social sphere, whereas this is more specifically political.

For the rodeo participants, the rodeo's purpose or significance consists mostly in competition, winning prize money, fellowship with other participants, fellowship with the horses, and continuing family traditions within the games. For the spectators – the *theoroi,* as the ancient Greeks called festival spectators – the Stampede is a mixed bag. For many, the ten-day festival is bacchanalian. It is said that the wedding bands of many Calgarians are removed from fingers during that time. Alcohol and other intoxicants, including country music that most never listen to at other times of the year, lubricate the overturning of the *nomoi* that usually accompanies festivals. For many others, the festival is simply a time to enjoy spectacles, the animals, the carnival atmosphere, and (according to a venerable tradition) being served pancakes by one's social superiors. For others, especially those from eastern parts of Canada, the Stampede is a tasteless exercise in kitsch, a nostalgia play based on what Marxist historian Eric Hobsbawm called an "invented tradition." From that perspective, the Stampede is simply bread and circuses created by an oligarchy to pacify the dispossessed masses. Thus, discerning meaning in the festival, beyond mere pleasure or "tradition," is not easy to do.

Yet, as Max Foran observes, it is not the images or spectacle per se that makes the Stampede; it is the act of one's participation in it. "I learned my first and probably most important lesson about the Stampede that day [of his first Stampede]: it had more to do with the act of participation than with offered opportunities. Paradoxically, it has been this capacity to embody a significance that transcends the sum of its various components that explains in part why the Stampede is held in such high and low regard."[8] Thus, keeping in mind Foran's observation of how participation helps one enucleate the inner meaning of the Stampede, let us proceed in the same spirit in which Pythagoras says we should view festivals: "Life … is like a festival; just as some come to the festival to compete, some to ply their trade, but the best people come as spectators [*theatai*], so in life the slavish men go hunting for fame [*doxa*] or gain, the philosophers for truth."[9]

In celebrating the cowboy, the Calgary Stampede celebrates the humble and stoic virtues of the cowboy and his work. It celebrates calf-roping,

8 Max Foran, *Icon, Brand, Myth: The Calgary Stampede*, ix.

9 Pythagoras, quoted by Diogenes Laertius, *Lives of Philosophers* 8.8, in Kirk and Raven, eds., *The Presocratic Philosophers*, 228.

bull riding, horse riding, and, unique to southern Alberta, chuckwagon racing. It transforms the workaday world of the ranch worker into a playful celebration of universal humanity, our relationship with the animal world, and the cosmos. This festival is also a synthesis of free play and compulsion. It is expected that participants will dress in western wear, however gaudy. Indeed, I always find it marvelous when I see Canadians of non-European descent dressed up in cowboy wear. These outfits complement their turbans and they figure out how to fit their cowboy hats on top of their hijabs.

Guy Weadick, along with his main backers, Patrick Burns, George Lane, A.E. Cross, and Archibald McLean (the so-called Big 4), inaugurated the first Calgary Stampede in 1912 to celebrate the western way of life in the form of rodeo, and specifically to recollect the time before the closing of the frontier, which had occurred some thirty years before. Weadick wished to put together "the greatest gathering of men who participated in the laying of the foundation of the present great Western development."[10] This comment hints at a deep ambivalence regarding the project, because to celebrate the frontier was to commemorate an era that had passed. It is for this reason that the Big 4 thought the first Stampede would also be the last. At the same time, it also marked "the present great Western development." So the Stampede is an alchemic mix that celebrates the freedom of the frontier and the virtues of the cowboy – his risk-taking, cooperation, and manliness in particular – along with the "development" that takes place after the closing of the frontier, after the "wire" that carved up the open range into private lots. This alchemy of, or perhaps translation between, prehistory and history can be seen in the way that modern risk-takers identify with the risk-taking of the cowboy: "The myth of the pioneer, especially of the pioneer as risk taker, remains a central part of Calgary's and Alberta's view of itself. It is remarkable how slight a shift has been required to extend an appreciation of the homesteader's perceived rural character and perseverance into a justification of the activities of Calgary capitalists. The notion of risk has now become central in the idealization of the Stampede."[11]

So the cowboy is an independent risk-taker who is also cooperative. This embodies both liberty and the specific manner in which cooperation is manifest in the modern liberal regime, namely volunteerism,

10 Foran, "The Stampede in Historical Context," in *Icon, Brand, Myth*, 7, quoting Guy Weadick.

11 Donald G. Wetherell, "Making Tradition: The Calgary Stampede, 1912–1939," 41–2. For more details on Alberta political culture, see Richard Avramenko, "Of Homesteaders and Orangemen: An Archeology of Western Canadian Political Identity."

which Harvey Mansfield suggests is in a middle position between the passive citizen and the permanent revolutionary.[12] The cowboy's liberty is ordered liberty, leavened with obedience to the rhythms of nature, including the harsh continental climate of western Canada, and the cowboy's companion, his horse. By celebrating the horse, the Calgary Stampede is in a long line of horse cultures that goes back to the anonymous communities along the banks of the Oxus, the river that separates central Asia and Persia, as well as to the artists in southern France who painted their horses on the walls of caves, their cathedrals. The Stampede connects post-industrial and post-historical humanity with history and prehistory. It is a universal festival.

J. Edward Chamberlin's family ranched along the Milk River Ridge in southern Alberta. For horses this is the "belly button" (*omphalos*) of North America, on account of being located at the centre of the continent, where the rivers that flow into the Pacific, Atlantic, and Arctic Oceans originate. Chamberlin reflects that life with a horse is a life between freedom and necessity, and between civilization and barbarism, in which freedom is experienced as a gift: "Horses need watching. They let you wander, but they made you settle down."[13] Horses "embody the in between, not only in between wandering and settling down but also in between the fence and the free."[14] Reflecting on freedom, Chamberlin states, "it's a gift of grace, a form of forgiveness; and when a wild horse is tamed, or a young horse is trained, we take custody of that gift and catch a glimpse of that generosity."[15]

Of course, in rodeo, the bucking broncos are not tamed, which is the point of cowboys wishing to test themselves by riding on their backs. Yet the in-between tension of life with horses obtains here too. The archetypical pose of the bronco rider, with one hand waving free, is "both concentrated and cavalier ... bringing together the clarity of a flying change of leads with the mystery of how it happened, and hovering between surrender and control."[16] Their ride is a cosmic dance, the Stampede version of the choreut dance in Plato's *Laws*. As one philosopher-cowboy told me, "The very act of riding is metaxic, one sits with another life between one's knees, between earth and heaven." Cowboys speak lovingly about their horses, their counterparts in the action.

12 Mansfield, *America's Constitutional Soul*, 133.

13 Chamberlin, *Horse: How the Horse Has Shaped Civilizations*, 241. On *omphalos* as symbolic center of the cosmos, see Voegelin, *Israel and Revelation*, 27–9.

14 Chamberlin, *Horse*, 250.

15 Ibid., 251.

16 Ibid., 53.

Indeed, while horses frequently get killed at the Stampede, especially in its famous chuckwagon races,[17] the cowboys respond that competing with those horses is a means of raising them up. If they did not compete, they would go to the glue factory.[18] As a world-historic festival of the horse, Stampeders have what Voegelin termed a primary experience of the cosmos that also engages their universal humanity. The Stampede celebrates the in-between, the *metaxy*. Thus, the lesson of the Stampede is the direct opposite of the lesson of that other great horseman, Napolean, as described by Hegel: "I saw the Emperor – this world-soul – riding out of the city on reconnaissance. It is indeed a wonderful sensation to see such an individual, who, concentrated here on a single point, astride a horse, reaches out over the world and masters it ... this extraordinary man, whom it is impossible not to admire."[19] Instead of seeing world history sitting astride reality in a pose of domination, as if history had ended and all possibilities exhausted, the Stampeder views the cowboy as trying to attain gyroscopic balance atop the primordial forces of nature, with the recognition that if he lasts eight seconds, he – and we, the spectators, the *theoroi* – will have received the gift of freedom. Born out of the expectation that the closure of the frontier – the "wire" – would end history, the Stampede in fact stands as a forceful reminder of the full amplitude of humanity's historical existence.

Chuckwagon racing is an Albertan innovation with roots, one can imagine, in Roman chariot races. The original chuckwagons were the portable kitchen wagons, or "Conestogas," used in the US Civil War and then in the great cattle drives of the second half of the nineteenth century. Naturally, someone realized that great fun could be had racing them. Today's Stampede races involve four wagons, each pulled by a team of four horses with a driver, and two outriders responsible for placing the kits inside the wagons who accompany their wagon teams through the initial figure eight before racing the "half mile of hell" around the racetrack. What appears as a chaotic sprint is actually a carefully choreographed team effort.

17 "Horse Collapses, Dies After Calgary Stampede Chuckwagon Race," *Global News*, July 13, 2013, http://globalnews.ca/news/715288/horse-collapses-dies-after-calgary-stampede-chuckwagon-race/.

18 More frequently than by the cowboys, the case is made by the annual Stampede editorial by a cowboy Voegelinian. Barry Cooper, "Vancouver Critic of Rodeo Should Pipe Down," *Calgary Herald*, July 10, 2013, http://www.calgaryherald.com/opinion/columnists/Cooper+Vancouver+critic+rodeo+should+pipe+down/8636888/story.html.

19 Hegel, letter to F.P.I. Niethammer, quoted in Terry Pinkard, *Hegel: A Biography*, 228.

Aritha Van Herk explains the cultural significance of the chuckwagon races: "The chuckwagon cowboys personify the co-operative spirit of Western Canada … [they] remain independent spirits in a communal enterprise. And their sport, which embodies team sportsmanship, community, and collaboration, is an apt mirror of the Canadian West and a symbol of the character of western Canadians."[20] Van Herk goes on to explain the "symbol of character":

> For chuckwagon racing is about staring at mortality, the possibility of death always hovering, the thunder of hooves an apocalypse. Jim Nevada recounts, "I was fifteen years old, it was my second show outriding, and I was nervous. Veteran driver Orville Strandquist said to me, 'Jim, when your card's laid, it's played. It could be on the racetrack or in a car on your way to Calgary, but as long as you're doing something you like, that's what you do. You don't know when you're going to die, and don't push it, but when your card's played, you're dead"… Such fatalism might belong to the world of unpredictability, but it also speaks to an acceptance of danger as a companion to the adrenaline of risk … Every race articulates a hope that out of the complicated danger of these competitions will come a gently persuasive story. This legend might indeed hark back to the ancient chariot races, but it also echoes a yearning to witness the long-lived haunting of a western tradition.[21]

Spectators witness chuckwagon races as cooperative exercises that entail deadly risk. Racers cooperate with one another – outriders with outriders, and outriders with the wagon driver – but they also cooperate with their horses. It is not uncommon for a chuckwagon horse to perish in the races, and racers face a similar risk. At the core of the race, for driver and for spectator, is the experience of playing your card and having your cards played within a specific set of cultural and even family traditions that they embody. The outcome of life's endeavours are uncertain. Liberty involves risk. Our cooperative exercise in the regime is a risky endeavour. The Stampede is marked, then, by a topsy-turvy dance, but one that is balanced on a point. It is metaxic dancing. It is neither Apollonian nor Dionysian, but Hermetic. After all, Hermes, the patron of friendship and political societies, was also the original cattle rustler.

In 1967, the *Calgary Herald* editorialized: "The Stampede is by and of the citizens of Calgary. It is for the world."[22] The Calgary Stampede is a festival that embodies the core principles of liberty and cooperation of

20 van Herk, "The Half Mile of Heaven's Gate," 247, quoting Glen Mikkelson.

21 van Herk, "The Half Mile of Heaven's Gate," 248–9.

22 *Calgary Herald*, July 5, 1967, cited in Foran, "The Stampede in Historical Context," 2.

the modern liberal regime, which makes it a festival of universal humanity, and thus tolerance. It is also a festival of a specific place, with its own practices and local traditions. Its spectators are able to see in it, and through it participate in, a key set of cultural and political attributes that they regard as central to their lives as citizens. As a universal festival, it welcomes outsiders and practises hospitality. Indeed, in the early days Guy Weadick disobeyed federal officials to permit Indians to attend and participate in the Stampede; it was illegal for Indians to leave their reserves for fear that partaking in festivals would corrupt them. Indians have always been an integral part of the Stampede.[23] Today, one witnesses Muslim girls wearing cowboy hats atop their hijabs, as they reconcile their religious practice with the civil religion of their home.

The Stampede, then, is a public commemoration of the kind of spiritual tension that seems to be central to numerous faith traditions. It seems that the bronc riders, chuckwagon drivers, and their spectators, share the same spiritual tension that Voegelin notices in Plato's myth of the Last Judgment and in Islamic prayer exercises, which Calgary city officials accommodated for the city's Muslim taxi driver population.[24] Voegelin writes: "When I want to pray, says the rule, I go to the place where I wish to say my prayer. I sit still until I am composed. Then I stand up: The Kaaba is in front of me, paradise to my right, hell to my left, and the angel of death stands behind me. Then I say my prayer as if it were my last. And thus I stand, between hope and fear, not knowing whether God has received my prayer favorably or not."[25] The chuckwagon driver, bronc and bull rider, spectator, Muslim, Christian, Platonist, all pray the same prayer.

And no public funds were necessary to build the tent used for the Muslim taxi drivers, as it was paid for by the taxi driver association.

FRIENDS DWELLING TOGETHER

This book has attempted to demonstrate how "sunaisthetic" friendship, as the "crest of the crest" of human excellence, informs political friendship; and to show that festivity is the paramount expression in politics of

23 Hugh A. Dempsey, "The Indians and the Stampede," 57–61. However, Indians participated as cowboys and in cowboy games, not in Indian games.

24 Kelly McParland, "Calgary Shows Tolerance in Accommodating Muslim Cabbies During Ramadan," *National Post*, 10 July 2013, http://fullcomment.nationalpost.com/2013/07/10/calgary-shows-toleration-in-accommodating-muslim-cabbies-during-ramadan/.

25 Voegelin, *Science, Politics, and Gnosticism*, 312–3.

that higher friendship. Necessarily, because the discussion has focused on the perfection of human and political action, there is something idealistic about my claims. Indeed, the authors of the texts I consider admit as much. In the *Politics,* Aristotle claims that the best possible regime is something for which one prays, but which one should not really expect. Similarly, the bringing into existence of Magnesia in Plato's *Laws* is conducted as if in a dream. But the idealism of these plans should not take away from their import as moral standards for politics, because, for both Aristotle and Plato, the practice of politics implies them.

Central to these philosophers' reflections is the political problem of how to reconcile dissimilars. The Athenian Stranger suggests as much when he proposes that political rule aims at "reconciling [*diallagon*] them by laying down laws for them for the rest of time and thus securing their friendship for one another" (*Laws* 627e). Reconciliation is the mystery that Plato's appeal to Hermes aims at clarifying, and, at its deepest expression, involves the "safe cable" that assists us mortals to cross the "rather swift and perhaps almost unfordable" argument establishing the political rule of Nous.

One of the main criticisms of Plato's and Aristotle's ideas on friendship is that they restrict its practice to Greek aristocratic males. However, we have seen how both set forth an educational agenda that promotes the capacity of individuals to discern intellectual and moral character, as distinct from biology, gender, class, ethnicity, and even citizenship. We saw in chapter 2 how Aristotle shows sunaisthetic friendship to involve the discernment of courage or justice in the soul of another. We saw in chapter 3 how Aristotle sees *philanthropia* as one of the main educational goals of tragedy, with Oedipus, king of Thebes and eternal enemy of Athens, as his primary example. In chapter 4 we saw Socrates philosophizing outside the walls of his city and making oaths to an Egyptian god. In chapters 5 to 7 we saw the Athenian Stranger, whose own name suggests a peculiar relationship with foreigners, evoking Nous as the order of politics. The inter-Greek alliance between him, Kleinias, and Megillus is to be the primary carrier of Nous, but Nous also judges it. This is not to suggest that Plato and Aristotle were cosmopolitans in the sense that they thought human beings could organize an international community, or even that such an international community could be an ethical standard for particular polities. Nor did they think that human differences could be very easily collapsed. The most extreme example of this is the difference between master and slave. Slavery is part of Magnesia and of Aristotle's best regime, but Aristotle's distinction between "natural" slaves (those incapable of reason) and "conventional" slaves (those defeated in wars) should be noted, as should the Athenian Stranger's comment that slaves in Magnesia can be freed if they perform noble actions. Finally, Plato and Aristotle were not Christians for whom *caritas* both deepens friendship and unsettles political friendships. The self-annihilation of the Athenian Stranger, or even of Socrates, does not reach as far as that of Jesus, who was annihilated as a person on account of the absolute loss of his dignity.[26]

In each of these examples of discerning virtues apart from their instantiations, we see an ideal or universal that points beyond their mere "Greekness." Still, at the same time, the ideal or universal is inseparably embedded within particulars. This is the difference between the *philanthropia* cultivated by the spectacle of Oedipus, and the "humanity" evoked by Victor Hugo, as seen in chapter 3. This is the significance of Socrates in the *Lysis,* walking and philosophizing just outside the walls of Athens – his own kin, as he describes them in his statement to the Athenian jury, used as the epigraph of this conclusion. Following Socrates, Plato and Aristotle wish to philosophize with just about anyone, but "more so" with their townsmen, inasmuch as they "are closer to me in kin."

Our "kin" are not simply our family connections. They are those with whom we have been brought together, for reasons beyond our comprehension; they are those with whom we dwell and for whom we have the deepest responsibility, and they for us. They are those "sculptor" friends upon whom we place our "impress" and who place theirs upon us, under the light of the "bloom of well-being" that is the good. We share and we are one another's stories, interspersed in moments of "effortful holding of oneself in readiness." With our friend we share "consciousness of his existence and this would come through living together and sharing conversation and thinking; for this would seem to be what living together means in the case of human beings" (*NE* 1170b10–12).

26 See David Walsh, "Dignity as an Eschatological Concept," 255, and the reflections of Kierkegaard in *Works of Love,* 274–9.

Bibliography

PRIMARY SOURCES

The Perseus Digital Library (Classics Department, Tufts University) has been used for the Greek texts used in this study (http://www.perseus.tufts.edu/hopper/). I have used the English translations listed below.

Aeschylus. *Persians.* Translated by Janet Lembke and C.J. Herington. Oxford: Oxford University Press, 1991.

– *Prometheus Bound.* Translated by J. Scully and C.J. Herington. Oxford: Oxford University Press, 1975.

Alter, Robert. *Genesis: Translation and Commentary.* New York: W.W. Norton and Company, 1996.

Apollodorus. *Library.* In *Apollodorus' Library and Hyginus' Fabulae: Two Handbooks of Greek Mythology,* translated by Stephen Trzakoma and R. Scott Smith, 1–94. Indianapolis: Hackett, 2007.

Aquinas, Thomas. *Summa Theologica.* Translated by the Fathers of the English Dominican Province. 5 vols. Westminster, MD: Christian Classics, 1948.

Aristotle. *The Complete Works of Aristotle.* Edited by Jonathan Barnes. 2 vols. Princeton: Princeton University Press, 1984.

– *Nicomachean Ethics.* Translated by J. Sachs. Newburyport, MA: Focus Publishing, 2002.

– *On Poetics.* Translated by Seth Benardete and Michael Davis. South Bend, IN: St Augustine's Press, 2002.

– *On the Soul and On Memory and Recollection.* Translated by J. Sachs. Santa Fe, NM: Green Lion Press, 2001.

– *Poetics.* Translated by Joe Sachs. Newburyport, MA: Focus Publishing, 2006.

– *Politics.* Translated by C. Lord. Chicago: University of Chicago Press, 1984.

Augustine. *Confessions.* Translated by F.J. Sheed. Indianapolis: Hackett, 2006.

Austen, Jane. *Pride and Prejudice*. Edited by James Kinsley. Oxford: Oxford University Press, 2004.

Boesche, Roger, ed. *Alexis de Tocqueville: Selected Letters on Politics and Society*. Berkeley: University of California Press, 1985.

Byron, Lord. "L'Amitie est l'Amour sans Ailes." In *The Oxford Book of Friendship*, edited by D.J. Enright and David Rawlinson, 151–2. Oxford: Oxford University Press, 1991.

Callimachus. *The Hymns*. Translated by Susan A. Stephens. Oxford: Oxford University Press, 2015.

Cappon, Lester J., ed. *The Adams-Jefferson Letters*. Chapel Hill: The University of North Carolina Press, 1987 [1959].

Churchill, Winston. *The Churchill War Papers*. Vol. 2. Edited by Martin Gilbert. New York: W.W. Norton, 1985.

– *The Gathering Storm*. London: Thomas Allen, 1948.

– *History of the English Speaking Peoples* . Vol. 4. Toronto: McLelland and Stewart, 1958.

– *Marlborough: His Life and Times*. 2 vols. Chicago: University of Chicago Press, 2002.

– "Moses: The Leader of a People." In *Thoughts and Adventures*, edited by James W. Muller, 299–314. Wilmington, DE: Intercollegiate Studies Institute, 2009.

– *My Early Life*. New York: Scribner's, 1958.

– *The River War*. 2 vols. London: Longmans, Green, 1899.

Cicero, Quintus Tullius. *How to Win an Election: An Ancient Guide for Modern Politicians*. Translated by Philip Freeman. Princeton: Princeton University Press, 2012.

Clarke, Charles Cowden. "Recollections of Keats." In *Recollections of Writers*, 120–57. London: Sampson Low, Marston, Searle, & Rivington, 1878.

Clausewitz, Carl von. *On War*. Translated by Michael Howard and Peter Paret. Princeton: Princeton University Press, 1989.

Colville, John. *Fringes of Power*. London: Lyons Press, 2002.

Descartes, René. *The Passions of the Soul*. Translated by Stephen H. Voss. Indianapolis: Hackett, 1989.

Diodorus. *The Library of History*. Vol. 3. Translated by C.H. Oldfather. Loeb Classical Library. Cambridge: Harvard University Press, 1939.

Durkheim, Émile. *Elementary Forms of the Religious Life*. New York: MacMillan, 1915.

Eliot, T.S. *Collected Poems, 1909–1962*. New York: Faber and Faber, 2002.

Euripides. "Helen." In *Euripides: Medea, Hippolytus, Electra, Helen*, translated by James Morwood, 119–68. Oxford: Oxford University Press, 1997.

Grant, George. "Thinking about Technology." Chapter 1 in *Technology and Justice*. Toronto: House of Anansi Press, 1986.

Herodotus. *The History.* Translated by David Grene. Chicago: University of Chicago Press, 1987.

Hesiod. *Theogony/Works and Days.* Translated by C.S. Morrissey, foreword by Roger Scruton, afterword by Eric Voegelin. Vancouver: Talonbooks, 2012.

Hobbes, Thomas. *Leviathan.* Edited by Richard Tuck. Cambridge: Cambridge University Press, 1996.

Homer. *The Iliad.* Translated by Robert Fagles. New York: Penguin, 1990.

Homer. *The Odyssey.* Translated by Robert Fagles. New York: Penguin, 1996.

Hyginus. *Fabulae.* In *Apollodorus' Library and Hyginus' Fabulae: Two Handbooks of Greek Mythology,* translated by Stephen Trzakoma and R. Scott Smith, 95–182. Indianapolis: Hackett, 2007.

"Hymn to Hermes." In *Hesiod, The Homeric Hymns, and Homerica,* translated by Hugh G. Evelyn-White, 362–405. Cambridge: Harvard University Press, 1964 [1914].

Jouvenal, Bertrand de. *On Sovereignty.* Indianapolis: Liberty Fund, 1997.

Kant, Immanuel. "On a Newly Arisen Superior Tone in Philosophy." In *Raising the Tone of Philosophy: Late Essays by Immanuel Kant, Transformative Critique by Jacques Derrida,* edited by Peter Fenves, 51–82. Baltimore: The Johns Hopkins University Press, 1998.

Keats, John. "On First Looking into Chapman's Homer." http://www.poetryfoundation.org/poem/173746.

Kierkegaard, Søren. *Either/Or: Parts I and II.* Edited and translated by Howard V. Hong and Edna H. Hong. Princeton: Princeton University Press, 1987.

– *Papers and Journals: A Selection.* Edited by Alastair Hannay. New York: Penguin, 1996.

– *Philosophical Fragments/Johannes Climacus.* Edited and translated by Howard V. Hong and Edna H. Hong. Princeton: Princeton University Press, 1985.

– *Works of Love.* Edited and translated by Howard V. Hong and Edna H. Hong. Princeton: Princeton University Press, 1995.

Kirk, G.S. and J.E. Raven, eds. *The Presocratic Philosophers.* Cambridge: Cambridge University Press, 1957.

Lewis, C.S. *The Four Loves.* London: HarperCollins, 1960.

Lincoln, Abraham. "Temperance Address." http://www.abrahamlincolnonline.org/lincoln/speeches/temperance.htm.

Lucretius. *On the Nature of Things.* Translated by W.H.D. Rouse and Martin F. Smith. Loeb Classical Library. Cambridge: Harvard University Press, 1924.

Malouf, David. *Ransom.* New York: Vintage, 2009.

Mann, Thomas. *Joseph and His Brothers.* Translated by John E. Woods. New York: Alfred A. Knopf, 2005.

Montaigne, Michel de. "Of Friendship." In *The Complete Essays of Montaigne,* edited by D.M. Frame, 135–44. Stanford: Stanford University Press, 1976.

Nonnos. *Dionysiaca*. Vol. 1. Translated by W.H.D. Rouse. Loeb Classical Library. Cambridge: Harvard University Press, 1940.

Pausanias. *Description of Greece*. Translated by W.H.S. Jones. 4 vols. Cambridge: Harvard University Press, 1964.

Plato. *Apology*. In *Four Texts on Socrates: Plato's Euthyphro, Apology, and Crito and Aristophanes' Clouds*, translated by T.G. West and G.S. West, 63–98. Ithaca, NY: Cornell University Press, 1984.

– *Gorgias*. Translated by James Nichol. Ithaca, NY: Cornell University Press, 1998.

– *The Laws of Plato*. Translated by T.L. Pangle. Chicago: University of Chicago Press, 1988.

– *Letter VII*. Translated by L.A. Post. In *The Complete Dialogues of Plato*, edited by Edith Hamilton and Huntington Cairns, 1574–98. Princeton: Princeton University Press, 1961.

– *Lysis*. In *Plato's Dialogue on Friendship: An Interpretation of the* "Lysis," *with a New Translation*, translated by D. Bolotin, 17–61. Ithaca, NY: Cornell University Press, 1979.

– *Phaedrus*. Translated by J.H. Nichols, Jr. Ithaca, NY: Cornell University Press, 1998.

– *Philebus*. Translated by R. Hackforth. In *The Complete Dialogues of Plato*. Edited by Edith Hamilton and Huntington Cairns, 1086–1150. Princeton: Princeton University Press, 1961.

– *Plato's* 'Statesman.' Translated by S. Benardete. Chicago: University of Chicago Press, 1986.

– *Plato's* 'Symposium.' Translated by S. Benardete. Chicago: University of Chicago Press, 2001.

– *Republic*. Translated by Joe Sachs. Newburyport, MA: Focus Publishing, 2007.

– *Socrates and the Sophists: Plato's Protagoras, Euthydemus, Hippias Major, and Cratylus*. Translated by Joe Sachs. Newburyport, MA: Focus Publishing, 2011.

Plutarch. "Of Garrulity, or Talkativeness." In *Plutarch's Morals, Vol. 4*, translated by several hands, corrected and revised by W.W. Goodwin, with an introduction by R. Waldo Emerson. Boston: Little, Brown, 1878. Online Library of Liberty Edition. http://oll.libertyfund.org/titles/1214/92421.

Rilke, Rainer Maria. *The Sonnets to Orpheus*. Oxford: Oxford University Press, 2011.

Rousseau, Jean-Jacques. *Discourse on the Origin and Foundations of Inequality Among Men*. In *Basic Political Writings*, translated by Donald A. Cress, 27–92. Indianapolis: Hackett, 1987.

Schelling, F.W.J. *Historical-Critical Introduction to the Philosophy of Mythology*. Translated by Mason Richey and Markus Zisselsberger. Albany: State University of New York University Press, 2008.

Smith, Adam. *An Inquiry into the Nature and Causes of the Wealth of Nations*. Edited by R.H. Campbell and A.S. Skinner. Indianapolis: Liberty Fund, 1982.

Smith, F.E. [Lord Birkenhead]. *Contemporary Personalities*. London: Cassel, 1924.

Sophocles. *Oedipus the King*. Translated by Stephen Berg and Diskin Clay. Oxford: Oxford University Press, 1978.

Thucydides. *History of the Peloponnesian War*. Translated by Rex Warner. New York: Penguin, 1972.

Tocqueville, Alexis de. *Democracy in America*. Translated by Harvey Mansfield and Delba Winthrop. Chicago: University of Chicago Press, 2000.

Virgil. *Georgics*. Translated by Peter Fallon. Oxford: Oxford University Press, 2009.

Xenophon. *Memorabilia*. In *Memorabilia. Oeconomicus. Symposium. Apologia*, translated by A.C. Marchant and O.J. Todd, 1–359. Loeb Classical Library. Cambridge: Harvard University Press, 1923.

SECONDARY SOURCES

Addison, Paul. "Destiny, History and Providence: The Religion of Winston Churchill." In *Public and Private Doctrine: Essays in British History Presented to Maurice Cowling*, edited by Michael Bentley, 236–50. Cambridge: Cambridge University Press, 1993.

Agamben, Giorgio. "Friendship." *Contretemps*, no. 5 (December 2004): 2–6.

Anderson, Benedict. *Imagined Communities: Reflection on the Origin and Spread of Nationalism*. London: Verso, 1983.

Anderson, Warren. *Ethos and Education in Greek Music*. Cambridge: Harvard University Press, 1966.

Arendt, Hannah. *Men in Dark Times*. New York: Harcourt Brace, 1995.

– *The Human Condition*. Chicago: University of Chicago Press, 1958.

Auerbach, Erich. *Dante: Poet of the Secular World*. Chicago: University of Chicago Press, 1961.

Avramenko, Richard. "Of Homesteaders and Orangemen: An Archeology of Western Canadian Political Identity." In *Hunting and Weaving: Empiricism and Political Philosophy*, edited by Thomas Heilke and John von Heyking, 41–64. South Bend, IN: St Augustine's Press, 2013.

Barker, Andrew. "The *Laws* and Aristoxenus On the Criteria of Musical Judgment." In *Performance and Culture in Plato's Laws*, edited by Anastasia-Erasmia Peponi, 392–416. Cambridge: Cambridge University Press, 2013.

Benardete, Seth. *Plato's "Laws": The Discovery of Being*. Chicago: University of Chicago Press, 2000.

Beneviste, Emile. "The Notion of 'Rhythm' in its Linguistic Expression." In *Problems in General Linguistics*, translated by Mary Elizabeth Meek, 281–8. Miami: University of Miami Press, 1973.

Berns, Laurence. "Aristotle's *Poetics.*" In *Ancients and Moderns: Essays on the Tradition of Political Philosophy in Honor of Leo Strauss,* edited by Joseph Cropsey, 70–87. New York: Basic Books, 1964.

Bertrand, J.-M. *De l'écriture à l'oralité: Lectures des Lois de Platon.* Paris: Publications de la Sorbonne, 1999.

Bishirjian, Richard J. "Daimonic Men." *Modern Age,* Winter 1996: 159–63.

Bloom, Allan. *Love and Friendship.* New York: Simon and Schuster, 1993.

Brann, Eva. *The Music of the Republic: Essays on Socrates' Conversations and Plato's Writings.* Philadelphia: Paul Dry Books, 2004.

– *Open Secrets/Inward Prospects: Reflections on World and Soul.* Philadelphia: Paul Dry Books, 2004.

– *Paradoxes of Education in a Republic.* Chicago: University of Chicago Press, 1979.

– "A Reading of Lincoln's 'Gettysburg Address.'" In *Homage to Americans: Mile-High Meditations, Close Readings, and Time-Spanning Speculations,* 135–92. Philadelphia: Paul Dry Books, 2010.

– *The World of the Imagination: Sum and Substance.* Lanham, MD: Rowman and Littlefield, 1991.

Brown, Christopher. *Singing the Gospel: Lutheran Hymns and the Success of the Reformation.* Cambridge, MA: Harvard University Press, 2005.

Burden, Hamilton. *The Nuremberg Party Rallies, 1923–39.* New York: Praeger, 1967.

Burger, Ronna. *Aristotle's Dialogue With Socrates: On the* Nicomachean Ethics. Chicago: University of Chicago Press, 2008.

Burkert, Walter. *The Greek Religion.* Translated by J. Raffan. Cambridge: Harvard University Press, 1985.

Burrell, David B. *Friendship and the Ways to Truth.* Notre Dame: University of Notre Dame Press, 2000.

Butterworth, Edric Allan Schofield. *The Tree at the Navel of the Earth.* Berlin: Walter de Gruyter, 1970.

– *Some Traces of the Pre-Olympian World in Greek Literature and Myth.* Berlin: Walter de Gruyter, 1966.

Calame, Claude. "Choral Practices in Plato's *Laws*: Itineraries of Initiation?" In *Performance and Culture in Plato's Laws,* edited by Anastasia-Erasmia Peponi, 87–108. Cambridge: Cambridge University Press, 2013.

Caldwell, Gail. *Let's Take the Long Way Home: A Memoir of Friendship.* New York: Random House, 2010.

Carey, George. "Social Friendship in the Founding Era." In *Friendship and Politics: Essays in Political Thought.* Edited by John von Heyking and Richard Avramenko, 248–67. Notre Dame: University of Notre Dame Press, 2008.

Carpenter, Edward. *Cantuar: The Archbishops in Their Office.* London: Mowbray, 1971.

Chamberlin, J. Edward. *Horse: How the Horse Has Shaped Civilizations.* Toronto: Vintage, 2006.

Charnwood, Lord [Godfrey Rathbone Benson]. *Abraham Lincoln.* New York: Pocket Books, 1939 [1916].

Cherry, Kevin, and E.A. Goerner. "Does Aristotle's Polis Exist by Nature?" *History of Political Thought* 27, no. 4 (Winter 2006): 563–85.

Clay, Jenny Strauss. *The Politics of Olympus: Form and Meaning in the Major Homeric Hymns.* Princeton: Princeton University Press, 1989.

Cooper, Barry. "'A Lump Bred Up in Darknesse': Two Tellurian Themes in the *Republic.*" In *Politics, Philosophy, Writing: Plato's Art of Caring for Souls,* edited by Zdravko Planinc, 80–121. Columbia: University of Missouri Press, 2001.

Cornford, Francis. "Hermes, Pan, Logos." *Classical Quarterly* 3, no. 4 (October 1909): 281–4.

Crosson, Frederick. "Structure and Meaning in St. Augustine's *Confessions.*" In *The Augustinian Tradition,* edited by Gareth B. Matthews, 27–38. Berkeley: University of California Press, 1999.

Cunningham, J.V. *Woe or Wonder.* Denver: Swallow Press, 1960.

Dancy, R.M. *Plato's Introduction of Forms.* Cambridge: Cambridge University Press, 2004.

Davis, Michael. *The Poetry of Philosophy: On Aristotle's Poetics.* South Bend, IN: St Augustine's Press, 1992.

Dempsey, Hugh A. "The Indians and the Stampede." In *Icon, Brand, Myth: The Calgary Stampede,* edited by Max Foran, 47–72. Edmonton: Athabasca University Press, 2008.

Dunbar, Robin. *How Many Friends Does One Person Need?* New York: Faber and Faber, 2011.

Duriez, Colin. *Tolkien and C.S. Lewis: The Gift of Friendship.* Mahwah, NJ: HiddenSpring, 2003.

Eden, Kathy. *Friends Hold All Things In Common: Tradition, Intellectual Property, and the Adages of Erasmus.* New Haven: Yale University Press, 2001.

Ehrenreich, Barbara. *Dancing in the Streets: A History of Collective Joy.* New York: Metropolitan Books, 2007.

El Murr, Dimitri. "*Philia* in Plato." In *Ancient and Medieval Concepts of Friendship,* edited by Suzanne Stern-Gillet and Gary M. Gurtler, 3–34. Albany: SUNY Press, 2014.

Epstein, Joseph. *Friendship: An Exposé.* New York: Houghton Mifflin, 2006.

Ferrante, Elena. *Those Who Leave and Those Who Stay.* New York: Europa Editions, 2013.

Flakne, April. "Embodied and Embedded: Friendship and the Sunaisthetic Self." *Époche* 10, no. 1 (2005): 37–63.

Foran, Max, ed. *Icon, Brand, Myth: The Calgary Stampede.* Edmonton: Athabasca University Press, 2008.

Foran, Max. "The Stampede in Historical Context." In *Icon, Brand, Myth: The Calgary Stampede*, edited by Max Foran, 1–20. Edmonton: Athabasca University Press, 2008.

Friedländer, Paul. *Plato: The Dialogues, First Period*. Vol. 2. Translated by H. Meyerhoff. New York: Pantheon Books, 1964.

Gadamer, Hans-Georg. *Dialogue and Dialectic: Eight Hermeneutical Studies on Plato*. New Haven: Yale University Press, 1980.

Gennep, A. van. *The Rites of Passage*. Translated by M.B. Vizedom and G.L. Caffee. Chicago: University of Chicago Press, 1960.

Georgiades, Tharsybulos. *Greek Music, Verse and Dance*. Translated by E. Benedikt and M.L. Martinez. New York: Merlin Press, 1956.

Gibbs, Nancy, and Michael Duffy. *The Presidents Club: Inside the World's Most Exclusive Fraternity*. New York: Simon and Schuster, 2012.

Gilbert, Martin. *Finest Hour, 1939–1941*. Vol. 6 of *Winston S. Churchill*. London: Heinemann, 1983.

Goerner, Edward A. "The Political Ethics of the Rule of Law Versus the Political Ethics of the Rule of the Virtuous." *Review of Politics* 45, no. 4 (October 1983): 553–75.

Goodwin, Doris Kearns. *Team of Rivals: The Political Genius of Abraham Lincoln*. New York: Simon and Schuster, 2005.

Grier, Peter. "An Insider Look at George W. Bush," review of *Dead Certain: The Presidency of George W. Bush*, by Robert Draper. *Christian Science Monitor*, September 18, 2007, http://www.csmonitor.com/2007/0918/p13s01-bogn.html.

Gonzalez, Francisco. "How to Read a Platonic Prologue: *Lysis* 203a–207d." In *Plato as Author: The Rhetoric of Philosophy*, edited by A. Michelini, 15–44. Leiden: Brill, 2003.

– "Plato's *Lysis*: An Enactment of Philosophic Friendship." *Ancient Philosophy* 15 (1995): 69–90.

Griffith, M. "Brilliant Dynasts: Power and Politics in the '*Oresteia*.'" *Classical Antiquity* 14, no. 1 (1995): 62–129.

Haden, J. "Friendship in Plato's *Lysis*." *Review of Metaphysics* 37, no. 2 (1983): 327–56.

Halliwell, Stephen. *The Aesthetics of Mimesis: Ancient Texts and Modern Problems*. Princeton: Princeton University Press, 2002.

Harrison, Jane E. *Epilegomena to the Study of Greek Religion and Themis: A Study of the Social Origins of Greek Religion*. New Hyde Park, NY: University Books, 1962 [1912, 1921].

Hewitt, Anne. "Aristotle's *Poetics* as an Extension of His Ethical and Political Theory." *History of Political Thought* 27, no. 1 (2006): 10–26.

Heyking, John von. *Augustine and Politics as Longing in the World*. Columbia: University of Missouri Press, 2001.

– "Befriending Those No Decent Person Would Talk To." *C2C Journal*, June 25, 2012, http://c2cjournal.ca/2012/06/befriending-those-no-decent-person-would-talk-to-2/.
– *"Comprehensive Judgment" and "Absolute Selflessness": Winston Churchill on Politics as Friendship*. South Bend, IN: St Augustine's Press (forthcoming).
– "Friendship and Its Language." *The Cresset* 70, no. 3 (2007): 21–27. http://thecresset.org/2007/Heyking_L2007.html.
– "Friendship as Precondition and Consequence of Creativity in Politics." In *The Primacy of Persons in Politics: Empiricism and Political Philosophy*, edited by John von Heyking and Thomas Heilke, 79–106. Washington, DC: Catholic University Press, 2013.
– "Hermes as Eros in Plato's *Lysis*." *History of Human Sciences* 26, no. 5 (2013): 134–156.
– "The Intermediaries of the Eranos Festival: Orpheus and Hermes." In *The Eranos Movement: A Story of Hermeneutics*, edited by Tilo Schabert, 57–72. Würzburg: Königshausen & Neumann, 2015.
– "Liberal Education Embedded in Civic Education for Responsible Government: The Case of John George Bourinot." In *Liberal Education And Canadian Political Culture: The Legacy, The Need, And The Prospects*, edited by David Livingstone, 44–76. Montreal: McGill-Queen's University Press, 2015.
– "The Luminous Path of Friendship: Augustine's Account of Friendship and Political Order." In *Friendship and Politics: Essays in Political Thought*, edited by John von Heyking and Richard Avramenko, 115–38. Notre Dame: University of Notre Dame Press, 2008.
– "'The Sum Total of Our Relationships to Others': Kant on Friendship." In "The Luminosity of Modernity: Essays on the Political Thought of David Walsh," edited by Rouven Steeves and Steven McGuire. Unpublished manuscript.
– "'Sunaisthetic' Friendship and the Foundations of Political Anthropology." *International Political Anthropology* 1, no. 2 (2008): 179–93.
– "Tolerance in Festivity." *Convivium 3*, no. 16 (October–November 2014), http://www.conviviummagazine.ca/article/4508/faith-and-festivity.

Heyking, John von, and Richard Avramenko, eds. *Friendship and Politics: Essays in Political Thought*. Notre Dame: University of Notre Dame Press, 2008.

Heyking, John von, and Thomas W. Heilke, eds. *Hunting and Weaving: Empiricism and Political Philosophy*. South Bend, IN: St Augustine's Press, 2013.

Himmelfarb, Gertrude. *The Moral Imagination: From Adam Smith to Lionel Trilling*. Lanham, MD: Rowman and Littlefield, 2012.

Holland, Matthew S. *Bonds of Affection: Civic Charity and the Making of America; Winthrop, Jefferson, and Lincoln*. Washington, DC: Georgetown University Press, 2007.

Howland, Jacob. "Aristotle on Tragedy: Rediscovering the Poetics." *Interpretation* 22, no. 3 (Spring 1995): 359–403.

Huizinga, Johannes. *Homo Ludens: A Study of the Play Element in Culture.* Boston: Beacon Press, 1971.

Jaffa, Harry. "Aristotle and the Higher Good." *New York Times*, July 1, 2011. http://www.nytimes.com/2011/07/03/books/review/book-review-aristotles-nicomachean-ethics.html.

– "Can There Be Another Winston Churchill?" *Claremont Review of Books*, February 2004. https://www.claremont.org/basicPageArticles/can-there-be-another-winston-churchill/.

James, William. *The Varieties of Religious Experience.* New York: Modern Library, 1999.

Janssens, David. "Easily, At a Glance: Aristotle's Optics." *Review of Politics* 72, no. 3 (Summer 2010): 385–408.

Jardin, A. *Tocqueville: A Biography.* Translated by L. Davis and R. Hemenway. Baltimore: Johns Hopkins University Press, 1988.

Johnston, S. Iles. "Myth, Festival, and Poet: The 'Homeric Hymn to Hermes' and Its Performative Context." *Classical Philology* 97, no. 2 (2002): 109–32.

Jones, Kathleen B. "Hannah Arendt's Female Friends." *LA Review of Books*, November 12, 2013. http://lareviewofbooks.org/essay/hannah-arendts-female-friends.

Kellow, Geoffrey. "The Wisdom of the Commons: The Education of Citizens from The Republic to The Wealth of Nations." Unpublished manuscript.

Kerényi, Karl. *Hermes: Guide of Souls; The Mythologem of the Masculine Source of Life.* Translated by M. Stein. Dallas: Spring Publications, 1986.

– *The Religion of Greeks and Romans.* New York: E.P. Dutton, 1962.

Keys, Mary M. *Aquinas, Aristotle, and the Promise of the Common Good.* Cambridge: Cambridge University Press, 2006.

King, Preston. *The Challenge to Friendship in Modernity.* Portland, OR: Frank Cass, 2000.

– ed. *Friendship in Politics: Theorizing Amity In and Between States.* New York: Routledge, 2008.

Kochin, Michael. *Gender and Rhetoric in Plato's Political Thought.* Cambridge: Cambridge University Press, 2002.

– "The Unity of Virtue and the Limitations of Magnesia." *History of Political Thought* 19, no. 2 (1998): 125–41.

Kosman, Aryeh. "Aristotle on the Desirability of Friends." *Ancient Philosophy* 24, no. 1 (2004): 135–54.

– "Metaphysics Λ 9: Divine Thought." In *Aristotle's Metaphysics Lambda: Symposium Aristotlelicum*, edited by M. Frede and D. Charies, 307–26. Oxford: Oxford University Press, 2000.

Kowalzig, Barbara. "Broken Rhythms in Plato's *Laws*: Materialising Social Time in the Chorus." In *Performance and Culture in Plato's Laws,* edited by Anastasia-Erasmia Peponi, 171–211. Cambridge: Cambridge University Press, 2013.

Kurke, Leslie. "Imagining Chorality: Wonder, Plato's Puppets, and Moving Statues." In *Performance and Culture in Plato's Laws,* edited by Anastasia–Erasmia Peponi, 123–70. Cambridge: Cambridge University Press, 2013.

Lachterman, David. *The Ethics of Geometry: A Genealogy of Modernity.* New York: Routledge, 1989.

Leibiger, Stuart. *Founding Friendship: George Washington, James Madison, and the Creation of the American Republic.* Charlottesville: University Press of Virginia, 1999.

Leibovitch, Mark. *This Town: Two Parties and a Funeral in America's Gilded Capital.* New York: Blue Rider, 2013.

Lewis, V. Bradley. "Aristotle, the Common Good, and Us." *Proceedings of the American Catholic Philosophical Association* 87 (2014): 69–88.

– "Gods for the City and Beyond: Civil Religion in Plato's Laws." In *Civil Religion in Political Thought: Its Perennial Questions and Enduring Relevance in North America,* edited by Ronald Weed and John von Heyking, 19–46. Washington, DC: Catholic University of America Press, 2010.

– "The Nocturnal Council and Platonic Political Philosophy." *History of Political Thought* 19 (1998): 1–20.

Lockwood, Thornton. "Is There a *Poetics* in Aristotle's *Politics*?" In *The Poetics in its Aristotelian Context,* edited by Malcolm Heath and Dana Munteanu. Cambridge: Cambridge University Press (forthcoming).

Longo, Oddone. "The Theater of the Polis." In *Nothing to Do with Dionysos? Athenian Drama in its Social Context,* edited by John J. Winkler and Froma I. Zeitlin, 12–19. Princeton: Princeton University Press, 1990.

Lonsdale, Steven H. "Dance and Play in Plato's *Laws*: Anticipating an Anthropological Paradigm." In *Dance and Play in Greek Religion,* 21–43. Baltimore: Johns Hopkins University Press, 1993.

Lord, Carnes. *Education and Culture in the Political Thought of Aristotle.* Ithaca, NY: Cornell University Press, 1982.

Lynch, J.P. *Aristotle's School: A Study of a Greek Educational Institution.* Berkeley: University of California Press, 1972.

MacIntyre, Alasdair. *After Virtue.* Second Edition. Notre Dame: University of Notre Dame Press, 1984.

Manent, Pierre. *A World Beyond Politics?* Translated by Marc LePain. Princeton: Princeton University Press, 2006.

Mansfield, Harvey. *America's Constitutional Soul.* Baltimore: Johns Hopkins University Press, 1991.

McClain, Ernest. *The Pythagorean Plato: Prelude to the Song Itself.* Stony Brook, NY: Nicolas Hays, 1978.

McMenomy, M. "Roles of Hermes in Athenian Drama." PhD diss., University of Pennsylvania, 2006.

Meacham, Jon. *Franklin and Winston: An Intimate Portrait of an Epic Friendship.* New York: Random House, 2004.

Minar, Edwin L. "Pythagorean Communism." *Transactions and Proceedings of the American Philological Association* 75 (1944): 34–46.

Miller, James L. *Measures of Wisdom: The Cosmic Dance in Classical and Christian Antiquity.* Toronto: University of Toronto Press, 1986.

Mitchell, Joshua. "It Is Not Good for Man to Be Alone: Tocqueville on Friendship." In *Friendship and Politics: Essays in Political Thought,* edited by John von Heyking and Richard Avramenko, 268–86. Notre Dame: University of Notre Dame Press, 2008.

Morrow, Glenn. *Plato's Cretan City.* Princeton: Princeton University Press, 1960.

Nagy, Gregory. *Pindar's Homer: The Lyric Possession of an Epic Past.* Baltimore: Johns Hopkins University Press, 1997. http://www.press.jhu.edu/books/nagy/PH.html.

Nails, Debra. *The People of Plato.* Indianapolis: Hackett, 2002.

Neer, Richard. *The Emergence of the Classical Style in Greek Sculpture.* Chicago: University of Chicago Press, 2010.

Nelson, Christopher. "The Things of Friends Are Common." Convocation address, St John's College, Annapolis, MD, August 26, 2009. http://www.theimaginativeconservative.org/2012/03/things-of-friends-are-common.html.

Newell, Waller. *Tyranny: A New Interpretation.* Cambridge: Cambridge University Press, 2013.

Nichols, Mary. *Citizens and Statesmen: A Study of Aristotle's Politics.* Savage, MD: Rowman and Littlefield, 1992.

– *Socrates on Friendship and Community: Reflections on Plato's Symposium, Phaedrus, and Lysis.* Cambridge: Cambridge University Press, 2009.

Nicholson, Adam. *The Mighty Dead: Why Homer Matters.* London: William Collins, 2014.

Novak, Michael. *The Joy of Sports: End Zones, Bases, Baskets, Balls, and the Consecration of the American Spirit.* New York: Basic Books, 1976.

Oakeshott, Michael. *Rationalism in Politics and Other Essays.* Indianapolis: Liberty Fund, 1991.

Ober, Josiah, and Barry Strauss. "Drama, Political Rhetoric, and the Discourse of Athenian Democracy." In *Nothing to Do with Dionysos? Athenian Drama in its Social Context,* edited by John J. Winkler and Froma I. Zeitlin, 271–313. Princeton: Princeton University Press, 1990.

O'Donovan, Oliver. *Common Objects of Love: Moral Reflections on the Shaping of Community.* Grand Rapids, MI: Eerdmans, 2002.

O'Grady, William. "About Human Knowing." *St. John's Review* 37, no. 1 (1986): 37–43.

Onians, R.B. *The Origins of European Thought: About the Body, the Mind, the Soul, the World, Time and Fate.* Cambridge: Cambridge University Press, 1988.

Otto, W.F. *The Homeric Gods.* Translated by M. Hadas. New York: Pantheon, 1954.

Ozouf, Mona. *Festivals and the French Revolution.* Translated by Alan Sheridan. Cambridge: Harvard University Press, 1988.

Pangle, Lorraine S. *Aristotle and the Philosophy of Friendship.* Cambridge: Cambridge University Press, 2003.

Pangle, Thomas L. *Aristotle's Teaching in the Politics.* Chicago: University of Chicago Press, 2013.

Peterson, Merrill D. *Adams and Jefferson: A Revolutionary Dialogue.* Oxford: Oxford University Press, 1976.

Peponi, Anastasia–Erasmia, ed. *Performance and Culture in Plato's Laws.* Cambridge: Cambridge University Press, 2013.

Pieper, Josef. *In Tune With the World: A Theory of Festivity.* South Bend, IN: St Augustine's Press, 1971.

– *Leisure: The Basis of Culture.* Translated by A. Dru. Indianapolis: Liberty Fund, 1952.

Pinkard, Terry. *Hegel: A Biography.* Cambridge: Cambridge University Press, 2001.

Planeaux, Christopher. "Socrates as Unreliable Narrator? The Dramatic Setting of the 'Lysis.'" *Classical Philology* 96, no. 1 (2001): 60–8.

Planinc, Zdravko. *Plato's Political Philosophy: Prudence in the Republic and the Laws.* Columbia: University of Missouri Press, 1991.

– *Plato Through Homer: Poetry and Philosophy in the Cosmological Dialogues.* Columbia: University of Missouri Press, 2003.

– "Tracking the Good in Plato's *Republic*: The Literary and Dialogic Form of the Sun, Line, and Cave Imagery." In *Hunting and Weaving: Empiricism and Political Philosophy*, edited by Thomas Heilke and John von Heyking, 154–78. South Bend, IN: St Augustine's Press, 2013.

Prauscello, Lucia. "Patterns of Chorality in Plato's *Laws*." In vol. 1 of *Music and Cultural Politics in Greek and Chinese Societies*, edited by Dimitrios Yatromanolakis, 133–58. Cambridge: Harvard University Press, 2012.

– *Performing Citizenship in Plato's Laws.* Cambridge: Cambridge University Press, 2014.

Rawson, Beryl. *The Politics of Friendship: Pompey and Cicero.* Sydney: Sydney University Press, 1978.

Rhodes, James. *Eros, Wisdom, and Silence: Plato's Erotic Dialogues.* Columbia: University of Missouri Press, 2003.

– "Platonic *Philia* and Political Order." In *Friendship and Politics: Essays in Political Thought*, edited by John von Heyking and Richard Avramenko, 21–52. Notre Dame: University of Notre Dame Press, 2008.

Rorty, Amélie Oksenberg. "The Psychology of Aristotelian Tragedy." In *Essays on Aristotle's Poetics*, edited by Amélie Oksenberg Rorty, 1–22. Princeton: Princeton University Press, 1992.

Rose, Jonathan. *The Literary Churchill: Author, Reader, Actor.* New Haven: Yale University Press, 2014.

Rosen, Stanley. *The Quarrel Between Philosophy and Poetry: Studies in Ancient Thought.* New York: Routledge, 1988.

Rothkopf David. "This Man is an Island," *Foreign Policy* 5, November 5, 2014. http://foreignpolicy.com/2014/11/05/this-man-is-an-island-2.

Rowe, Jonathan Y. *Sons or Lovers: An Interpretation of David and Jonathan's Friendship.* New York: Bloomsbury T & T Clark, 2012.

Salkever, Stephen. "Taking Friendship Seriously: Aristotle on the Place(s) of *Philia* in Human Life." In *Friendship and Politics: Essays in Political Thought*, edited by John von Heyking and Richard Avramenko, 53–83. Notre Dame: University of Notre Dame Press, 2008.

Saul, John Ralston. *Louis-Hippolyte LaFontaine and Robert Baldwin.* Toronto: Penguin, 2010.

Schabert, Tilo. "Chaos and Eros: On the Order of Human Existence." *Diogenes* 42, no. 165 (1994): 111–32.

– "A Classical Prince: The Style of François Mitterand." In *Philosophy, Literature, and Politics: Essays Honoring Ellis Sandoz*, edited by Charles Embry and Barry Cooper, 234–57. Columbia: University of Missouri Press, 2005.

– "Eric Voegelin's Workshop: A Study in Confirmation of Barry Cooper's Genetic Paradigm." In *Hunting and Weaving: Empiricism and Political Philosophy*, edited by Thomas Heilke and John von Heyking, 232–51. South Bend, IN: St Augustine's Press, 2013.

– *How World Politics Is Made: France and the Reunification of Germany.* Edited by Barry Cooper. Translated by John Tyler Tuttle. Columbia: University of Missouri Press, 2002.

– "The True Form of Governments: The Constitutional Movements of Power." In *The Primacy of Persons in Politics: Empiricism and Political Philosophy*, edited by John von Heyking and Thomas W. Heilke, 3–22. Washington, DC: Catholic University of America Press, 2013.

Schall, James. "On the Seriousness of Sports, Watchers All." *Vital Speeches of the Day* 49 (February 15, 1983): 271–4.

Schütz, Alfred. "Making Music Together." In *Collected Papers.* Vol. 2, *Studies in Social Theory.* Edited by Arvid Brodersen, 159–78. The Hague: Martinus Nijhoff, 1964.

Scruton, Roger. *The Face of God.* London: Continuum, 2012.

– *I Drink Therefore I Am.* London: Continuum, 2009.

– *Understanding Music.* London: Continuum, 2009.

Smidchens, Guntis. *The Power of Song: Nonviolent National Culture in the Baltic Singing Revolution.* Seattle: University of Washington Press, 2014.

Smith, Thomas W. "Aristotle on the Limits for and Conditions of the Common Good." *American Political Science Review* 93, no. 3 (September 1999): 625–36.

– *Revaluing Ethics.* Albany: SUNY Press, 2001.

Sokolowski. Robert. "Friendship and Moral Action in Aristotle." *Journal of Value Inquiry* 35 (2002): 501–20.

– "The Phenomenology of Friendship." *Review of Metaphysics* 55 (2002): 451–70.

– *Phenomenology of the Human Person.* Cambridge: Cambridge University Press, 2008.

Spaemann, Robert. *Happiness and Benevolence.* Translated by Jeremiah Alberg. Notre Dame, IN: University of Notre Dame Press, 2000.

Stern-Gillet, Suzanne. "Souls Great and Small: Aristotle on Self-Knowledge, Friendship, and Civic Engagement." In *Ancient and Medieval Concepts of Friendship,* edited by Suzanne Stern-Gillet and Gary M. Gurtler, 51–83. Albany: SUNY Press, 2014.

Strauss, Leo. *The Argument and Action of Plato's Laws.* Chicago: University of Chicago Press, 1975.

– "Churchill's Greatness." *Weekly Standard* 5, no. 3 (January 4, 2000). http://www.weeklystandard.com/article/11653#.

– *What is Political Philosophy? and Other Studies.* Chicago: University of Chicago Press, 1988.

Stroud, R.S. "The Gravestone of Socrates' Friend, Lysis." *Hesperia* 53, no. 3 (1984): 355–60.

Swanson, J. "The Political Philosophy of Aeschylus' *Prometheus Bound.*" *Interpretation: A Journal of Political Philosophy* 22, no. 2 (1994–5): 215–46.

Sweeny, Alastair. *George-Étienne Cartier.* Toronto: McClelland and Stewart, 1976.

Telfer, Elizabeth. "Friendship." In *Other Selves: Philosophers on Friendship,* edited by Michael Pakaluk, 250–67. Indianapolis: Hackett, 1991.

Thomson, Clare. *The Singing Revolution: A Political Journey through the Baltic States.* London: Michael Joseph, 1992.

Trivigno, F.V. "Philosophy and the Ordinary: On the Setting of the *Lysis.*" *Greek, Roman, and Byzantine Studies* 51 (2011): 61–85.

Tuan, Yi-Fu. "Community, Society, and the Individual." *Geographical Review* 92, no. 3 (2002): 307–18.

Tusty, James, Maureen Castle Tusty, and Mike Majoros. *Singing Revolution.* DVD. Directed by James Tusty and Maureen Castle Tusty. Los Angeles: Universal Studios Home Entertainment, 2009.

van Herk, Aritha. "The Half Mile of Heaven's Gate." In *Icon, Brand, Myth: The Calgary Stampede,* edited by Max Foran, 235–50. Edmonton: Athabasca University Press, 2008.

Velasquez, Eduardo A., ed. *Love and Friendship: Rethinking Politics and Affection in Modern Times.* Lanham, MD: Lexington, 2003.

Vernon, Mark. "The Ambiguity of Friendship: Is the Western Tradition Friend or Foe to Amity?" Paper presented at the Friends and Foes Conference, Belfast, Northern Ireland, November 2007.

Vlastos, Gregory. *Platonic Studies.* Princeton: Princeton University Press, 1973.

Voegelin, Eric. *Anamnesis: On the Theory of History and Politics.* Vol. 6 of *Collected Works of Eric Voegelin.* Edited by David Walsh. Translated by M.J. Hanak and Gerhart Niemeyer. Columbia: University of Missouri Press, 2002.

– "In Search of the Ground." In *Published Essays, 1953–1965.* Vol. 11 of *Collected Works of Eric Voegelin.* Edited by Ellis Sandoz, 224–52. Columbia: University of Missouri Press, 2000.

– *In Search of Order.* Vol. 5 of *Order and History.* Baton Rouge: Louisiana State University Press, 1987.

– *Israel and Revelation.* Vol. 1 of *Order and History.* Baton Rouge: Louisiana State University Press, 1956.

– *Modernity Without Restraint: The Political Religions; The New Science of Politics; and Science, Politics, Gnosticism.* Vol. 5 of *Collected Works of Eric Voegelin.* Edited by M. Henningsen. Columbia: University of Missouri Press, 1999.

– *Plato and Aristotle.* Vol. 3 of *Order and History.* Baton Rouge: Louisiana State University Press, 1956.

– "Reason: The Classic Experience." In *Published Essays, 1966–1985.* Vol. 12 of *Collected Works of Eric Voegelin.* Edited by Ellis Sandoz, 265–91. Baton Rouge: Louisiana State University Press, 1990.

– *The World of the Polis.* Vol. 2 of *Order and History.* Baton Rouge: Louisiana State University Press, 1956.

Wall, John. "Phronesis as Poetic: Moral Creativity in Contemporary Aristotelianism." *Review of Metaphysics* 59 (December 2005): 313–31.

Walsh, David. "Dignity as an Eschatological Concept." In *Understanding Human Dignity,* edited by Christopher McCrudden, 245–58. Proceedings of the British Academy. Oxford: Oxford University Press, 2013.

– *Guarded By Mystery.* Washington, DC: Catholic University of America Press, 1999.

– "Hope Does Not Disappoint." In *Hunting and Weaving: Empiricism and Political Philosophy,* edited by Thomas W. Heilke and John von Heyking, 252–71. South Bend, IN: St Augustine's Press, 2013.

– *The Modern Philosophical Revolution: The Luminosity of Existence.* Cambridge: Cambridge University Press, 2008.

Watkins, C. "Studies in Indo-European Legal Language, Institutions, and Mythology." In *Indo-European and Indo-Europeans,* edited by G. Cardona and H. Hoenigswald, 321–54. Vol. 9 of Haney Foundation Series. Philadelphia: University of Pennsylvania Press, 1970.

Wetherell, Donald G. "Making Tradition: The Calgary Stampede, 1912–1939." In *Icon, Brand, Myth: The Calgary Stampede*, edited by Max Foran, 21–46. Edmonton: Athabasca University Press, 2008.

Woodruff, Paul. "Aristotle on *Mimesis*." In *Essays on Aristotle's Poetics*, edited by Amélie Oksenberg Rorty, 73–96. Princeton: Princeton University Press, 1992.

Wycherley, R.E. *The Stones of Athens*. Princeton: Princeton University Press, 1978.

Yarbrough, Jean M. "Politics and Friendship in the Adams-Jefferson Correspondence." In *Friends and Citizens: Essays in Honor of Wilson Carey McWilliams*, edited by Peter Dennis Bathory and Nancy L. Schwartz, 67–79. Lanham, MD: Rowman and Littlefield, 2001.

Young, Kenneth. *Churchill and Beaverbrook: A Study in Friendship in Politics*. New York: James H. Heineman, 1966.

Zuckert, Catherine. *Plato's Philosophers*. Chicago: University of Chicago Press, 2009.

Index